Harry Mount's Odyssey

Ancient Greece in the Footsteps of Odysseus

BLOOMSBURY

LONDON · OXFORD · NEW YORK · NEW DELHI · SYDNEY

Bloomsbury Continuum

An imprint of Bloomsbury Publishing Plc

50 Bedford Square
London
WC1B 3DP
UK

1385 Broadway
New York
NY 10018
USA

www.bloomsbury.com

**Bloomsbury, Continuum and the Diana logo are trademarks of
Bloomsbury Publishing Plc**

First published 2015
Paperback 2016

British Library Cataloguing-in-Publication Data
A catalogue record for this book is available from the British Library.

Library of Congress Cataloguing-in-Publication data has been applied for.

ISBN: HB: 978-1-4729-0467-6
PB: 978-1-4729-3596-0
ePDF: 978-1-4729-0469-0
ePub: 978-1-4729-0468-3

2 4 6 8 10 9 7 5 3 1

Typeset by Integra Software Services Pvt. Ltd.

Printed and bound in Great Britain by CPI Group (UK) Ltd, Croydon CR0 4YY

To find out more about our authors and books visit www.bloomsbury.com.
Here you will find extracts, author interviews, details of forthcoming events and the
option to sign up for our newsletters.

To S, the face that launched a single ship

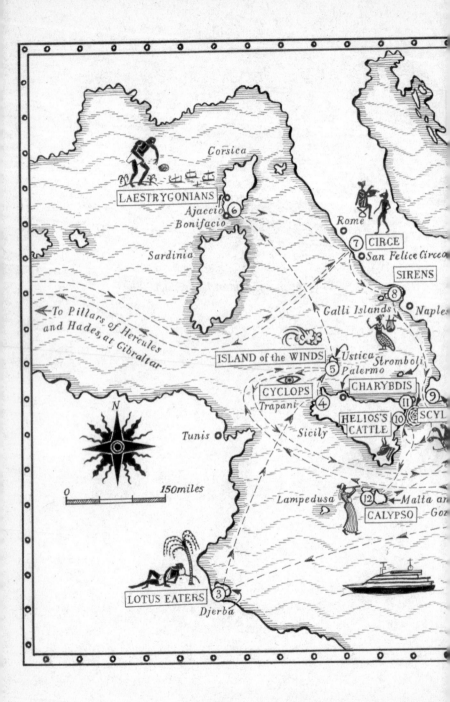

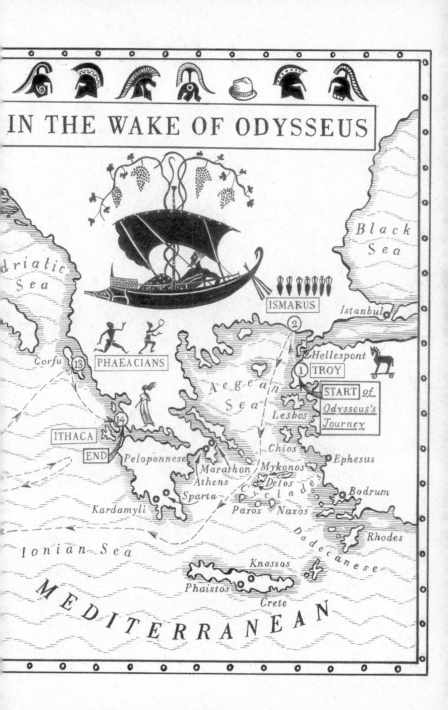

IN THE WAKE OF ODYSSEUS

Black Sea

Adriatic Sea

ISMARUS

Istanbul

Corfu ⑬ PHAEACIANS

Hellespont

① TROY

Aegean Sea

START of Odysseus's Journey

Lesbos

Chios

Ephesus

ITHACA ⑭

END Peloponnese

Marathon
Athens
Sparta

Mykonos

Delos

Cyclades

Bodrum

Kardamyli

Paros · Naxos

Rhodes

Dodecanese

Ionian Sea

Knossos

Phaistos

Crete

MEDITERRANEAN

The sea, autumn mildness, islands bathed in light, fine rain spreading a diaphanous veil over the immortal nakedness of Greece. Happy is the man, I thought, who, before dying, has the good fortune to sail the Aegean Sea. To cleave that sea in the gentle autumnal season, murmuring the name of each islet, is to my mind the joy most apt to transport the heart of man into paradise.

NIKOS KAZANTZAKIS, ZORBA THE GREEK

Now the sea is the Argonauts' sea, and in the dawn Odysseus calls the commands, as he steers past those foamy islands. Wait, wait, don't bring the coffee yet, nor the pain grillé. The dawn is not off the sea, and Odysseus's ships Have not yet passed the island, I must watch them still.

D. H. LAWRENCE, THE ARGONAUTS

List of Illustrations

Chapter 7

Chapter 8

Chapter 9

Chapter 10

Chapter 11

Chapter 12

Chapter 13

Chapter 14

A Potted History of Ancient Greece

2000–1600 BC – Minoan Crete.

1600–1150 BC – Mycenean Greece.

1200 BC – Rough date of the Trojan War, lasting ten years. Odysseus criss-crossed the Mediterranean for another decade.

1150–800 BC – The Dark Ages.

776 BC – The first Olympic Games.

c. **750 BC** – The Greek alphabet was invented.

c. **750–725 BC** – Homer wrote *The Iliad* and *The Odyssey*.

508 BC – Cleisthenes created democracy.

490 BC – The Battle of Marathon. The Athenian underdogs beat the Persians.

480 BC – The Battle of Thermopylae. The Persians beat the Greeks, despite a heroic last stand by Leonidas and his 300 Spartans.

480 BC – The Battle of Salamis. The Greeks beat the Persians.

461–429 BC – Pericles in charge of Athens.

460–445 BC – The First Peloponnesian War, fought by Sparta against Athens. Resulted in the Thirty Years' Peace.

458 BC – Aeschylus's *Oresteia*.

447 BC – The Parthenon was begun.

442 BC – Sophocles's *Antigone*.

431–404 BC – The second Peloponnesian War, between Athens and Sparta. Athens lost.

429 BC – Pericles died.

399 BC – Socrates executed.

357 BC – Birth of Alexander the Great.

323 BC – Alexander died at Babylon.

146 BC – Rome destroyed Corinth and took over Macedon.

27 BC – The last vestiges of ancient Greece yielded to Rome, as southern Greece became the Roman province of Achaea.

Contents

Introduction:
from Heathrow to Troy

Odysseus began his journey home to Ithaca on the windswept plain beneath the burning ramparts of Troy, by the banks of the meandering River Scamander.

Edward Gibbon embarked on *The History of the Decline and Fall of the Roman Empire* in the ruins of the Roman Capitol, while the barefoot friars were singing vespers in the Temple of Jupiter.

I started my odyssey in the Pret a Manger at Terminal 5 in Heathrow Airport. I was waiting for a BA flight to Istanbul – the nearest major international airport to Troy.

Odysseus never had to ask the girl behind the counter at Pret a Manger for a receipt for £5.26. Keeping an efficient record of tax-deductible expenses wasn't a priority for distinguished Trojan War veterans.

He was too broad-minded to bother paying the VAT-free takeaway price – for a Pret smoked salmon sandwich, an apple juice and an apple – and yet sit in the customer seating area all the same. Still – another small victory over the taxman. Never to be sniffed at.

Odysseus didn't have any Factor 50 Boots sunblock in his spongebag, either. Looking at my face in the mirror a few days earlier, I'd noticed a faint corrugation to my upper lip – the ghost of a wrinkle. After eating my sandwich, I rushed to the skincare department of the Boots at Terminal 5.

Over the last 15 years, age had made pretty good inroads into the ephebic good looks of my youth – ephebes were Greek citizens, aged 18 to 20, usually hard at work on garrison duty.

I bet Odysseus's olive skin was less wrinkled than mine, even after a decade baking in the salty, Mediterranean sunshine under the sloping, towering walls of Troy.

He wouldn't have needed my sunhat. Later in my journey, even the weakening October sun in Mycenae was enough to turn my bald pate an angry shade of red, after I'd lost my hat – a much-loved stingy brim I'd got near the Fulton Fish Market in New York seven years earlier. I had worn it on every sunny day of my journey – so often that the bottom half of my face was tanned a freckly cappuccino colour; the top half, from the bottom of my eyes up, remained a pasty off-white.

I'd parted from my hair a decade before. I certainly had less of the stuff than Odysseus. Homer refers to Odysseus's abundant head of hair when he's shipwrecked, naked, on the shores of Corfu, on the final leg of the journey to Ithaca. There he is discovered, shielding his crotch with a leafy branch, by the gorgeous Princess Nausicaa, while she tosses a beach ball at her singing handmaidens. The Greeks were the first to develop modern beach activities – surviving Minoan paintings on Crete show women in bikinis as early as 2000 BC.

To make the shipwrecked Odysseus look more attractive to Nausicaa, Athene, Odysseus's guardian goddess, transformed his scurfy, salty hair into curls that looked like 'huakinthino' – hyacinths. These days, I can't scrape a single lock of hair together, let alone a full hyacinth's worth.

At 42, the bell was tolling for my youth – and how I minded the whirring-by of the years.

Odysseus was enviously indifferent to the passage of time as he whiled away the hours with Nausicaa; or a whole year with the foxy witch, Circe, on the island of Aeaea, now a peninsula off the Italian coast near Anzio, about 50 miles south of Rome.

Yes, 20 years was a painfully long time for him to be away from his adored wife, Penelope. But he did spend seven of those years nestling in a secret love cave with the seductive sea-nymph Calypso, on the island of Ogygia – thought to be Gozo, Malta's neighbour.

He was washed up on Calypso's shore – fully clothed this time – clinging to a single timber, the only remnant of his shipwrecked boat. I eventually tracked down Calypso's cave on Gozo – no knockout nymph was there to greet me.

Odysseus was the original eurotrash Latin – or Greek – lover, that annoyingly good-looking man with the screaming jet ski on the beach in Crete. However tight the Speedos, however thickly matted the chest hair, they never put off the smokin' hot chick in the G-string, crouched on the back of the jet ski, reaching round to rummage in that chest hair with her elegant talons.

He was a thoroughly southern Mediterranean soul – the complete reverse of me. Majestically unworried – except when he's being attacked by things like cannibalistic Laestrygonians, which seem worrying enough – Odysseus really took his time getting home, having all those steamy affairs along the way.

You can still see that lack of worry across the Mediterranean. As I travelled around Greece, the bankrupt country was almost as troubled as when it went to war with the Trojans 3,000 years ago. But, even as continental Europe was falling apart during the economic crisis, it was hard to spot any overt sign of anxiety in its southern peoples – so much thinner, better-looking and better-dressed than us neurotic, fat, pasty, northern types. And so untroubled-looking.

That innate calm is bred into the southern Europeans at a young age. I saw it in the way Spanish-looking, English-speaking ten-year-old boys rode their bikes around Gibraltar, the site of Homer's underworld: swaggering, swinging their bikes from side to side, standing up, straight-legged, hovering over the saddle, oblivious to passing traffic.

I noticed it, too, one early evening in the town square of Sartène, Corsica, in October 2014, on my way to the home town of those man-eating Laestrygonians: Bonifacio, on the southern tip of the island.

In the town square, unworried parents chatted, drank red beer and didn't even glance at their unworried children climbing lamp posts, doing handstands, spitting and playing football with nimble, loose-hipped coordination.

All this easy insouciance was beyond me as a child – and nowadays, too, with my super-cautious sensitivity. Rather than bothering the waiter that evening in Sartène – and going through all the stage-managed pantomime of getting his attention – I left a €5 note on a €3 and 20 centime bill. My natural parsimony was defeated by the greater fear of making a fuss – and the desire to hurry my trip, and my life, along, even though I had all the time in the world to get to Bonifacio that evening.

I should have been less worried – and more grateful to Odysseus for leading me to such lovely places. He was always good at picking the big Mediterranean islands: Sicily, Corsica, Malta and Corfu were all on his itinerary. But he was also good at choosing idyllic backwaters for his romantic minibreaks – which invariably turned into maxibreaks if the witch or nymph in question was attractive enough.

Odysseus – and I – ended up doing a pretty thorough tour of the Mediterranean. Among his top destinations were the Sirenusas – also known as the Galli Islands, off the holiday island of Capri – named after the bewitching Sirens, who tried to lure Odysseus to his death with their honeyed voices.

His men stuffed their ears with beeswax to shut out the noise. Odysseus was so determined to hear their song that he kept his ears unblocked, but he had his sailors strap him to the mast to stop him buckling. He was never one to turn down a pleasure.

More recently, the Sirenusas have become the acme of hyper-idyllic, gazillionaire holiday hotspots. The islands provided the backdrop to the Dolce & Gabbana Light Blue fragrance campaign, in which superhunk David Gandy, wrapped around a pouting babe, lounged on a boat in his tighty whities. The babe changed in the three different campaigns – in 2007, 2010 and 2013 – but Gandy was ever-present in all three, as were the photographer, Mario Testino, and the Sirenusas.

On the coast opposite the islands, the pretty little resort of Positano also claimed the Sirens as its own, not least at the upmarket boutique hotel, Le Sirenuse: its emblem shows two knockout, topless Sirens, bearing a little hotel in their hands.

Did the holiday destinations develop in these places because Odysseus visited them? Or did Homer consciously pick already prominent places in eighth-century BC Greece to despatch his hero to? Or did holiday resorts invent their Odysseus associations to lure the punters in? My journey would enlighten me.

Back at Terminal 5, I was growing increasingly irritated at the 90-minute delay that had just been announced. I sat at Gate A13, staring at the departures screen. Why did it take me almost as long to get the 15 miles from my north

London flat to my seat on the plane (two hours and 20 minutes) as it did to fly the 1,500 miles from Heathrow to Istanbul: three and a half hours?

My God, I would have been irritated by Odysseus's terrible delays. The Trojan War lasted ten years, and Odysseus spent another decade criss-crossing the Mediterranean, in one of the most catastrophic navigation exercises in maritime history.

Even in 1200 BC – when *The Iliad* and *The Odyssey* are roughly thought to be set – you could sail from Troy, on Turkey's western Asian coast, to Ithaca, off the north-western shore of the Peloponnese, in a couple of weeks.

In Aeschylus's *Agamemnon*, the fall of Troy was communicated from the city, 500 miles across the Aegean, to Agamemnon's murderous wife, Clytemnestra, in Mycenae, in a matter of minutes, thanks to a series of fire beacons.

It's only around 500 miles from Troy to Ithaca, as the crow flies; double that, when you had to dip down under the Peloponnese, in the days before the Corinth Canal was built in 1893. You can now do the journey from Troy to Ithaca in a souped-up gin palace in less than a week, whichever route you take.

Lecturing on a cruise ship in 2014, following very roughly in Odysseus's footsteps, we went from Dubrovnik to Istanbul, and back to Venice. On our way out, we took the short route through the Corinth Canal. On the way back, we sailed, in Odysseus's wake, to Ithaca, around the bottom of the Peloponnese.

And still, moving at a leisurely pace, stopping off to look at sights all day, only travelling at night, we did the equivalent of at least two odysseys in three weeks. My whole journey – which expanded beyond Odysseus's itinerary to take in the non-Homeric sights of ancient Greece, and involved plenty of trips back to London – took only three years.

OK – our cruise ship, the *Corinthian*, had an engine. My dedication to recreating the Odyssey was nothing compared to Tim Severin, the writer who followed the route in the 1980s. He sailed in the *Argo*, a boat that approximated as closely as possible to Odysseus's primitive craft.

In 1819, another British writer, William Goodison, was even more daring, travelling around Ithaca's coast in a flimsy copy of an ancient raft, built by a one-eyed local called Captain Odysseus.

But, still, even with the shortcomings of thirteenth-century BC ocean travel, Odysseus's black, tar-smeared ship – unnamed in *The Odyssey* – should have managed the journey in a couple of months at most. Mediterranean ships were equipped with sails from around 2,500 BC – that gave ancient sailors 1,300 years or so to come up with some pretty quick yachts, before the Trojan War got going.

Odysseus's son, Telemachus, does say that other Greeks died on the perilous journey home from Troy. But none of the Greek leaders took quite so long to get back, even if, on their return, they got a pretty rough reception.

According to Aeschylus's *Oresteia*, Agamemnon was killed in the bath when he got home to Mycenae. The murderer was Agamemnon's wife, Clytemnestra. Clytemnestra also murdered Agamemnon's girlfriend, Cassandra – Priam's poor daughter, given the power of prophecy but also blighted by the curse that no one ever believed her predictions; like the unluckiest of Fleet Street columnists.

Agamemnon's children, Electra and Orestes, later avenged their father by killing Clytemnestra and her boyfriend, Aegisthus. The dead couple were buried outside the walls of Mycenae, polluted as they were by their shameful affair. Electra was so traumatised by the aftermath of the war that she starred in not one, but two plays called *Electra*, written by Euripides and Sophocles. Just as Freud came up with the Oedipus complex, Carl Gustav Jung devised the Electra complex – where a daughter vies in psychosexual combat for the attentions of her father.

The Trojans had a tough time after the war ended, too. Euripides's *Trojan Women* told the story of Hecuba, Priam's queen, and Andromache, Hector's wife, and their enslavement by the Greeks after the Trojan War.

So, other returning warriors had their dysfunctional families – and a fabulous selection of psychological conditions – to wrestle with. But they didn't suffer from Odysseus's navigational difficulties. For all his wily genius, he was the world's most accident-prone, unfaithful and heroic traveller: Eddie the Eagle meets Warren Beatty.

To be fair to Odysseus, he wasn't responsible for most of the delays. Poseidon, the god of the sea, had it in for him for blinding his son Polyphemus, the Cyclops, on the coast of Sicily. And so Poseidon's various monsters and whirlpools played havoc with Odysseus's schedule.

Even the naturally untroubled Odysseus was driven to the depths of despair by all this. His lowest point was in Book 5: *The Odyssey*, like *The Iliad*, was divided up into 24 books long after Homer composed the epics. This is the moment he was shipwrecked on Corfu's western shore – just before he meets the lovely Nausicaa.

That erotomaniac, Calypso, had reluctantly let Odysseus go from her sex cave on Ogygia. For 18 days after fleeing her clutches, Odysseus sailed perfectly happily, east towards Ithaca, on gentle breezes. That's until angry old Poseidon spotted him, whipped up the sea with his triton, and recruited all the winds to give Odysseus a good battering. Odysseus, flung into the sea by the storm, had to strip off all his swanky clothes – a present from Calypso – because they weighed him down. All the same, he was dashed upon the rocks, ripping his skin on them. Homer compared the scene to the torn suckers a cuttlefish leaves behind on pebbles when you pull it out of a hole.

Poor Odysseus was left naked, stranded in the shoals, his flesh swollen and torn, water pouring from his mouth and nostrils. Homer wrote, *Hali gar dedmeto philon ker*; or, to use the George Chapman translation Keats admired in 'On First Looking Into Chapman's Homer': 'The sea had soak'd his heart through.'

I could hardly claim any comparable levels of pain when I visited that same spot – Ermones Beach, now a little holiday resort on Corfu's western coast, with low-rise tower blocks climbing up the steep hill behind the beach.

In fact, I could hardly claim any real pain at all on my odyssey – except for the time I stood up too quickly to answer the phone in the London Library while researching this book. I hit my forehead on the leading edge of a low metal bookshelf. Blood poured down my face as I rushed down the stairs to the members' loo. I still bear the tiny scar to this day. Can a library injury be heroic?

I'd got to Ermones Beach by hire car from Corfu Town, the island's capital, where the *Corinthian* docked for the day. My biggest hardship was forgetting to bring my trunks. So I had to swim in my black pants, from Tesco's cheapo F & F range. I suppose I was nearly as naked as Odysseus, but in much calmer waters.

The beach was a little pebbly, it's true, but the pebbles weren't jagged enough to tear the skin off my feet like a cuttlefish's suckers; certainly not enough to put off several middle-aged Russian ladies, rocking on their backs in the warm water of early autumn, gossiping away. Wrapped in voluminous, all-in-one, black swimsuits, they did not bear much resemblance to my vision of Nausicaa.

A stiff westerly breeze whipped the water up into cream-peaked waves where it hit the beach – but, still, it was nothing the Russians and I couldn't handle. The breeze didn't even make for good drying conditions for my pants when I stretched them out on a sun lounger; I had to dump them in a bin on the beach and drive back to the ship commando-style. It was too windy, though, for the sort of beach ball played by Nausicaa and her handmaidens.

Not that I ever faced the kind of winds Odysseus had to deal with. Like him, I did come smack up against the meltemi – the northerly wind that still blows across the Aegean in summer when the hot air above the sea rises and cold air sweeps in from the north to replace it.

We were hit by the meltemi later that evening, as the *Corinthian* headed north from Corfu into Croatian waters. Blowing at force 7 for ten hours straight, the 35 mph wind rattled the cocktail glasses at pre-dinner drinks but failed to knock them over – hemmed in as they were by neat little plastic fences on the zinc bar.

Only a few old salts could face dinner that night, laughing and drinking their way through the small hours, buoyed by mutual reassurances of bravery, while the rest of us took to our cabins. It didn't do much for my stomach to see sick bags stuffed behind the banisters on every landing as I descended to my cabin on the Ariadne Deck. In my cabin, I broke the cheese-paring habits of a lifetime and splashed out on room service for an austere dinner – a club sandwich, soup and sparkling water.

The wind can still rip great chunks out of the Greek coastline and drown hundreds of desperate migrants sailing from Turkey to the Greek island of Lesbos. Earlier in my odyssey, a whole beach, freshly laid for the grand reopening of the Santa Marina Hotel in Mykonos, was whipped away by a freak southerly wind.

I spent a thoroughly enjoyable afternoon, lying on my sun lounger at the hotel's Bay View Beach Restaurant, watching the Bay View Beach being carefully reassembled. A quarter of a mile out to sea, a dredger sucked up sand from the seabed and sent it back to the rocky foundations of the old, vanished beach, via a huge, snaking, ribbed pipe. The sight of a beach being created in an afternoon was enough to make up for the whiff of briny sewage that accompanied the freshly dredged sand.

But even that storm was nothing compared to the typhoons that blasted poor old Odysseus from side to side of the Mediterranean, like a demented wasp in a jam jar. However low my fortunes got on my trip, I was cushioned by technology, money and comfort. After that dip in my pants on Ermones Beach, I had a chilled Nescafé frappé at the beachside café.

If I hadn't had to rush back from Ermones Beach to catch the *Corinthian* before sailing, I would have had lunch at the Taverna Nausika, a nice, elevated spot on the side of the beach, overlooking the sea. It was just before midday, but already three more plump Russian babushkas, in all-in-one black swimsuits, were installed at the bar. If only I could have hung around for calamari on the grill – or even the Greek 'folklore dancing' on Wednesdays at 9 p.m. – as displayed in the taverna's handwritten advert on the beach; luxuries not open to Odysseus.

Unlike Odysseus, I could also nip back home at irregular intervals. I was only ever a day's travel from my north London flat, not ten years away. My three-year-long journey around Greece, Italy, Turkey, Corsica, Malta, Albania, Croatia and Gibraltar was punctuated by trips home for journalism commissions, unmissable birthdays and family gatherings.

Where Odysseus's desperate heart was soaked through with the sea, I went in more for the kind of niggling, pointless irritation I felt at Heathrow Terminal 5. I was to Odysseus like the soulless, bookish narrator is to big-hearted, life-is-for-living Zorba in Nikos Kazantzakis's *Zorba the Greek*, the 1946 novel turned into the 1964 film.

At one point in the film, the narrator, a half-Greek, half-English intellectual, played by a shy, diffident Alan Bates, admits he'd prefer to read a book about a man falling in love than actually fall in love himself. Horrifyingly true of me.

The Alan Bates figure desperately asks Anthony Quinn's Zorba to teach him to dance, and break him out of his pompous crustiness. Zorba duly teaches him – on Stavros Beach, near Chania in Crete – to the accompaniment of Mikis Theodorakis's theme tune, based on traditional Cretan music.

I was in acute need of someone to teach me to dance.

Nausicaa's Taverna, Ermones Beach, Corfu – Odysseus was washed up naked on the beach in front of Princess Nausicaa, as she played beachball on the sand with her handmaidens.

1

Bye-bye, Penelope

When I set out for Troy, I was a dried-up husk of a person, with a dry-as-dust attitude to the ancient world. They should have stuck me in a glass case, alongside the mummies in the ancient galleries of the British Museum.

'The last vestige of a cloistered public school tradition,' the curator's caption on the glass case would read. 'This specimen devoted his youth to Latin and Greek but never did the racy things the ancients did: dance like a wine-crazed maenad, wrapped in snakes; drink till you're sick; have as much sex as possible – with both sexes. This individual spent a lot more time learning the third person singular of the perfect passive of *luo* – "I loose".'

I could hardly criticise Odysseus for mooching around in the backwaters of the Mediterranean with nubile beach babes, and generally not getting on with his life. When I set off to follow in his footsteps – or in his wake – I was, at 42, much the same age as Odysseus was at the end of his odyssey. There the resemblance ended.

By the time he'd reached his early forties, Odysseus had packed quite a lot into his life. Scholars suggest he was in his mid- to early thirties when he won the Trojan War. The victory was all thanks to his invention, the Trojan horse – which should really be called the Greek, or Ithacan, horse, in honour of its inventor's origins.

The horse wasn't mentioned in *The Iliad*, and was referred to in *The Odyssey* only briefly in Books 4 and 8. The story was told at much greater length in Book 2 of *The Aeneid* – another example of how Rome adopted, revered and altered Greek culture.

Odysseus was a clever one – the brightest of the Greeks, as Homer made clear in the first lines of *The Odyssey*: 'Tell me, O muse, of that ingenious hero who travelled far and wide after he had sacked the famous town of Troy.'

The word Homer used for 'ingenious' was *polytropon* – literally, 'many-faceted'. Odysseus was also called, at different moments, *polymetis* ('many-skilled'), *polytlas* ('much enduring') and *polymechanos* ('most ingenious').

'Poly-' comes from *polus*, meaning many, as in polygamy ('many times married'), polyglot ('many tongues') and hoi polloi. This literally means 'the many' – that's why you say hoi polloi, never *the* hoi polloi. Otherwise, you're guilty of tautology – from *tautos logos*, 'same word'.

Unlike Odysseus, I wasn't really poly-anything. I had no wars to my name and few significant travels, apart from a brief 18 months as the New York correspondent for the *Daily Telegraph*. I was a freelance journalist, recently parted from an adored girlfriend.

I was becoming a cold, desiccated, unengaged man. Unengaged, in every sense of the word. I certainly wasn't polygamous.

Marriage may rapidly be becoming a middle-class cult in twenty-first-century Britain, but that didn't stop me feeling like a child unless and until I was married. I wouldn't have gone down well in ancient Greece – under Athenian law, you were fined if you weren't married by the age of 35.

Homer wouldn't have approved of me, either. In *The Odyssey*, he said of marriage, 'Nothing is stronger or better than this, that a man and his wife live together, sharing one heart and one mind, a great grief to their enemies and a joy to their friends; but best of all they know it themselves.'

I had become a male Bridget Jones: desperate to get married but unable to find, or temperamentally incapable of finding, a wife. I wasn't sure which.

Just the mention of the word 'marriage' got me in a panic. In autumn 2014, I read an admirable *Spectator* article by John Hurt about a charity that helped disfigured children in Ethiopia have operations that meant they could 'go to school, get married'. That set off a little mad jag of jealousy for the poor, mutilated children and their future spouses.

When I read, shortly afterwards, that the singer Susan Boyle had found her first boyfriend – an American doctor – at the age of 53, I felt another screaming burst of jealousy.

Most of my friends were now married – including the druggies, the alcoholics and the gays. Friends referred to me more and more as a bachelor, no longer bothering to ask whether there was a girlfriend on the scene; or to set me up at dinner parties with fellow awkward singletons.

I'm not quite the last bachelor standing. My bachelor friends, I was beginning to notice, shared several of my characteristics: selfishness; a desire for the perfect relationship; the inability to compromise.

Those characteristics were gradually leading to their natural conclusion. The selfishness morphed into misery and loneliness – and buckets of self-pity. More eagle-eyed readers will already have noticed that self-pity is not entirely absent from these pages. The novelist Anthony Powell said immense self-pity was an almost essential adjunct of the bestseller. Fingers crossed.

On the whole, I had got pretty good at getting on with a life of self-contained despair; a restrained despair, only occasionally interrupted by heaving tears at moments of intense heartbreak, drunkenness or hangover.

I was half in love with melancholy – an ideal excuse for backing away from engagement with real life. One evening, soon after splitting up with my ex-girlfriend, I stared at myself in the bathroom mirror, secretly rather pleased at the depths of my sadness, while I wept fat tears and listened to the double CD *Love Hurts*.

The CD cover showed a single tear rolling down the velvet-skinned, gently contoured cheekbone of a lovely brunette who looked like a young Posh Spice. My favourite tracks on the album included Chris Rea's 'Fool (If You Think It's Over)' and Foreigner's 'I Want To Know What Love Is'.

Oh, for some misfortune to blame my oddness and unhappiness on! But I can hardly claim this is much of a misery memoir – a spoiltness memoir, perhaps, or a coming-of-middle-age memoir.

I am well-off and well-educated; expensively educated, too, at Westminster School, Magdalen College and the Courtauld Institute. I also trained as a banker and a barrister, running through the professions like a golden boy on speed. I don't think of myself as an insider – but run your finger down my CV and you will tick off plenty of Establishment boxes. It's one sign of privilege to do gilded, professional jobs. It's an even bigger sign to give them up, just because you find them boring.

If I were looking for a good title for my misery memoir, I could have called it not *Broken* or *Smashed*, but *Indulged*, *Over-educated* or simply *Posh*. Or *Bullingdon Boy*, perhaps. As if my life wasn't spoilt enough, I'd been a member of that bowel-shrinkingly embarrassing club at Oxford, the ultimate signifier of elitism in early twenty-first-century Britain. Oh, and David Cameron's my second cousin, too. And I was in that silly club at the same time as George Osborne.

I'd even been appointed as a sort of unofficial posh correspondent for the papers. When the *Daily Mail* wanted an article attacking *The Riot Club* – the awful 2014 film about the Bullingdon – they called me. When the *Telegraph* wanted something on Annabel's, the grand nightclub, moving from its posh basement in Mayfair in 2015, I was their man.

I suppose I am upper middle class, if you're looking for an identifiable slot in the ever-shifting sands of the British class system. I find it hard to believe anyone living in a flat in Kentish Town, a shabby-genteel corner of north London, can be anything higher than middle class. But my ancestry is sprinkled with earls, barons and field marshals.

As I've made clear, at some length, in several posh correspondent newspaper articles, Robert Peel is a direct ancestor; the Duke of Wellington is my great-great-great-great-uncle. My cousin Archie likes to call me the family archivist; I'm not sure I'm not the family snob.

My parents, brother and sister are happily married. I can claim no real problems, apart from a mild addiction to dry white wine that leaves me slightly itching with irritation at around half past six if I don't have a drink. Unlike some of my easier-going, drunker, druggier friends at school and university, I was too neurotic and competitive to go off the rails properly.

All my trials were self-created. In a 1944 letter to an old friend, Coote Lygon, Evelyn Waugh explained his thinking behind *Brideshead Revisited*, published the following year: 'I am writing a very beautiful book, to bring tears, about very rich, beautiful, high-born people who live in palaces and have no troubles except what they make themselves and those are mainly the demons, sex and drink.'

I may have lived in a maisonette in Kentish Town rather than a palace, but otherwise I was as self-indulgent as the Flytes of Brideshead. I, too, made my own troubles for myself.

I had developed a capacity for being on my own for extended periods of time. But I was also distressed by the absence of companions – and a close companion in particular. Twice on my odyssey, I even invented a pretend wife.

The first time was at Napoli Centrale railway station, on the way to find the Sirens at Positano. While I waited for the 1.55 p.m. express train to Salerno, a gypsy, with her baby in a pushchair, asked me for some of my lunch. I offered her my half-eaten provolone. She turned that down and demanded my prosciutto, still in its unopened packet, peeping out of the top of my unzipped leather holdall.

'C'e per mia moglie,' I pleaded.

Why invent an imaginary wife? Couldn't I have just said no? She didn't even take the provolone.

I invented another wife when I was flying back with easyJet from Bonifacio in Corsica.

One of the Mediterranean's great natural harbours, Bonifacio sits at the head of a steep-sided, flooded valley. Odysseus landed here in that catastrophic visit to the cannibalistic Laestrygonians and their grotesque wives – described by Homer as being 'as big as a mountain peak'. Corsican ladies are more attractive these days.

Odysseus sent several scouts out to ask the Laestrygonians for help – and they promptly became the Laestrygonians' dinner. As Odysseus and his surviving men fled, the Laestrygonians hurled boulders at their ships, sinking all of them except for Odysseus's.

I found it almost as difficult to get away from Corsica. I'd got to the airport in good time, racing at dawn over the spine of the island from Bonifacio. But years of travel had taught this old hand to wait until the last possible moment to board; to wait for all queues to dwindle to one or two people. So, comfortably installed at Ajaccio's airport café, I stared intermittently for two hours at the only queue in the terminal. My iPod buds were bolted into my ears, blocking out all announcements.

Ten a.m. – my departure time – came and went. I was still sitting in the café, isolated from the world, as I glanced out of the plate-glass windows towards the runway. There was my plane, loading its passengers off the baking hot tarmac. I craned my head and saw, beyond the unmoving queue, the bright orange easyJet part of the terminal – just round the corner from where I was sitting.

Racing to the desk, I pleaded with the easyJet girl. But I was too late. She and I watched, mute, through the big, plate-glass windows, as the last passengers climbed the mobile stairs, 500 yards away across the tarmac apron. Seconds later, the plane's front door closed and the mobile stairs were moved slowly away.

It was then that I invented another wife; well, two of them, actually.

'My wife is on the plane,' I pleaded.

Genuinely concerned, the girl called her supervisor over.

'I understand your wife is on the plane,' said the slightly older, equally concerned supervisor.

Oh God! They'd be able to trace my wife – or, more precisely, the absence of my wife – on the plane.

'Ah no – bit of a mix-up, sorry – she's not on the plane,' I said. 'My fault – I wasn't clear. She's back in London … pregnant.'

I don't know where that last detail came from. Dr Freud would have had a field day. Still, they didn't let me on board.

At that moment, I realised, with a stab to the heart, that my blunder made no real difference to my life. Annoying as it was to burn £300 on two more flights – to Bordeaux and London – there was no one waiting for me at home.

In my lonely, selfish life, hermetically sealed from the rest of the human race, my life had no knock-on effect on anyone else's. I was seeing *Gone Girl* with a friend that afternoon; I just postponed it till the evening.

I wasted six hours at Ajaccio Airport. But all I did in the departure lounge was what I would have done at home, anyway: read and write. My life could be lived anywhere with a laptop and a Wi-Fi signal. I could pick up sticks and go to Corsica, Naples, Ithaca – anywhere on the Odyssean trail – on a whim, and never tell anyone.

You might call it pure freedom. It was also pure selfishness; pure loneliness, too.

What could be nicer than sailing the Aegean, writing a book in the southern sun? Wonderful for expanding the brain, too. Better than a proper job. But I'm not sure my horizons weren't narrowing, the more I travelled in this self-indulgent way, free from a genuine, life-expanding life of a wife, children and real responsibilities.

Time was running out. 'Only the young can be alone freely,' wrote Philip Larkin. And only the young can naturally fall into friendships with people when they're travelling. On my journey, I often went days without talking to anyone other than hotel receptionists and waiters, without saying anything other than *Kalemera* or *Ena koriatike ke ena kalamari*.

Only the confident can travel without fretting about the noise of the lift in the Hotel Villa Taormina, or the arthritic plumbing in the Hotel Kalamitsi; without thinking they should be back in London, doing a proper job.

What was I doing chasing a mythical figure – or, perhaps, a real-life one – while my contemporaries were off being solicitors, bringing up children and, in my second cousin's case, running the country? While they accumulated families, and built up full, complete existences, I was fleeing responsibility, sleepwalking through life without touching the sides.

Once a mean hoarder, I had even tired of accumulating possessions, and took pleasure in getting rid of them. I threw books in the bin in the hotel room as soon as I'd finished them. I took my most frayed shirts in that leather holdall to Istanbul and binned them, too, when they got too stained around the collar with suntan lotion. Others accumulated souvenirs as they travelled; I used my trips to get rid of as many things as possible.

The only time my obsessive light packing has let me down was at Ben Gurion Airport in Tel Aviv a few years ago. Security were so astonished by my lack of luggage that they were convinced I was a suicide bomber.

My packing hero was a former Tory politician my father told me about. Flying together to Spain for a conference – and waiting at the luggage carousel for his suitcase – my father was amazed at the size of the politician's tiny plastic bag.

'All I need is this spare pair of pants,' the politician said cheerily, brandishing his little bag.

This light-travelling master only ever took this one spare pair of pants on foreign trips. He slept in the pants while his shirt, suit and other pair of pants were laundered overnight. It didn't just show an awesome devotion to travelling light; it also revealed a deep faith in the reliability of hotel laundries.

I hadn't always been this ultra-detached figure, desperate to be free of all baggage, emotional or otherwise. Only a year before my odyssey began, my husk had been at its least dried-up in its 40-year-long existence – thanks to that girlfriend, now an ex-girlfriend, who came up with the idea of my odyssey.

I'd dumped her. As a wincingly honest friend once told me, 'You always dump people and then behave like they dumped you.' But then I'd realised the error of my ways, and asked her to reconsider.

Another friend once gave me some advice on how to deal with an ex-girlfriend you're still in love with.

'It's always worthwhile telling them,' he said, 'Who knows what they're thinking. You might be looking back over your shoulder – and she might just be looking back over hers, too, at the same time.'

Well, I looked back and, for instantly understandable reasons, she wasn't.

So Odysseus was heading back to a woman he loved; I was fleeing one.

From time to time, I fooled myself into thinking my trip was an Iliad, not an Odyssey. Was I just on a brief journey from the adored one to battle wondrous foes, while she dutifully waited for my return in London?

Erm, no – Penelope wouldn't be leaning over the public barrier at Terminal 5 when I got home. In fact, she's more a Helen of Troy, with her captivating beauty and power to dominate the mind. But the Helen of Bayswater wouldn't be waiting for me at Terminal 5, either.

The Odyssey was unusual among the Greek myths, which were so crammed with mutilated brothers thrown off the backs of triremes, with sons killing fathers and marrying mothers. It had a happy ending. Not so with my odyssey, it seemed.

The *Eat, Pray, Love* arc of the film of this book would have led me back to her. But I am not Julia Roberts and my life arc is not Hollywood-friendly. *Eat, Feel Sorry for Self, Drink Quite a Lot of Dry White Wine* – anyone interested at 20th Century Fox?

I wasn't in a good way. When Evelyn Waugh was cuckolded by his first wife, also called Evelyn, he wrote to Harold Acton, saying, 'I did not know it was possible to be so miserable and live but I am told that this is a common experience.' I increasingly thought it wasn't possible to live and not be so miserable.

Shrinks call it a 'geographical' – when you move countries to get over a failed relationship. Well, my journey was a temporary geographical. A good reason to take off – the best, maybe. It's not that I'd be any less miserable – absence makes the heart grow sombre. My gloom was deepened by the fact that a modern odyssey was her idea; except the original idea was that we'd do it together.

Still, at least I'd be doing something interesting while feeling miserable. And it would be better than moping around familiar haunts redolent of her. We'd only been out with each other for 11 months. But 11 months – in a city as big as London – is enough to soak dozens of cafés and restaurants, and hundreds of streets, in agonising associations.

Not that the coasts of the Mediterranean were that different to the streets of London. They were less history-crammed places on the ancient, watery motorway around the sea; more the haunting ghosts of doomed minibreaks with her. That restaurant with the cold chips by the Athenian agora; the hotel in Naples, where I couldn't sleep because of the New Year fireworks ... each of them frozen in the memory, each a bitter-sweet Proustian madeleine, half pleasurable to remember, half caustic agony.

The *millefeuille* layers of memories that come with age were crowding out the dwindling brain space needed to treat new places with the appropriate level of enthusiasm. I was an acute sufferer of Lot's Wife syndrome – the constant urge to look back. Overloaded with wistfulness, my mind was a tired, slow, old computer, so stashed full with old information that it could barely deal with new things.

Is there a moment in the mind when it's so full of regret, sadness and exhaustion that there's no room left for fresh, uplifting thoughts? Medically incorrect, I imagine, but utterly convincing to me at that utterly low time. A melancholy overdose.

At least Odysseus was facing his monsters and his whirlpools afresh. I dealt with severe nostalgia – 'the pain of return' – every time I returned to the sites of previous holidays with her, from Istanbul to the Cyclades. I could date my past by a series of heartbreaks: 2011–12, when I went out with her; 2012–now, when I wasn't getting over her.

A return to Istanbul was a return to the night I'd spent worrying about the stuffy heat in the Four Seasons in Sultanahmet. Do you put up with the noise of the intermittently operative air-con, or open the window and let that sewage smell waft in off the Bosphorus? That particular conundrum had me calling in the hotel's engineer at two in the morning. Even the most sainted, deep-sleeping woman in the world – she was both – couldn't be expected to sleep through the sound of a panel being ripped out of the bedroom ceiling, in the quest for a temperamental air-conditioning pipe.

In one upmarket hotel on the western Turkish coast, near Bodrum, I couldn't get to sleep because the curtains were too flimsy – not something Odysseus ever complained about.

The break-up had wounded me deeply. The Greek for wound is *trauma* – an ideal word for that strange mixture of mental torture and near-physical pain brought on by heartbreak. Now, as I embarked on my journey, the scar tissue was accumulating. I was growing deadened to the pain, and less likely to engage in any future relationships.

When I got to Lesbos on my travels, a line from Sappho – the bisexual Greek poet from the island, who bequeathed the word 'lesbian' to the world – became my credo. She said of painful relationships, 'Let there be no honey or bee-sting for me.' It sounds particularly melodious in Greek: *Mete moi meli mete melissa*. That lovely name, Melissa, is Greek for 'honey bee'. Melodious also comes from *meli* – ancient and modern Greek for honey.

I was all washed up – but at least I had some place to go, a place mercifully free of the girl who plied me with honey and bee stings. Lots of places to go, in fact.

I urgently needed to harvest some of the enthusiasm for a modern odyssey, as recommended by the Greek poet Constantine Cavafy in his stirring 1911 poem, 'Ithaca', a favourite of President Kennedy's and Jackie O's:

As you set out for Ithaca,
hope the voyage is a long one,
full of adventure, full of discovery.
Laestrygonians and Cyclops,
angry Poseidon – don't be afraid of them:
you'll never find things like that on your way
as long as you keep your thoughts raised high,

as long as a rare excitement
stirs your spirit and your body.

My spirits weren't in great shape, it's true, but they had at least stirred my body from its musty bachelor nest in Kentish Town.

The too-loud, distorted Heathrow PA had just announced the delayed departure of the Istanbul flight; those spirits were about to lift me above Terminal 5 and send me across Europe, to the banks of the Hellespont.

Not necessarily a lesbian – Sappho, with her lyre, on Lesbos.

The author with Charlie Byron on the Gallipoli peninsula before swimming the Hellespont, in the wake of his ancestor, Lord Byron. We are on Turkey's European coast. Turkey's Asian coast and Troy are on the horizon.

2

From Europe to Asia – by Breast Stroke

You might have thought Lord Byron wasn't really the sporting type. The poet is better known for his club foot, heavy drinking and sleeping with his half-sister, Augusta Leigh, rather than any athletic skills.

In fact, he was extremely robust. One of his many mistresses, Lady Caroline Lamb, said Byron was 'mad, bad and dangerous to know'. She might have added, '… and pretty good at breast stroke'.

I began my odyssey by trying to emulate Byron's feat of swimming the Hellespont – the three-mile-wide stretch of water that separates Europe from Asia. Unlike Byron, I had a wetsuit, goggles, swimming cap, trunks, anti-chafe talc around the neck – and a bucketful of that Boots Factor 50 sunscreen on my face, hands and feet.

There were 42 safety boats, crammed with doctors, lifeguards and chocolate biscuits, tracking my every move on the charity swim. 139 other swimmers were gathered alongside me on the pebbly beach at Eceabat, a little Turkish town on the European side of the straits. The swimmers were mostly British, with a smattering of Americans and New Zealanders, and a lone Finn.

All Lord Byron had was a pair of trousers and the company of an old friend, Lieutenant Ekenhead – inspiration for one of the weaker sections of *Don Juan*. Byron writes of Juan:

> A better swimmer you could scarce see ever,
> He could perhaps, have pass'd the Hellespont,
> As once (a feat on which ourselves we prided)
> Leander, Mr Ekenhead, and I did.

Like Byron, I was also swimming the Hellespont with an old friend – called Ned.

According to Greek myth, Leander swam every night from Asia to Europe to visit his lover Hero, who lit a lamp to guide Leander to a regular night of passion. It all went fine in summer. But when the winter storms came, Hero's lamp was blown out; Leander lost his way and drowned. Despite his failure, Leander bequeathed his name to the Leander Club, the elite Thames rowing club founded in 1818.

I wasn't just following in the footsteps of Byron, Leander and Mr Ekenhead. The Hellespont, aka the Dardanelles – which connects the Black Sea with the Aegean, via the Sea of Marmara and the Bosphorus – is the most famous stretch of water in ancient history.

Because the thin channel connects Europe to Asia, it has always been a strategic spot. On the Asian side of the strait perches Troy, its ruined citadel still commanding the fertile headland near the entrance to the Hellespont; on the European side lies Gallipoli, the site of the Allies' 1915 humiliation.

The channel has been regularly crossed since time immemorial – and not just by humans.

Two hundred miles north-east from Eceabat, the strait narrows down to the half-mile-wide Bosphorus, straddled by Istanbul. The Bosphorus got its name from the legend of Jupiter's lover, Io. Juno was so jealous of drop-dead gorgeous Io that she turned her into a cow and hounded her across the world with a horsefly. The horsefly goaded her to cross from Europe to Asia. The spot where the cow forded the strait was called 'Cow's Ford' – 'Bosphorus' in Greek.

Jason also sailed the *Argo*, packed with his Argonauts, up the strait – from Iolchos, his home town in Thessaly, Greece, in search of the Golden Fleece at Colchis, on Georgia's Black Sea coast. Among the Argonauts was Laertes, Odysseus's father.

In 480 BC, Xerxes, the Persian king, crossed the Hellespont, using a pontoon of ships joined together with papyrus and flax cables. First time round, his men failed to link the pontoon. Xerxes ordered the sea to be whipped 300 times and branded with hot irons in revenge. Not something that appealed much if I failed to complete the crossing.

The Persians ultimately lost to the Athenians that same year, at the Battle of Salamis, an island ten miles west of Athens. Athenian supremacy didn't last long. In 405 BC, at the Battle of Aegospotami – a few miles north of where I was about to begin my swim – the Spartans beat the Athenians in the decisive sea battle of the Peloponnesian War. Athens surrendered a year later.

Byron did the swim to prove the Leander story was possible, concluding afterwards: 'Any young man in good health and of tolerable skill in swimming might succeed in it.' More than 170 years after Byron, Paddy Leigh Fermor managed the crossing at the age of 70. Despite being 30 years younger than Leigh Fermor when he did it, I wasn't to find it quite so straightforward.

In my defence, Byron was 22 at the time – 20 years my junior – and, as his descendant, the current Lord Byron, told me before the swim, he had far more to prove.

'I think he was always trying to make up for the club foot,' said Lord Byron, then 60, a shipping lawyer. He was there by the banks of the Hellespont to support his son – and Byron lookalike – Charlie, 19, an architecture student at Oxford Brookes University, also attempting the swim.

Lord Byron took an hour and ten minutes to do the whole thing. Even now, two centuries on, the record for the crossing is not that much quicker, at 48 minutes. When I did it, the British winner, Colin Hill, finished in an hour and 27 minutes. Whatever else he might have been, Byron was no softy.

'He loved swimming,' continued the current Lord Byron. 'He swam lots at Cambridge, and then swam across the Tagus [the longest river in Spain], and from the Venice Lido to Venice. But, still, he wasn't very tall and he drank too much.'

I am six foot two, take regular exercise and am not too much of a heavy drinker … and yet the swim was pure torture.

It started off well enough, as I plunged into the calm water on the European side, making good headway alongside the other swimmers. To begin with, it was almost pleasant – a leisurely holiday swim in Torquay.

For a couple of hours, the channel was officially closed to the mammoth oil tankers that inch their way down the Hellespont from the Black Sea. For a brief moment, Vladimir Putin's financial blood supply was cut off and the water was as empty as it had been when the Greeks landed on the Trojan shore opposite 3,000 years ago.

Ahead of me, the hump-backed, pine-fringed hills of Asia disappeared into the milky-grey, south-western horizon where the Hellespont meets the Aegean. This was Achilles's view as he dragged Hector's corpse round the walls of Troy in his three victory laps.

To attach the body to his chariot, Achilles threaded leather thongs through the sinews of poor Hector's heels. Ever since I read that as a child, I've always thought I'd prefer an Achilles's Heel to a Hector's Heel. As a grammar pedant, Achilles' Heel always annoyed me, anyway: Achilles's Heel may sound clumsy, but it's right.

It was an ideal day – around 85 degrees – although the water, flowing south from the Black Sea, was unusually icy for May, at just 55°F. That southerly current explained why we splashed into the water at Eceabat, a mile or so north-west of our target, the town of Çanakkale on the Asian side of the strait. The Hellespont is only just under a mile wide at its narrowest point – between Çanakkale and Kilitbahir, on the European side – but, there, the strangulated channel produces a lethal current. Better to aim north and let the current take you south in a gentle curve, in an upside-down J pattern.

The Mediterranean only has three places with strong surface currents: the Hellespont, the Strait of Messina and the Strait of Gibraltar. It can't be a coincidence that Odysseus sailed to all three spots: the killer whirlpool of Charybdis is said to be at Messina; Hades at Gibraltar; and Troy is on the banks of the Hellespont. It backs up the idea that Odysseus's route was retrospectively transplanted by critics – long after Homer wrote the epic – on to the most prominent, and difficult to sail, parts of the Mediterranean.

Only a third of the water lost by the Mediterranean to evaporation is replaced by the rivers that flow into it. Some of the shortfall was now flowing alongside me, south down the Hellespont from the Black Sea.

The rest comes in from the Atlantic, south of the Rock of Gibraltar, where the surface water gushes in at around two knots. The Med is saltier than the Atlantic: the denser, saltier Mediterranean water sinks to the bottom as fresh Atlantic water glugs in above it. In a miraculous flushing system, this heavier water drifts westwards, through the Strait of Gibraltar, at the bottom of the sea; meanwhile, the easterly Atlantic inflow continues, from the surface down for the first 408 feet. This serendipitous swap means the Mediterranean is completely renewed every couple of years.

Along with the southerly current, there was the choppy water to deal with, beating against me from the Asian side. Like Byron, I did the breast stroke. I'd like to say I did it out of historical accuracy. The real reason was I didn't like having my head underwater for as long as the pros. They started powering away from me the moment we clambered into the shallows. Each breast stroke took me forwards a yard, only for the waves to send me back three-quarters of a yard. The target we'd been told to aim at – a red-and-white transmitter mast on the Asian side – wasn't getting any bigger.

The orange swimming caps of Charlie Byron and Ned – doing the more effective front crawl – were getting smaller. More annoyingly, so were the yellow swimming caps worn by the other members of the press – I was writing about the swim for the *Daily Mail*. These were not your porky, boozy journalists of Fleet Street legend. They were a trim, virtuous bunch with lean tummies, trapezoid chests, and muscular arms and legs that beat the Hellespont with much more efficiency – and less anger – than silly old Xerxes.

And then the cramp hit. A kind 39-year-old triathlete from Camberwell had given me some salt tablets at lunch; cramp is caused by lack of salt, sweated out by exercise. I hadn't taken enough of them. A flashing pain shot up my right calf. Following the advice we'd been given before the race, I dangled my leg loosely in the water and struggled on for a bit. Ten minutes later, the cramp hit again in the right calf and then in the left. I was done for.

I made the agreed distress signal with my right hand, a semi-circular wave from right to left, not unlike the royal wave. Within seconds, a Turkish fishing boat sailed to my side. Once I'd scrambled aboard the stern, a doctor from Çanakkale took my pulse and said, in a gentle, indulgent way, as if he was calming down one of the more paranoid elderly ladies in his surgery, 'You are absolutely fine.'

Dr Mumtaz Piringciler, my saviour, gave me a chocolate biscuit, a glass of water and a towel. His assistant, a local lifeguard, gently massaged my cramp-ridden right calf. My humiliation was complete, as our pretty little wooden boat chug-chugged into Çanakkale port, past the bobbing, orange swimming caps of tougher competitors.

I tried to console myself – at least the yellow swimming caps of the press were towards the back of the group coming in to shore. And perhaps Leander suffered a touch of cramp, too, on his last lover's pilgrimage. Is that what killed him? Did Byron's club foot magically protect him from cramp?

The only convincing conclusion I came to was that Byron, as well as being highly motivated by his disability, was extremely fit. Even then, I'm clutching at straws – this was the poet who wrote, 'Let us have wine and women, mirth and laughter, sermons and soda water the day after.' It's hardly the stuff of austere fitness regimes.

I headed off to the Cafeka bar in Çanakkale to follow Byron's advice. There I drank several Efes beers and watched the yellow-hatted hacks making landfall on the Asian continent.

Alongside them was Ned. He was in touching distance of Asia when he was fished out of the water – the shipping lanes had to be reopened to let the oil tankers come down from the Black Sea. Putin's blood supply started circulating again. Homer's wine-dark sea was once more striped with the long, white wake of the tankers. Ned climbed out of the Hellespont and sat on the stern of the launch for a few seconds before thinking better of it, diving back in and reaching Asian soil.

Two hundred years after his famous ancestor proved it was possible, Charlie Byron did the swim in two hours, raising £2,000 for Help for Heroes in the process. Like his ancestor, he was now entitled to say,

He could perhaps, have pass'd the Hellespont,
As once (a feat on which ourselves we prided)
Leander, Mr Ekenhead, Ned and I did.

And I didn't. Thank God, Becky from the *Guardian* didn't, either.

Tourists stream out of the belly of the Trojan Horse in the car park at Troy, near Çanakkale, Turkey.

Byron in traditional Albanian costume, by Thomas Phillips, 1813. Byron bought the outfit in 1809 in Epirus, on the modern Albanian-Greek border, when he was on a Grand Tour of Southern Europe.

3

Greece 1 Rome 0

Byron's name isn't celebrated much in Turkey today. In Greece, it's a different matter – the man who fought for Greek independence almost 200 years ago is still a hero.

When the travel writer, Robert Byron, drove to Greece in 1925, he was treated like a king, thanks to his name, even though he was only a distant relation of the poet. Little boys wore sailor hats in Athens then, with the words 'Lordos Byron' on the rim.

A century after the poet's death, Robert Byron was assured that any member of the poet's family – or even someone with the same surname – could aspire to high political office if they cultivated 'a certain measure of self-advertisement'.

Byron is still referred to as *megalos philellen* – a great Greece-lover. A recent Greek children's book by Petros Bikos is called *Lord Byron – the Supreme Philhellene*. It even has a pull-out poster of the great man. Byron's verse is still transposed into traditional 15-syllable metre, too, transforming him into a Greek poet.

In the Athens National History Museum, the Homeric helmets Byron had made in Genoa for his battles for independence – along with his sword, pistol and the camp bed he died on – are on show. An Athenian street and neighbourhood are both named after Byron. There's a statue of him on the corner of Zappeion Gardens, behind the Greek Parliament.

When I was there in 2015, Syntagma Square, in front of the parliament, still bore the scars of five years of protest against the economic crisis. But in the gardens behind the parliament, all was calm and untouched. The statue of the poet stares up appreciatively at a bare-bosomed Hellas, who crowns him with a laurel wreath.

No wonder Byron's still so popular. Not only did he die in the cause of Greek independence. He was also furiously opposed to the Elgin Marbles being stripped from the Parthenon. The new Mrs George Clooney, Amal Alamuddin, is not the first British media darling to get plus points for wanting to return the marbles.

In *Childe Harold's Pilgrimage*, written in 1810, the year he swam the Hellespont, Byron wrote of Lord Elgin, 'Of all the plunderers of yon fane [the Parthenon] ... the last, the worst, dull spoiler, who was he? Blush, Caledonia, such thy son could be!'

Addressing the Parthenon, Byron put Amal Alamuddin's case perfectly:

Dull is the eye that will not weep to see
Thy walls defaced, thy mouldering shrines removed
By British hands, which it had best behoved
To guard those relics ne'er to be restored.
Curst be the hour when from their isle they roved,
And once again thy hapless bosom gored,
And snatch'd thy shrinking gods to northern climes abhorred!

Still, Byron failed to deal with the question that now bedevils Mrs Clooney's finely honed legal mind: is modern Greece the natural successor to the city state of Athens that commissioned them?

Greeks today certainly think so. That was the line put by Antonis Samaras, then the Greek prime minister, in December 2014. The Elgin Marbles statue of the river god Ilissos – named after a river that still runs through Athens – had just been lent by the British Museum to the Hermitage in St Petersburg. 'We Greeks are at one with our history and civilisation, which cannot be broken up, loaned out, or conceded,' Samaras said.

Taki, the *Spectator*'s High Life correspondent, agrees with Samaras. He likes to tease his British readers by saying we were living off roots and scratching our furry parts while Greece was building the Parthenon. True enough – but

I'm afraid the geniuses of ancient Athens have mixed with quite a few furry-part-scratchers over the past 2,500 years.

Athens, and much of Greece, was under Ottoman rule for 400 years. By the time Greece rebelled against Ottoman rule in the 1820s, its peasant economy had missed out on the Enlightenment altogether.

The Venetians, too, occupied many of the Greek islands, and bits and bobs of the mainland, for centuries. The ancient Greeks took over Sicily and much of southern Italy; the northern Italians returned the favour several thousand years later.

Many Greeks from the Ionian Islands – conquered by the Venetians, not the Turks – remain Catholic, thanks to Venetian occupation. Among them is Taki. He has written warmly of the Venetians for selling titles to the Greeks in return for their conversion to Catholicism.

Not everyone agrees that modern Greeks are the natural cultural descendants of ancient Greece. The decline of modern Greece is at the heart of the 1960 hit film *Never on Sunday*. Melina Mercouri plays a good-time girl/prostitute – *porne* in ancient Greek; thus pornography, from *pornographos*, 'someone who illustrates prostitutes'.

Mercouri's character, Ilya, plies her trade in the Athenian port of Piraeus. An American classicist from Connecticut – Homer Thrace – sees in her the collapse of ancient Greek values, and tries to redeem her through literature. For a fortnight, she gives up prostitution and turns to self-education, only to give it all up when scholarly life proves too dull. It's a Greek version of *My Fair Lady* or, further back, *Pygmalion* – itself inspired by Ovid's story of Pygmalion, a Cypriot sculptor who fell in love with his lifelike, staggeringly beautiful, ivory statue of Galatea.

However great the chasm between ancient and modern Greece, the modern country is still largely defined, in foreign eyes, by its ancient inheritance. It might well have been saved by that inheritance, too.

At the Potsdam Conference in Berlin in 1945, Winston Churchill claimed to have rescued Greece from disappearing behind Stalin's Iron Curtain. After the war, Russia grabbed the Balkans and most of Eastern Europe, except for Greece. 'This brand I snatched from the burning on Christmas Day,' said Churchill.

In his 1946 Iron Curtain speech in Fulton, Missouri, Churchill hinted why he chose to save Greece – because of its ancient inheritance. Talking of the countries behind the curtain, Churchill said, 'Athens alone – Greece with its immortal glories – is free to decide its future at an election under British, American and French observation.'

In fact, Greece went through some pretty undemocratic phases over the next 30 years: a civil war between Communists and anti-Communists, the 1967 coup by the colonels, who held power until 1974, and the abolition of the monarchy in 1973. And, despite Churchill's best efforts, Greece still feels more eastern than European, not least thanks to the considerable influence of the Greek Orthodox Church.

Greece has been in and out of trouble ever since it got independence from the Ottomans in 1832. In 1893, only three years before the glory of the first modern Olympiad in Athens, Greece went bankrupt. The latest economic crisis is nothing new.

It was Greece's ancient inheritance, too, which meant German politicians were keen for Greece to join the EEC in 1981. What better imprimatur for the European ideal than to admit the country that invented democracy? Later, John Major recalled that, when the subject of Greece joining the euro cropped up, other leaders insisted, 'You cannot say no to the country of Plato.' Major added, 'Maybe not, but every European is now paying the price for admitting an economically unfit nation to compete in the eurozone.'

Like a son growing up in the shadow of his famous father, Greece hasn't entirely benefited from its pre-eminent ancient ancestor. But it is still Homer's view of ancient Greece that dominates the modern view of Greek civilisation. Tourists are still drawn to classical ruins by the wine-dark sea; olive oil remains the biggest export from the Peloponnese, as it was in Homer's time.

When Taki refers to Athens as the Big Olive, he knows whereof he speaks. Greece's vegetation alters as you go north – from the dryness of southern Chios to the tropical jungle of Corfu in the north – but the whole country is rich in olives. The olive belt runs out not long after you move above Greece's northern latitudes.

Ancient Greece still dominates the political and commercial view of the modern country, too. At the height of the Greek crisis, in early 2015, the *Economist* got into hot water for its cover. It showed the Venus de Milo statue pointing a gun, above the caption, 'Go ahead, Angela, make my day.' When a cartoonist wants to signify modern Greece, he draws ancient Greece.

There's a shop opposite the British Museum, It's All Greek, selling Greek souvenirs. Except it's not all Greek – it's all ancient Greek. The windows are packed with copies of ancient artefacts – early Cycladic figures; the Horse of Selene from the pediment of the Parthenon; a charming little Mycenean piglet; a gold-sprayed olive wreath.

Olive wreaths were genuinely used for winners at the Olympic Games. That's why Hitler, hardly the most peaceful of men, received an olive branch from Olympia after the lighting of the eternal flame at the 1936 Berlin Olympics. Laurel wreaths – in honour of the laurel tree Apollo was born under on Delos – were used at Delphic competitions; pine wreaths at Isthmian games; and flimsy celery wreaths at Nemean ones.

At It's All Greek, there are some Etruscan vases from pre-Roman Italy in the window. But that's the latest it gets: there's absolutely nothing from modern Greece, or anything from the last 2,000 years. It's as if Greece stopped exporting its values at the end of the Athenian golden age.

The same goes for the Greek influence on architecture. There are no buildings in Britain inspired by modern Greece. But there are literally millions of terraced houses whose classical proportions are derived from the ancient world; not least the British Museum itself, with its giant Ionic portico, just across the road from It's All Greek.

Byron was thoroughly aware of Greece's decline from greatness. In *Childe Harold's Pilgrimage* he wrote,

Fair Greece! sad relic of departed worth!
Immortal, though no more; though fallen great!

Byron died for the Greece of Homer and Pericles. In the only poem he wrote in Greece – 'On this day, I complete my 36th year' – Byron produced more stirring, philhellenic lines, only three months before his death on Greece's behalf:

The sword, the banner – and the field –
Glory and Greece around me see!
The Spartan, borne upon his shield,
Was not more free.
Awake – not Greece. She is awake!
Awake, my spirit!

That reference to the Spartan's shield came from the legend that Spartan women said to their sons when they went off to fight, 'Come back with your shield – or on it.' To surrender – and give up your shield – was the ultimate disgrace.

Byron's devotion to the Greek cause was total. He gave a large chunk of his fortune to the Greek fleet, and commanded the Byron Brigade – hardened Souliot warriors from north-west Greece.

In a celebrated painting – *The Reception of Lord Byron at Missolonghi* by Theodoros Vryzakis – Byron greets his Greek soldiers in very modern-looking, civilian clothes: white trousers and shirt, black jacket and boots, all wrapped in what looks like an ancient Greek toga. In fact, Byron had that same tailor in Genoa run up a scarlet military uniform for him, to give the impression of a man of action.

There wasn't much time for action. Byron planned to attack the Turks 20 miles east from Missolonghi, at Lepanto – site of the 1571 Battle of Lepanto, the great Holy League victory over the Ottoman Empire.

Before he could join battle, Byron fell ill – in Easter Week, when local Greeks put off their usual celebrations out of concern for him. When Byron died on Easter Monday, 19 April, the Easter celebrations were cancelled altogether, replaced by three weeks of mourning.

Romantics claim that, if Byron had lived and beaten the Turks, he'd have been made King of Greece. As it was, he wasn't even buried in Greece. His body was taken back to England. Refused a place in Westminster Abbey because of his scandalous exploits, he was buried in the family vault in St Mary Magdalene, Hucknall Torkard, Nottinghamshire.

The real King of Greece – George I, a Danish prince and Queen Alexandra's brother, picked as king in 1863 – paid for the church's marble plaque, with Greek laurel wreaths inscribed in brass around Byron's name.

Byron studied both Latin and Greek at Harrow and Cambridge – but there was no doubt which language, and which civilisation, he thought superior. In 'The Isles of Greece', Byron made quite clear what he thought of the Roman victory over the Greeks:

But Turkish force and Latin fraud
Would break your shield, however broad.

This contrary idea – that the earlier, defeated civilisation was more sophisticated than the later one – went right back to the Romans themselves. Perhaps it had something to do with the Trojan War. Aeneas, Rome's mythical founder, was a Trojan – second cousin once removed of Priam, King of the Trojans, no less. And the Trojans lost to the Greeks; a fact that Homer, a Greek, never exulted in.

Wouldn't the Romans have preferred Mycenae – home town of Agamemnon, the Greek leader – to be Rome's parent, rather than that iconic Loserville, Troy? The idea of Trojan condoms always slightly worries me, too – wouldn't Greek condoms be a more reliable bet? The phrase 'He fought like a Trojan' also seems a bit odd. Wouldn't you prefer to fight like a Greek winner?

Rome got its revenge for the Trojan defeat in its ultimate victory over Greece. And yet the Romans went on indulging the Greek civilisation they'd conquered.

There's very little anti-Greek feeling in Latin literature, except for the most famous of Hellenophobe quotations, 'Beware of Greeks bearing gifts.' This appears in *The Aeneid*, Book 2, when the Trojan priest, Laocoön, warns the Trojans not to accept the horse.

Equo ne credite, Teucri! says Laocoön. *Quidquid id est, timeo Danaos et dona ferentis*: 'Don't trust the horse, Trojans! Whatever it is, I fear the Danaans [or the Greeks], even when they're bringing gifts.'

Long after Greece was conquered by Rome, it retained its hold over Roman culture. As the Roman poet Horace wrote, in his first-century BC *Epistles*, 'Captive Greece took her savage victor captive, and brought the arts into rustic Latium [the heartland of the Roman Empire].'

It isn't surprising Horace was such a philhellene. His first language might well have been Greek; and he was the first poet to combine Latin verse with the full range of archaic Greek music. Still, he did say, in the same letter, that Greece had lost its way in recent centuries:

> Once she'd finished her wars, Greece became silly; slipped into bad habits in the easy times. She fell in love, now with athletes, now with horses; her passion was for sculptors and carvers; she fixed her mind and soul on painted panels; she was besotted with flautists and tragic actors; like a baby girl playing with her nurse, she flung away the toys she begged for.

That idea of Greeks as weak aesthetes to Rome's tough guys lingered into the modern age. In his Winston Churchill biography, Boris Johnson wrote that, if Britain had capitulated to Germany in the war, it would have been 'fundamentally effete: Greeks to the Nazi Rome'.

Still, the feeling survived that those effete Greeks were more culturally sophisticated than the Romans. In the 1940s, Harold Macmillan – who got a first in his Classics Mods at Balliol – said, 'You will find the Americans much like the Greeks found the Romans: great, big, vulgar, bustling people more vigorous than we are and also more idle, with more unspoiled virtues but also more corrupt.'

Whether they were effete or not, the Greeks certainly lost their grip on the number one skill: fighting. That's why Rome conquered Greece – thanks to the superiority of the Roman legion over the Greek phalanx formation. A phalanx – Greek for 'finger' – marched in a single block of infantry, armed with pikes and spears. A legion was a vast group of 5,400 infantrymen and cavalrymen, divided into ten nimble maniples or cohorts. Because of Roman military supremacy, the writing was on the wall for the Greeks by the third century BC.

In 279 BC, Pyrrhus, a Greek leader, beat a Roman consul, Publius Decius Mus, at the Battle of Asculum in southern Italy. Still, the victory was so costly for the Greeks that Pyrrhus said of it, 'If we are victorious in one more battle with the Romans, we shall be utterly ruined.' Thus a Pyrrhic victory.

The final Roman conquest of old Greece came at the Battle of Corinth in 146 BC, when the Roman province of Achaea was created out of southern Greece. By the time of the battle, ancient Corinth was held up as the height of riches, luxury and laziness – paid for by the toll fees they charged for crossing the Corinthian isthmus, before the canal was built. On the proceeds of all that cash, the Corinthians went sex mad. Their Temple of Aphrodite was so crammed with courtesans that Aristophanes referred to sex as Corinthing.

Five hundred years later, the Corinthians were still on the job. In his first letter to the Corinthians, written in Ephesus, St Paul said, 'It is reported commonly that there is fornication among you.' This self-indulgent side of Corinth explains why 'Corinthian' was used in nineteenth-century Britain and America of rich, amateur sportsmen, particularly yachtsmen. And that sailing aspect explains why the cruise ship I lectured on was called the *Corinthian*. It couldn't have been anything to do with the sex addict side of things. I did no Corinthing in my three weeks aboard.

Only later did Corinthian come to mean those who played a game for the sheer, idealistic love of it – as in the Corinthian Casuals, the Surrey amateur football team – rather than for wicked money-grubbing reasons. A word meaning plutocratic self-indulgence performed a full backflip, to mean austere athleticism.

Once Corinth fell, Rome only had to mop up a few sad, effete fragments of the wreckage of ancient Greece. The last Hellenistic Greek kingdom to fall was Antony and Cleopatra's Ptolemaic Egypt, defeated in 31 BC at the Battle of Actium by Augustus. But, even as Greece gave way to Rome, Greek remained the ultimate in civilised languages for centuries to come.

ANCIENT SPARTA (RESTORED).

The glory that was Sparta – before the Spartans turned soft. (1890 drawing)

The Acropolis in 1810, when Athens was still under Ottoman control. In the fore-ground is the Temple of Olympian Zeus, the biggest temple in Greece in the Roman period. Begun in the sixth century BC, it was finished by the Emperor Hadrian in 132 AD.

The Greeks invented the Doric order of the Parthenon and the Corinthian order of the Temple of Olympian Zeus, as well as the Ionic order. The Romans could only come up with the Composite order – a combination of Ionic and Corinthian. (1810 picture)

4

Shakespeare's Classical Education

Julius Caesar's last words, as he bled to death on the floor of the Roman Senate, weren't, *Et tu, Brute*? They were, *Kai su, teknon* – 'You, too, my child?'

He wasn't the only Greek speaker in the Senate that day. Casca, the first assassin to attack Caesar, cried out to his conspirators, *Adelphe, boethei* – 'Brother, help.' Brutus and the rest of them knew their Greek, too: they duly piled in, daggers at the ready.

As for Cleopatra, she may have been the Egyptian Queen of the Nile and have fallen for the Roman general Mark Antony, but she had a Greek name – from *kleos*, 'glory', and *pater*, 'father'. She also spoke Greek – with a Macedonian accent.

Roman emperors continued to speak Greek long after they had conquered Greece. When Constantine converted to Christianity, he did it in Greek. On the night before the battle of the Milvian Bridge, in AD 312, he had a vision that changed the course of the Roman Empire – the world even – and ultimately turned Britain into a Christian country.

Looking above the heads of his marching soldiers, Constantine saw a burning cross of light above the sun, next to the Greek words, *en toutoi nika* – 'In this sign, you will conquer.' The following night, Christ appeared to Constantine in a dream, telling him to use the sign against his enemies. Constantine did as he was told. He stuck a cross on his army's shields, won the battle, killed his rival Maxentius, became undisputed Roman Emperor, and the rest is history – Christian history.

Throughout much of the Roman Empire, Greek remained the closest thing to a world language, particularly in imperial circles – a nod to the superior, older civilisation, in whose image the emperors shaped themselves. In the eastern Mediterranean, ancient Greek was the lingua franca from the fourth-century BC conquests by Alexander the Great until the ancient form shifted into Byzantine Greek, in around AD 600.

You begin to see why the Romans continued to revere their defeated enemy – again and again, the Greeks got there first; not just in literature, but in architecture, sculpture, art, history, economics, philosophy, political history, the natural sciences, maths, comedy, tragedy, drama, epic poetry, physics and metaphysics.

Of the four classical orders of architecture, three were invented by the Greeks – and the fourth, the only one the Romans could come up with, was the Composite order, a lazy combination of two of the Greek ones.

The Romans slavishly copied Greek statues. The most famous surviving Greek statues are Roman copies – from Myron's Discus-thrower to Pheidias's Wounded Amazon and Praxiteles's naked Aphrodite of Cnidus. Quintilian, the Roman rhetorician, was happy to acknowledge the mass Roman theft of Greek originals. *Satura quidem tota nostra est*, he said. 'At least satire is completely ours.'

Those uninspired Romans did at least dream up the novel; although Milan Kundera claimed the novel, too, was really the natural descendant of *The Odyssey*. The poor old Romans lose out again.

Even as Athens declined in importance, its cultural legacy lived on under centuries of Roman rule: the Athenian schools of philosophy weren't closed until AD 529, under the Edict of Justinian. Smart, young Romans went to Athens for their Grand Tour gap years, among them the little rich kids Horace, Cicero and Julius Caesar. Brutus moved to Athens when the political temperature got too hot in Rome after Caesar's assassination in 44 BC. A dip into Greek life was their version of university. As Philostratus said in his third-century AD *Life of Apollonius of Tyana*, 'Everything is Greece to the wise man.'

In AD 54, St Paul preached on the Areopagus – the great flat chunk of limestone next to the Acropolis that acted as the ancient Greek Court of Appeal. The Acropolis had been the site of Greek justice for half a millennium – it was on the Acropolis that Orestes was acquitted for the murder of his mother, Clytemnestra in Aeschylus's *Oresteia*. Here the Western European court was born. Athenian citizens acted as jurors in the Athenian courts – and that's what happens at the end of the *Oresteia*. Orestes is tried for matricide by the goddess Athena, one of a jury of 12 selected by Athena from the Athenian citizens.

Much of the infrastructure of ancient Greece was still in place when Paul arrived in Athens. The Epicureans and the Stoics – philosophy schools founded in the fourth century BC – collared him by the Areopagus. According to the New Testament, they were concerned – quite accurately as it turned out – that he was 'a setter forth of strange gods'.

'What will this babbler say?' the Epicureans and the Stoics asked.

Standing on the rock, St Paul answered them robustly: 'God that made the world and all things therein, seeing that he is Lord of heaven and earth, dwelleth not in temples made with hands.'

A bold thing to say in the shadow of the greatest handmade temple in the world: the Parthenon.

When the Emperor Hadrian got to Athens in the second century AD, he still revered the heroes of Greek legend. On his Arch of Hadrian – which still stands on the fringes of the ancient city – the emperor acknowledged the old supremacy of Greece. The inscription on the Acropolis side of the arch read, 'This is Athens, the ancient city of Theseus [the legendary founder of Athens].' On the new, Roman side, another inscription read, 'This is the city of Hadrian and not of Theseus.'

Back in Rome, there were so many Greek slaves that Greek was probably spoken more often than Latin. The Romans even produced a series of bilingual textbooks of conversation – called *Colloquia*, as in 'colloquial' – written in Greek and Latin. Young Romans learnt grammar and vocabulary through textbook stories in Greek and Latin – just as I did at Westminster, in the dying days of the classical tradition. Eighty of these *Colloquia* recorded a schoolboy's mind-numbingly dull lunchtime conversations and his visits to the baths:

> I awoke from sleep before dawn, got out of bed, sat down … and put on my shoes. I asked for water for my face: I washed my hands first, then I washed my face … I anointed my head and combed it … I left the bedroom with my pedagogue and nurse to say good morning to my father and mother. I greeted and kissed them both and then left the house and go to school.

Under the Roman Empire, Greece remained the architectural ideal. In *Description of Greece* – a second-century AD list of tourist sights – Pausanias lavished praise on the Parthenon but said nothing about the newly built Roman temple next to it. The country's first ever guidebook, *Description of Greece,* set the pattern for today's visitors. Pausanias mentioned Athens, Corinth, Delphi and the Temple of Apollo at Bassae – where the Corinthian order was used for the first time, in the mid-fifth century BC. All remain five-star sights for the modern tourist.

When Antipater, a Greek from Sidon, wrote a poem about the seven wonders of the world in 140 BC, there wasn't a single Roman building among them, even after Greece had been eclipsed by the new empire.

That idea of defeated Greece being the superior civilisation to victorious Rome lingered in Western Europe until half a century ago. In his 1623 ode to Shakespeare, Ben Jonson said the playwright 'hadst small Latin, and less Greek'. Jonson was, unwittingly, making the same point: Greek was the higher of the two callings, the necessary qualification for the civilised mind.

Shakespeare pre-empted Jonson in *Julius Caesar* – when Casca said of Cicero's unintelligible speech that 'It was Greek to me.' Casca's catchphrase survives today, in altered form – 'It's all Greek to me.' When I finished my odyssey in Ithaca, I was solemnly assured by a guide that the Greeks say, 'It's all Chinese to me' as their alternative.

For centuries, Greece remained a code word for the origins of Western European culture. The study of Classics was – and still is, to a fading degree – another code word for intelligence. Literally, in the case of the egghead code-breakers at Bletchley Park during the Second World War. When they went to the pub at lunchtime, it was ancient Greek that the real show-offs chatted in.

The academic deference to the classical world is clear even in that name, 'Classics'. The word retains its own inner boast; as do two of the names for the Classics course at Oxford – *Literae Humaniores* ('more humane letters') and Greats.

By the seventeenth century, Classics was at the heart of a sophisticated British education. When the erotic poet Lord Rochester went up to Wadham College, Oxford, in 1660, he was only allowed to speak Latin and Greek at lunch – bread and cheese with weak beer in Wadham's dining hall.

This idea didn't work when it was attempted on a commercial basis. Half a century later, Richard Hogarth, the painter's father, a Latin teacher, set up a Latin-only coffee house in Clerkenwell. He lost all his money and went to Fleet Prison for five years for debt.

Schools, too, were devoted to classical studies. When my old school, Westminster, was founded in 1560 by Queen Elizabeth I, it was expressly designed as 'A publique schoole for Grammar, Rhethorick, Poetrie, and for the Latin and Greek Languages'. The same went for hundreds of grammar schools across the country in the sixteenth century, including Shakespeare's school, the King's New School in Stratford, set up in 1533. And the grammar they learnt at those grammar schools was Greek and Latin grammar.

Until fairly recently, it remained a commonly held British belief that Greek was the foundation of the properly developed intellect. The educated Victorian Englishman – and it was usually a man – felt closer to, and knew more about, the ancient Greeks than the Anglo-Saxons.

Greek was so widespread among the intelligentsia of nineteenth-century Britain that the headmaster of Rugby, Thomas Arnold, could write to a friend in 1829 about his pupils: 'Being the sons of quieter parents, they have far less hubris [pride] and more euetheia [good nature] than the boys of any other school.'

Gladstone wrote three hefty books about Homer, doing much of the research while he was still prime minister – among them *Homeric Synchronism: An Enquiry into the Time and Place of Homer*. Rumours of his dangerous Homer obsession got out while Gladstone was in Downing Street. He quickly wrote a letter to the *Spectator*, denying the accusation that he started every day with 'his old friend Homer.'

The nineteenth-century elite even wrote to each other in Greek. In the 1880s, Heinrich Schliemann, the German archaeologist who excavated Troy, wrote a thank-you letter to the Marquess of Dufferin and Ava. Dufferin had been Viceroy of India, Ambassador to the Ottoman Empire and, in Schliemann's words, *toi philomousoi thaumastei tou theiou Homerou*, 'the Muse-loving admirer of the divine Homer'. 'As soon as I saw your handwriting in Greek,' Schliemann wrote, also in ancient Greek, 'I recognised it and I read it again and again.'

That expectation of a classical knowledge wasn't confined to scholars and obsessives. Schliemann fell in love with *The Iliad* as a teenager, when he heard a drunken miller recite 100 lines of Homer in the grocer's shop he worked in.

Thomas Hardy was confident enough of his readers' intellect to finish *Tess of the D'Urbervilles* with the line, 'The President of the Immortals, in the Aeschylean phrase, had finished his sport with Tess.' And Mary Anne Disraeli, the prime minister's wife, was mocked for saying she could 'never remember who came first, the Greeks or the Romans'.

Writers in search of a quintessential Victorian or Edwardian schoolmaster tend to plump for Classics teachers. Mr Chipping – as in *Goodbye, Mr Chips*; the teacher who remains at Brookfield School for half a century leading up to the First World War – is a Classics master. In Terence Rattigan's *The Browning Version*, Andrew Crocker-Harris, the elderly curmudgeon nicknamed 'the Crock', teaches Classics.

In both works, the poignant plot depends on their high-minded, classical crustiness being cracked by kindness: in Mr Chips's case, by a lovely wife 20 years his junior, who dies young; in the Crock's case, by the boy who gives him a copy of Robert Browning's translation – or version – of Aeschylus's *Agamemnon*.

Those odd, clever connotations of Classics loomed large in Mycroft Holmes, Sherlock Holmes's even more intelligent brother. When Mycroft set up a London club, he called it the Diogenes Club after the Greek philosopher, Diogenes the Cynic. The Diogenes was for the cleverest, oddest men in London. Diogenes the Cynic was certainly odd. Thinking all social conventions trivial, he took to living in a large ceramic jar – often mistakenly called a barrel – and masturbating in public.

Freedom was the Cynics' watchword: freedom of speech, freedom to rise above conventions, hardship and luxury, like Diogenes in his jar; the freedom of becoming a citizen of the world, or a *kosmopolites*, as in 'cosmopolitan'. And the freedom to have loads of sex. The Cynics got their name from *kunikos* – 'dog-like' – because they were rumoured to mate in the streets like dogs.

'It now contains the most unsociable and unclubbable men in town,' Sherlock Holmes said of the Diogenes Club. 'No member is permitted to take the least notice of any other one. Save in the Strangers Room, no talking is, under any circumstances, allowed, and three offences, if brought to the notice of the committee, render the talker liable to expulsion. My brother was one of the founders, and I have myself found it a very soothing atmosphere.'

The real-life London club for brainy people – dons and bishops – is Grecian, too: the Athenaeum, which takes its name from Athena, goddess of wisdom. Athena – and her Roman counterpart, Minerva – were often accompanied by an owl, the symbol of wisdom. Thus Hegel's line, 'Only when the dusk starts to fall does the owl of Minerva spread its wings and fly.'

Eighteenth- and nineteenth-century America inherited the British love of ancient Greece, not least in the university fraternities. The first eighteenth-century fraternity – set up in 1750 at the College of William and Mary in Williamsburg, Virginia – was a Latin one: the FHC society, short for *Fraternitas, Humanitas, et Cognitio*, 'Brotherhood, Humanity and Knowledge'. Among the first members of the FHC – nicknamed the Flat Hat Club – was one Thomas Jefferson.

The FHC was a kind of American Bullingdon Club, with members carousing with sailors and soldiers in the rough Raleigh Tavern in downtown Williamsburg. The disapproving university authorities sent out scouts to track down the members. To avoid the scouts, members came up with their own secret handshakes, oaths and passwords. These practices were copied by the first Greek society, the Phi Beta Kappa Society, founded in 1776; short for *philosophia biou kybernetes* – 'Philosophy is the helmsman of life.' Phi Beta Kappa was set up by students who couldn't get into the Flat Hat Club. The rejects' club, an altogether more serious organisation, began by calling itself a literary fraternity.

America quickly went Greek-mad, with chapters opening in universities across America. The Greek habit even spread to the Ku Klux Klan, set up in Pulaski, Tennessee, in 1865 by six Confederate veterans. You could call the Klan – named after the Greek word, *kuklos*, 'circle' – America's least agreeable Greek fraternity, worse even than John Belushi's Delta Tau Chi fraternity in *Animal House*.

After a lull during the Civil War, fraternities boomed again, and the growth has continued ever since, both in terms of the number of chapters and their members. The University of Illinois, the Greekest campus on earth, has 46 fraternities and 23 sororities.

Every year for the last decade, since 2005, the number of American frat members has increased by 4 per cent, despite the authorities cracking down on *Animal House*-style behaviour. At the University of Virginia, a frat heartland, new rules outlaw beer kegs and the consumption of pre-mixed drinks. Three 'sober monitors' pour all drinks and prevent amorous frat boys going upstairs with tipsy sorority girls.

Wall Street has its own Greek fraternity: Kappa Beta Phi, a mocking inversion of that original one, the Phi Beta Kappa. Since 1929, the club has gathered for the induction of new members. New members – mighty hedge-funders and chief executives – bellow the frat motto, *Dum vivamus edimus et biberimus*: 'While we live, we eat and drink.'

At a recent Kappa Beta Phi gathering in the St Regis Hotel in Manhattan, the new members, dressed in leotards, gold-sequinned skirts and women's wigs, did drunken skits. A hedgie, a CEO and a top investor did a financial parody of the Village People's YMCA. An executive from RBC Capital Markets sang a number called, 'Mama, Don't Let Your Babies Grow Up To Be Traders'.

Well into the twentieth century, Classics remained the crucial subject at British public schools. A century ago, all Oxford candidates sat a Greek entrance paper. Until 1931, all Yale applicants took a compulsory Latin exam. Oxbridge only removed Latin as a matriculation requirement in 1960. Louis MacNeice mocked the classical obsession of public schools and Oxbridge in a 1920s poem:

> Which things being so, as we said when we studied
> The classics, I ought to be glad
> That I studied the classics at Marlborough and Merton,
> Not everyone here having had
> The privilege of learning a language
> That is incontrovertibly dead,
> And of carting a toy-box of hall-marked marmoreal phrases
> Around in his head.
> We wrote compositions in Greek which they said was a lesson
> In logic and good for the brain;

We marched, counter-marched to the field-marshal's blue-pencil baton,
We dressed by the right and we wrote out the sentence again.
We learned that a gentleman never misplaces his accents,
That nobody knows how to speak, much less how to write
English who has not hob-nobbed with the great-grand-parents of English,
That the boy on the Modern Side is merely a parasite.

Parasite, by the way, was originally the Greek word for a fellow diner.

Thirty years after MacNeice wrote his poem, Classics still reigned supreme in British public schools, according to former *Private Eye* editor Richard Ingrams. Ingrams was taught Classics, to the exclusion of almost everything else: 'The only concession was divinity, and that consisted of reading the New Testament in Greek.'

Still, a slow decline in classical rigour had been setting in since the First World War. In 1913, Mr Chipping, that crusty 65-year-old Classics master in *Goodbye, Mr Chips*, realised he was one of the dwindling number of people who understood the classical references in short leaders in *The Times*. Even Mr Chips secretly thought of 'Latin and Greek far more as dead languages from which English gentlemen ought to know a few quotations than as living tongues that had ever been spoken by living people.'

Evelyn Waugh wrote about the decline of Greek in *Scott-King's Modern Europe*, his 1947 novella about a Greek master at a dim public school. Scott-King is invited to the Eastern European state of Neutralia to lecture on the even dimmer Renaissance Latin poet, Bellorius:

When Scott-King was a boy and when he first returned as a master, the school was almost equally divided into a Classical and a Modern side, with a group of negligible and neglected specialists called 'the Army Class'. Now the case was altered and, out of 450 boys, scarcely 50 read Greek.

Still, even in the post-war years of decline, Classics in translation did well; one translation of *The Odyssey* in particular, by E. V. Rieu. I still think E. V. Rieu's 1946 translation is the best, flowery and dated though it can be. The first Penguin Classic, it inspired the 1,300-strong Penguin Classics series, commissioned by Allen Lane, Penguin's founder. Rieu edited the series until 1964. In London, in the early years of the war, Rieu would sit after supper, as the Blitz was raging, and translate *The Odyssey* to his wife and children across the dining table. His translation sold three million copies. In 2003, his son, D. C. H. Rieu, revised his father's translation.

That respect for the supposed intellect of classicists hasn't entirely vanished today. When I was a *Daily Telegraph* leader-writer a decade ago, I was asked by the editor, Charles Moore, to write a whole editorial in Latin. The fact that few readers would understand it was neither here nor there. The *Telegraph* was showing it was still part of the hallowed group that conversed easily in Greek and Latin. No one ever wrote a leader in French, German or hieroglyphics.

The elite associations of ancient Greece – held so dear by the Romans – linger on today, in odd, little pockets. Banks still use Greek names for investment vehicles: from Artemis ('the Profit Hunter' – not one of her divine gifts, as far as I know) to Isis Equity Partners, Hermes Investment Funds Plc, Neptune ('Invest in Depth') and Troy Asset Management; not forgetting Ithaca Energy or Ithaka Harbors, the non-profit organisation that owns JSTOR, the digital academic library. In November 2014, incidentally, Isis Equity Partners changed its name to Living Bridge, in order not to be confused with the terrorist group. A banker friend tells me they're rapidly running out of classical names for their products: Hubris and Nemesis are still available.

Homeric myth survives in the strangest places. On 2 March 2014, the *Sunday Times* Style section devoted a page to the hip Helen of Troy look: 'It's time to launch your own thousand ships, starting with the gilded gloss of Helen of Troy… Terry Barber, director of make-up artistry at Mac, suggests using flecks of gold for a sunlit facial glow: "It's about pinpoint highlighting in all the right places – the centre of the lash line on the upper lid, the bridge of the nose and the cupid's bow."'

Even in mass culture, Greek originals echo down the millennia. At the time of writing, the latest schlocky superhero film in the cinemas is *Hercules*, the Roman name for the Greek hero, Heracles – another example of a Roman theft of a Greek original. Hollywood has constantly plundered ancient Greece for plotlines: from *Alexander the Great* (1956), which was really about corruption and juvenile delinquency in 1950s America, to *The 300 Spartans* (1962).

This told the story of the Battle of Thermopylae in 480 BC – when 300 heroic Spartans and their leader, Leonidas, were slaughtered in a narrow pass by the double-dealing Persians, who crept behind them through a secret route in the mountains. In an echo of Anglo-American post-war politics, the Spartans were played by Americans and their Greek allies by the British. In the 2007 film, *300*, the story was retold with the Middle East as the enemy.

For all its popular influence, the formal study of Greek has been pretty much eradicated from the British education system over the last half-century, a few private schools and grammar schools apart – and, even there, only in a few rarefied classes of eggheads and aesthetes. In March 2015, there came the sad news that Camden School for Girls in north London – the last non-selective state school to offer Greek at A-Level – was planning to stop teaching the subject to its three Greek A-Level students. Greek is now essentially extinct for the vast majority of pupils in the country.

The reason for the relative decline of Greek versus Latin is easy to explain: the different letters. That's why people who have studied ancient Greek are considered so brainy. That, and the fact that Greek has more inflections, or changing word endings, than Latin. The average Latin verb has over two hundred endings; English verbs rarely have more than five. Greek ones can have well over a thousand.

Greek has all sorts of forms not used in English, among them the optative – a type of verb used to express wish or desire. It also has the Dual – a word used only of two people or objects. Utterly useless in modern English – although the writer Stanley Johnson, father of Boris, once told me he longs for a Dual to counter his wife and one of his daughters when they gang up on him.

Greek has the same Indo-European origin as Latin – and, indeed, Sanskrit, Teutonic and Celtic. But, even though it came before Latin, it is more flexible in nuances of expression and meaning. It has more participles – ten to Latin's three – allowing for more subordinate clauses. And it has a whole pack of conjunctions that can flip sentences on their head and alter their meaning.

Ancient Greek also had different pitches – marked from the third century BC with circumflex, grave and acute accents – making the language extremely musical. Sappho's poetry had the devilish Mixolydian mode, with note pitches at quarter-tone intervals – and that was in the seventh century BC.

Long gone are the days when undergraduates knew the Mixolydian mode and the Dual. But that old-fashioned, high-minded, classical tradition was in full swing in the 1880s, when my great-grandfather studied Classics at Christ Church, Oxford. When he set off to fight at Gallipoli in 1915 – one of the oldest soldiers there, at 50 – he was longing to see Troy. He didn't get far beyond Gallipoli's killer beaches.

Work a classical look, as at Dolce & Gabbana.
Rococo Nail Apparel Gold Leaf Lacquer, £35;
uk.spacenk.com. Liz Earle Radiant Glow Bronzer, £17.
Lancôme Miracle Air de Teint foundation in 03, £30;
selfridges.com. YSL Glass Volupté in Gold, £21

HELEN OF TROY

It's time to launch your own thousand ships, starting with the gilded gloss of Helen of Troy, which was much re-created for this season. But it isn't only about bronzed limbs and Grecian curls. Terry Barber, director of make-up artistry at Mac, suggests using flecks of gold for a sunlit facial glow: "It's about pinpoint highlighting in all the right places — the centre of the lash line on the upper lid, the bridge of the nose and the cupid's bow." At Dries Van Noten, Peter Philips placed flakes of gold leaf into the models' partings and eyelashes; Pat McGrath blended elemental bronze V shapes into socket lines at Gucci; and at

Dolce, nymph-like models wore headdresses of Roman coins. Give the gilding a strong foundation by prepping skin thoroughly: massage dry areas with a hydrating essence, or mix a couple of drops of face oil into your foundation. "The complexion has to be summery, gorgeous and glowing," says Tom Pecheux, who maximised the glow by giving models a facial backstage at Balmain. Keep your base ethereally light: work a make-up-free look or stick to sheer formulations such as Lancôme Miracle Air de Teint (£29.50; selfridges.com). Apply it with your fingers so that it becomes one with the skin.

Beauty never goes out of fashion – the Sunday Times style section, March 2nd, 2014.

An empty grave – My great-grandfather's tombstone at Green Hill Cemetery, Gallipoli.

5

My Great-Grandfather's Cenotaph at Gallipoli

For someone who'd read Classics at Oxford, the sight of Troy must have been strangely moving.

As he sailed towards Gallipoli, my great-grandfather, the fifth Earl of Longford, could just make out a small mound commanding the flat plains of Ilion, the ancient site of Troy. Excavated only 40 years before by Schliemann, Troy had already reverted to its martial role: the Turks had dug a trench and set up a machine-gun post on top of Priam's citadel. Longford wrote back to his family in Ireland, saying how he had looked across to Troy from his ship and longed to visit it.

He wasn't the only one stirred by parallels between Gallipoli and the Trojan War. Just before Rupert Brooke died – at sea, of a mosquito bite infection, days before landing at Gallipoli – he wrote in his notebook,

> They say Achilles in the darkness stirred …
> And Priam and his 50 sons
> Wake all amazed, and hear the guns,
> And shake for Troy again.

When the Senegalese troops of the French 6th Colonial Regiment landed on the Asian side of the strait a century ago, they were the first foreign invasion force to draw up their ships on those beaches since Agamemnon's Greeks landed on them, 3,000 years earlier.

Only a few days after seeing Troy, Thomas Longford was killed at Gallipoli, on 21 August 1915. His last words to his second-in-command, who was crouching down to avoid the shells flying overhead, were, 'Please don't duck, Fred. It won't help you and it's no good for the men's morale.'

Soon after, advancing at the head of his Yeomanry Brigade troops with a map in one hand and a walking-stick in the other, he fell in a hail of rifle fire. 'Fred' – Fred Cripps, brother of Sir Stafford, the future Chancellor of the Exchequer – survived for another 60 years. He was one of the lucky few: 21 of the 28 officers and all Longford's staff were killed.

So heavy was the fire that bullet met bullet in mid-air – several of the squashed crosses of lead that were formed by these collisions are now in the Gallipoli Museum, which I visited the day before I failed to swim the Hellespont.

When I met Prince Harry at the centenary commemoration of Gallipoli in April 2015, I asked him what the protocol on ducking is now.

'You're allowed to duck,' he said, 'But there's a severe protocol against officers running away.'

Anzac Day, 25 April, marks the anniversary of the beginning of the Gallipoli campaign, when 1,500 Australians landed on the Turkish coast, 200 miles south of Istanbul. These were the first of 500,000 men who poured on to the Gallipoli peninsula over the next four months as part of Winston Churchill's ill-fated scheme to spring the deadlock of the Western Front with a push into Europe from the east. Half of them were wounded or killed. The survivors are long gone now. The last British survivor, Darcy Jones, a member of Longford's brigade, died in January 2000 at the age of 103.

After Longford's death, it wasn't possible to collect his body; it was lying too close to the Turkish guns. The survivors retreated and the corpses remained where they fell for three years, until the Armistice.

'My father had had his coat of arms tattooed on his chest in blue,' I was told by my great-aunt, Violet Powell, Longford's daughter and wife of the novelist, Anthony Powell. 'Because he knew how difficult it would be to tell the bodies apart.'

The family crest – 'An eagle displayed gules coming out of a mural crown or' – and the accompanying motto, 'Gloria Virtutis Umbra', had been punctured prominently on Longford's chest. But the tattooed flesh had long decayed by the time the men of the Allied War Graves Commission arrived in 1918 to bury the dead. The battlefields which had been craters and mud and dust were now covered with camel thorn, wild thyme, saltbush and myrtle, and it was near impossible to identify the bodies. All that remained were bones.

Of the 3,000 tombstones in the cemetery where Longford lies, 2,400 of them, including Longford's, are topped with the words, 'Believed to be buried in this cemetery'.

His empty tomb is literally a cenotaph, derived from *kenos taphos*, ancient Greek for 'empty tomb'. It was an ancient Athenian custom to include an empty coffin next to occupied ones, to salute the unburied dead. This Greek custom was echoed in Whitehall's Cenotaph. That cenotaph was a temporary timber structure, built for a military commemoration in 1919, but it proved so popular that Edwin Lutyens recreated it in stone a year later.

For a year after Longford's death, he was listed as missing in action. His wife persisted in thinking he might have been taken prisoner.

'She once called me to her room to write a letter to him because she had an idea that a child's letter might get through,' Mary Clive, my great-aunt and Longford's second-oldest daughter, told me before she died, aged 102, in 2010. 'It didn't get through; it was sent back and the following July she gathered us all together and said that he was dead. And then it was never mentioned by my mother for about 20 years.'

Longford was a career soldier who had served and been wounded in the Boer War. When not on duty, he returned to his houses in Oxfordshire and Ireland, where he was Lord Lieutenant of County Longford and a keen hunter. According to Fred Cripps, Longford 'was never happier than when he came home after a day's hunting, with his face covered with blood from swinging through an impenetrable "bull-finch" [a high hedge]'.

'He was also a literary man,' Aunt Violet said. 'He built up a large collection of books, as did my mother, who thought old books were unhygienic and so she always bought new ones.'

This literary streak was passed on to his children and grandchildren – the Pakenham clan of writers, among them Antonia Fraser, Thomas Pakenham and Rachel Billington. Thomas Longford published nothing, but he was a prolific letter-writer. On leaving for Gallipoli, he wrote a short card to Violet:

> Goodbye till we meet again. Do be a good girl.
>
> Your loving dada, Longford.

'I just remember him visiting us in the nursery to say goodbye,' said Aunt Violet, who was three at the time. 'Turning his back and going out of the door.'

The ship sailed for Gallipoli via Egypt. Longford's 2nd South Midland Mounted Brigade awaited the call to action in Cairo for four months. While they were there, the Waza – Cairo's red-light district – was burnt down by Australian troops in revenge for the venereal disease they had contracted in its brothels.

Even before the brigade left Cairo, it became clear that all was not going according to plan in Gallipoli. The first front, carved out by the Australians and New Zealanders at Anzac Cove, had not shifted for some weeks. The troops were securely dug into the lee of the slopes leading up from the coast, but they could progress no further without being fired upon by the Turks entrenched in the hills above them.

It was decided that a second front would be opened up to the north. The 10,000 horses shipped from England, including Longford's hunter, would not be needed; they were left in Egypt. Trained as cavalrymen, the men of the Mounted Brigade had less than a fortnight to turn themselves into infantry.

They sailed on towards Gallipoli, disembarking at the mouth of the Dardanelles, just south of the stretch of water Byron had swum across a century before; and that I didn't swim across two centuries later. The Dardanelles takes its name from Dardanos, ancestor of the kings of Troy. Not far from Troy is the ancient site of Dardania, supposedly the first city in the region.

Longford's brigade headed north towards the second front. Their route took them across a salt lake, dried in the August sun, leaving a great white bed of crystals. Before setting off across the lake, Longford beckoned to Cripps and said, 'I wanted to say goodbye to you, as we shall both inevitably be killed this afternoon.'

Walking across the stark, white salt bed, Longford and his men presented easy targets to the riflemen ensconced in the hills ahead of them. Shells burst in the sky above, showering the British with shrapnel. The men hurried towards the shelter of a bluff known as Chocolate Hill: even today, a few minutes' walk through this fertile region – rich in vines, tomatoes, wheat, olives and sunflowers – clogs the shoes with heavy, cocoa-coloured mud.

From this refuge, the survivors turned round to look at the dead and wounded. Among the casualties was Cripps, who had been hit in the leg and was unable to move. As the Westminster Dragoons came by, a Lieutenant Ferguson handed over his troop to his sergeant and went to Cripps's aid. Arm-in-arm, the two figures could just be picked out against the dust and the smoke. Bullets and shrapnel fell around the limping pair.

When they at last reached the safety of Chocolate Hill, Cripps produced a cigar case from his pocket and lit an outsized Corona. A cheer went up from the spectators. Longford took his brigade on towards the next significant Turkish outpost, the crescent-shaped Scimitar Hill.

A thick mist, unusual for the time of year, settled on the battlefield, and dusk was gathering. Sir John Milbanke VC, a colleague of Longford, was ordered 'to take a redoubt, but I don't know where it is and don't think anyone else knows either, but in any case we are to go ahead and attack any Turks we meet'. In this confusion and the now almost complete darkness, Longford was killed.

When I returned to the salt bed in September 2014, it was flooded, leaving a thin scimitar of soft white sand at its edge – the perfect beach, with only a German hippy, his pregnant girlfriend and their broken-down camper van to enjoy it.

'It always floods in September,' said my taxi-driver, after he'd offered to return with a vital engine part for the German hippy.

Perhaps my great-grandfather would have been OK if he'd landed a month later. With the salt bed flooded, he might have docked in the shelter of Chocolate Hill; he might have returned home safely; he might have brought up my grandmother, only one when he died …

Instead, the action of Scimitar Hill was, according to the regimental history, 'the most costly, in proportion to its size, and the least successful of all the Gallipoli battles'.

'The British losses, particularly of the Yeomanry and the 29th Division, were heavy and fruitless,' Churchill later wrote of the battle. 'On this dark battlefield of fog and flame, Brigadier-General Lord Longford, Brigadier-General Kenna VC, Colonel Sir John Milbanke VC, and other paladins fell.'

These words of praise were not enough to absolve Churchill from his part in the conception of the Gallipoli campaign. For a decade afterwards hecklers shouted, 'What about the Dardanelles?' whenever he stood for election. And Lady Longford never forgave him.

'It was the custom then,' said Aunt Violet, 'to invite the parents of your children's friends to their coming-out parties, although very few of them ever came. I remember my mother being horrified at the thought that Churchill might turn up with his daughter at one of her parties. It was rather lucky my mother didn't live to see him become saviour of the world.'

For a decade, Lady Longford could not bear to visit the supposed site of her husband's grave. She tried once, got as far as Istanbul, and then turned back, unable to face the ordeal. The next year, in 1926, she did get to the cemetery, accompanied by her daughter, Mary Clive.

The man in charge of the whole campaign, General Ian Hamilton, later wrote a tribute to the men of Gallipoli.

You will hardly fade away until the sun fades out of the sky and the earth sinks into the universal blackness. For already you form part of that great tradition of the Dardanelles which began with Hector and Achilles. In another few thousand years the two stories will have blended into one, and whether when 'the iron roaring went up to the vault of heaven through the unharvested sky', as Homer tells us, it was the spear of Achilles or whether it was a 100lb shell from Asiatic Annie won't make much odds to the Almighty.

It does, though, make a difference to today's tourists. The site of Troy is filled with coaches and parties of schoolchildren. Visitors pour into the café and playground – its main feature a large wooden horse; there's another wooden horse in Çanakkale, a gift from the producers of Brad Pitt's 2004 film, *Troy*.

But the immaculately kept cemeteries of Gallipoli are largely empty, except for a handful of cemeteries on the tourist bus trail, including Anzac Cove. In the day I spent wandering around the graveyards I saw nobody except for the

Commonwealth War Graves Commission gardeners, assiduously weeding and pruning away.

Each cemetery is surrounded by a bank of pines and planted with arbutus, rosemary, junipers, cypresses and Judas trees. A single purple flower grows next to my great-grandfather's tombstone. A botanist cousin and her expert friend identified it as Tulbaghia, also known as Pink Agapanthus or Society Garlic – 'A contradiction in terms,' my father said when he passed on the identification.

A year after Longford's death, a memorial service was held in St Mary's, Bryanston Square, in London. Violet Powell remembered wearing a posy of forget-me-nots. An extra verse was added by Lady Longford to one of the hymns, 'Within the churchyard':

And those who die away from home
Their graves we may not see
But we believe God keeps their souls
Where'er their bodies be.

My great-grandfather, Thomas Longford. His last words to his second-in-command, Fred Cripps, who was crouching down to avoid the shells, were, 'Please don't duck, Fred. It won't help you and it's no good for the men's morale.' Fred, brother of Sir Stafford Cripps, the future Chancellor of the Exchequer, survived for another 60 years.

Sophia Schliemann in the 'Jewels of Helen'. In fact, the jewels – discovered at Troy by her husband, Heinrich Schliemann, in 1873 – were made several centuries before the Trojan War. (Photograph c.1874)

6

In Search of Priam's Troy

Stand on top of Troy's ruined towers – on the Asian side of the Hellespont – and it's hard not to believe you're back in the world of *The Iliad*.

On the plain below me, I traced the trail Achilles carved on his chariot, dragging Hector's body round the city three times. Beyond Troy's walls snaked the meandering River Scamander, often mentioned in *The Iliad*, which takes its name from Ilion, as Homer called the city; Troy was his name for the surrounding area. A few hundred miles south flowed the River Maeander, the origin of that word 'meandering'.

Those walls beneath me were Cyclopean – built of such huge, irregular boulders that, so the legend goes, only the monstrous Cyclops could have lifted them. I could see the distinctive slope of the ancient walls, too – Homer wrote about how the walls sloped. In the western flank of the fortifications, I saw where those walls fell away – the same vulnerable spot Athena advised the Greeks to attack.

And there, stretching just below the horizon, beneath the Cape Helles Memorial to the British dead of Gallipoli, was Homer's wine-dark sea. He called it the *oinops pontos*; literally, the 'wine-faced sea'. James Joyce, a keen classicist at Clongowes Wood College, his boarding school in County Kildare, referred to the *oinops pontos* in *Ulysses* – a bit of an optimistic comparison for the Irish Sea on a gloomy, damp day.

The distant sea, viewed from the sloping walls of Troy, didn't look much like any wine I'd ever drunk. It ranged from sky blue at midday to a dark, inky blue as the sky darkened in the evening. I used to put the discrepancy down to the fact that there's no Homeric word for blue; or something to do with the sort of wine Homer drank – a rough concoction, mixed with plenty of water.

The Greeks thought undiluted wine was vulgar – the thuggish Macedonians liked to drink their wine neat. Soon after leaving Troy, Odysseus attacked the Ciconian coastline in northern Greece, near the modern Turkish border, and came away with 12 jars of the best Ismarian wine. He described the wine to King Alcinous as being 'mellow and unmixed'; he would have mixed it before drinking.

Sophisticated Greeks mixed wine with hot water in winter, cold in summer. They added honey and spice, too. In ancient Mycenae, they added pine resin – an early kind of retsina. It was rather weaker than our own wine: the 18 per cent alcohol content, when mixed with one part to two or three parts of water, was reduced to about the strength of a can of Stella Artois.

Later on my odyssey, I did see the sea turn a dark mauve, claret colour. It was during an evening walk by the Mediterranean shore, in the shadow of Paddy Leigh Fermor's old house in Kardamyli, in the Mani. Homer knew of Leigh Fermor's part of the world – in *The Iliad*, Agamemnon offered the citadel of Kardamyli to Achilles.

Homer's geography fits neatly on to the geography of modern Greece. Of the 164 places named in the Catalogue of Ships – the list of Greek ships taken to Troy, which appears in Book 2 of *The Iliad* – half of them have been identified today. They encompass much of modern Greece, from Cephalonia in the far west to Crete, Athens and Symi, by the coast of Turkey. Several real-life places – including the island of 'sacred Cythera', sacred to 'sweet-garlanded' Aphrodite Kytheria, the goddess of love – are mentioned for the first time in *The Iliad* and *The Odyssey*. Mycenean pottery has been found in all the places identified in the Catalogue of Ships. Troy, too, is rich in pottery from the Mycenean period – around 1600–1100 BC.

On top of all this, ancient records in Pylos – on the west coast of the Peloponnese, home to Nestor, oldest of the Greek leaders in the Trojan War – refer to Asian women being kept as slaves in the town a generation after the war. Were these Trojan captives? Surely Homer must have come to Troy to get all these details right? Surely this was Priam's citadel I was climbing?

There are varying degrees of romanticism about the myth. I am the full, wide-eyed romantic – and still believe there was a war between a Greek tribe and a non-Greek tribe. And I believe that war happened on the western coast of modern Turkey, where Troy is today. For what it's worth, Boris Johnson is a romantic, too.

'*The Iliad* must have happened,' he told me at the launch of his Churchill biography in the autumn of 2014. 'That description of the Trojans attacking like birds is so chilling, it must be true.'

Boris was referring to the beginning of Book 3 of *The Iliad*, where Homer described how the Trojans 'advanced with cries and clamour, a clamour like birds, cranes in the sky, flying from the winter's storm and unending rain, flowing towards the streams of the Ocean, bringing the clamour of death and destruction to pygmy tribes, bringing evil and strife at the break of day'.

Whether it's true or not, the story behind *The Iliad* and *The Odyssey* is actually pretty simple; particularly when compared to the complex shenanigans between the ever-warring, ever-shagging characters in the celestial soap opera up on Mount Olympus.

Paris, the good-looking Trojan prince, was asked to pick out the prettiest of the goddesses, Aphrodite, Athena and Hera. He gave the prize, a golden apple, to Aphrodite. She rewarded Paris by making the loveliest mortal in the world, Helen, wife of the Greek nobleman Menelaus, fall in love with him. Paris promptly whisked her off to Troy. In revenge, Agamemnon – Menelaus's brother and the King of Mycenae – took a Greek army off to Troy to get Helen back.

After ten years' fighting – fights take up half of *The Iliad*'s text – the Greeks won, thanks largely to Odysseus's Trojan horse, and they headed home, with Odysseus making rather a meal of the return journey.

That, in a nutshell, is the story of *The Iliad* and *The Odyssey*. So what's all the fuss about? The answer is that these two fully formed, unprimitive epics miraculously sprang out of nowhere, with nothing to match them in previous, surviving literature, and nothing to match them for several centuries after.

If there was a Trojan War, no one knows exactly when it happened – in the twelfth or thirteenth century BC, most modern scholars say. It could have been much later or much earlier. A precise date of 1184 BC was proposed by Eratosthenes of Cyrene, a third-century BC librarian at the Library of Alexandria, the scholarly heart of the ancient world. The library contained

490,000 ancient Greek works – the biggest known collection then, and the ultimate ancestor of all surviving Greek literature.

Eratosthenes worked out the date through precise calculations of the dates of the Olympic Games – or Olympic Game; the first competition in 776 BC only had one race, the 200m. More events were added over the next 1,000 years, including the 400m in 724 BC, and chariot-racing in 680 BC. The original Olympic Game was for individuals only, not teams.

You could argue that the roots of the games go back to Homer. Greco-Roman wrestling – still a modern Olympic pursuit – only appeared for the first time in the 18th Olympiad in 708 BC. But the earliest description of the sport is in *The Iliad* – when Odysseus wrestles with Ajax. With his wily genius, Odysseus used inspired tactics to overcome Ajax's thuggish strength; just as he designed the Trojan horse to bring down the toweringly strong walls of Troy.

In Ithaca, I was given an ultra-precise date for *The Odyssey* by a local tour guide, Dionyssia Trohoulia. She insisted on calling herself Denise, to be better understood by the tour group; how the brutish English language bastardises melodious Greek. Dionysus, too, sounds a little less divine in the English version: Denis. According to Denise, Penelope's suitors were killed on the evening of 16 April 1179 BC. That was the day a solar eclipse brought the cover of darkness for the long night of death mentioned in *The Odyssey*.

Ultimately, it's all speculation about dates – or facts – about the Trojan War. The huge stumbling block us romantics can't get around is the fact that there is no Homeric silver bullet – no contemporary document that expressly mentions the Trojan War, the wooden horse or Odysseus's epic journey home.

What is true is that, shortly after the supposed twelfth-century BC end of the Trojan War, the Mycenean age came to an abrupt end, for an unknown reason. *The Iliad* marked the beginning of Western European literature; the Trojan War marked the twilight of an earlier age, not the dawn of a later one.

During the Dark Ages that followed, most leading Mycenean and Minoan cities – including Troy, Mycenae, Pylos and Knossos – were destroyed, perhaps thanks to an enormous earthquake or volcanic eruption. There's an outlandish theory that the Trojan horse was an awkward analogy for an earthquake that destroyed Troy.

A black hole of lost history yawned wide open. You're fumbling in the dark when you try to join the dots between the Trojan War and Homer's lifetime, around 400 years later, with such a limited amount of information about the intervening centuries.

But, but, but... here, below my Chelsea boots, stood the sloping walls of a city that could well be Troy. Why shouldn't there have been a Trojan War? And why shouldn't all that happened to Odysseus after the war ended have a kernel of truth to it?

Certainly, the supposed site of Troy was at a critical point on Mediterranean trade routes. The site had its own natural harbour in the late Bronze Age, when the sea was 500 yards further inland than it is today. The city commanded the entrance to what was then the most important waterway in the world, leading through the Dardanelles up the Bosphorus into the Black Sea.

And people have been visiting the current site of Troy for so long that there's a thick vein of historical continuity between the original Troy and modern Troy.

In the early fifth century BC, Xerxes, the Persian king, took a pilgrimage to Troy and made a sacrifice. In 334 BC, Alexander the Great visited the supposed graves of Ajax and Achilles. Alexander kept a copy of *The Iliad* by his bedside on his conquests, annotated by his old tutor, Aristotle. It was thanks to his eastern conquests that *The Iliad* and *The Odyssey* were translated into Indian languages at an early stage.

When Alexander got to Troy, he raced, naked and oiled, round Achilles's tomb, while his companion, Hephaistion, ran, also naked, around the tomb of Patroclus, Achilles's great friend. Questions about the closeness of Alexander to Hephaistion, and of Achilles to Patroclus, linger on.

By the time Alexander the Great got to Troy, it was little more than a village. Julius Caesar – who liked to think he was descended from Aeneas – visited in 48 BC. According to Lucan, he 'walked around what had once been Troy, now only a name, and looked for traces of the great wall which the god Apollo had built. But he found the hill clothed with thorny scrub and decaying trees, whose aged roots were embedded in the foundations.'

Still, despite Troy's decline, it remained a near-holy spot. At the beginning of the third century AD, the Roman emperor, Caracalla, took a trip to the city.

He made a sacrifice to Achilles and also paraded around his tomb – not naked, but heavily armed.

It's always Achilles – the tragic strong man of *The Iliad* – they sacrifice to, rather than the leaders of either side, Agamemnon or Priam. The difference is that they survived the war; Achilles, shot in his Achilles's heel by Paris, didn't. The hero that dies is better box office than the leader who survives.

In the fourth century AD, Constantine the Great considered building his new Roman capital at Troy before opting for Constantinople. Even Sultan Mehmet II, the Ottoman victor over Constantinople in 1453 AD, came to Troy in 1462, making more sacrifices to Achilles.

Over the ruins, Mehmet II declared, 'It is to me that Allah has given to avenge this city and its people ... Indeed, it was the Greeks who devastated this city, and it is their descendants who, after so many years, have paid me the debt which their boundless pride had contracted to us, the people of Asia.'

The subtext is pretty obvious – the Muslim descendants of the Trojans had thumped the Christian descendants of the Greeks.

For centuries after the Muslim conquest, Troy slumbered on, accumulating thicker layers of topsoil. When Byron visited in 1810 he wrote, 'where I sought for Ilion's walls, the quiet sheep feeds, and the tortoise crawls'.

When Troy was finally excavated by Heinrich Schliemann, in 1873, it had been lost to the world – or thought never to have existed. Several archaeologists got to the mound of Troy before Schliemann, but none attacked it with such gusto. He removed 50 foot of debris, built up over the three thousand years or so since the Trojan War. Roman London, more than half as old as Troy, is only 20 feet below the street level of modern London.

The German archaeologist was a little too zealous, carving a thumping great trench through the site, destroying valuable artefacts. One scholar said he'd done what the Greeks had never been able to do – break the walls of Troy down to their foundations, without resorting to the trickery of the wooden horse.

It later turned out that Schliemann had dug far too deep. He had sliced into a pre-*Iliad* Troy of around 2,500 BC. Still, he had discovered the site of Troy – quite a find, even if the later city he dug through is not nearly as big as Homeric legend suggests. The citadel is just 200 yards by 150 yards. It's thought only the grandest Trojans lived there – while their dependants lived on the plain stretching away beneath my feet, at the bottom of those sloping walls.

Perhaps Troy's limited size explained why Schliemann had to sex up his dig. He claimed he'd found 'the Jewels of Helen' – earrings, a necklace and a gold diadem. Was this the jewellery that once adorned the face that launched a thousand ships? To ram the suggestion home, the 51-year-old Schliemann photographed Sophia, his gorgeous 21-year-old wife, in the jewels.

In 1881, Schliemann sold Helen's jewels to the Royal Museum of Berlin. There they stayed until the Second World War – when they were looted for a second time, from a bunker under Berlin Zoo, after the city fell to the Russians. In 1994, they turned up in the Pushkin Museum in Moscow.

Schliemann was a master of the PR stunt. He even stooped to inscribing swastikas on Trojan pottery to build a connection with swastikas found on early German pottery. All this was long before the Nazis, of course; but, still, a dodgy trick to link nineteenth-century Germany with the heroes of *The Iliad*.

In 1876, Schliemann pulled off a similar stunt at Mycenae in the Peloponnese, home to Menelaus, the husband of Helen of Troy. There he found a gold mask laid over a skull, its eyes and 32 teeth still intact. He immediately assumed the mask was Agamemnon's. 'I have gazed upon the face of Agamemnon,' he is wrongly reported as saying in a telegram to the King of Greece.

In fact, for all his PR skills, even the old conman had to hedge his judgement, saying, 'This corpse very much resembles the image which my imagination formed long ago of wide-ruling Agamemnon.' Clear as mud. In fact, the mask probably dated from the sixteenth century BC, three or four hundred years before the supposed date for the Trojan War.

Still, Schliemann's gambles kept paying off. And he was quite a gambler. He embarked on a huge dig at Orchomenos in Boeotia, northern Greece, purely on the back of a line from Achilles, referring to Orchomenos and Thebes, 'where treasures in greatest store are laid up in men's houses'.

He was so excited by his discoveries at Troy that he christened his children Agamemnon – after the leader of the Greeks – and Andromache, after Hector's Trojan wife. No taking sides there. Schliemann let them be baptised as Christians but insisted on holding a copy of *The Iliad* over their heads during the christening, while he recited a hundred Homeric hexameters.

Schliemann was later buried in an enormous show-off temple to his own memory: a Doric mausoleum in Athens's main cemetery, the Proto Nekrotafion Athinon, empty on the autumn day I visited. The caretaker pointed me in the direction of Schliemann's tomb – now rarely visited but still one of the grandest in the cemetery; before his archaeological career, Schliemann made a fortune in gold deals in California and armaments manufacturing in the Crimean War.

His mausoleum is decorated with classical bas-reliefs of the Trojan War. In among the heroic Greeks and Trojans, skewering each other with spears and making sacrifices to the gods in a tripod-mounted cauldron, Schliemann sticks out like a sore thumb in his modern dress. He's in a pith helmet – blackened today with Athenian soot – standing next to his child-bride, Sophia. As he recites a passage from *The Iliad*, he flamboyantly raises one hand. At the same time, he directs his workmen to lift the stones of Troy and carry Priam's vases.

As I clambered over the ruins of Troy, I was sneakily grateful that Schliemann dug right down to the city's foundations. Thanks to his bulldozer approach, I could see the 11 ancient cities built on top of each other at Troy, dating from 3,000 BC to AD 600. The ruins were dotted with little cards, reading 'VI' or 'VII' to denote which city you're looking at – the bigger the number, the later the city; the higher up in the archaeological sandwich.

It's a pretty good bet that Homer's city is somewhere in the sandwich. There's even a thrilling layer of finds that suggests one city was destroyed between 1250 and 1180 BC, just as Homer described. This layer – like the red layer of London soil where the city was burnt by Queen Boadicea in AD 60 – is crammed with scorched objects, arrowheads, skulls and butchered skeletons.

Nearby, vast, sunken soup jars have been found, embedded into a kitchen floor. Was this the soup kitchen kitted out to deal with a potential Greek siege? This was the layer Schliemann thought must contain 'the ruins and red ashes of Troy'. Later archaeologists were convinced the real Troy lay higher up, and later, in the sandwich.

'Helen's jewels' might have been worn by the great-great-grandmother of Priam, King of Troy. But they never rested – in Christopher Marlowe's lines from *Doctor Faustus* – beneath 'the face that launched a thousand ships and burnt the topless towers of Ilium'. Strictly speaking, she was even prettier than

Marlowe suggested: according to Homer, the Greeks brought 1,186 ships with them to Troy's topless towers.

For all these visits and digs over several millennia, there is still no concrete proof that Homer's Trojan War took place at this hallowed spot. But there's every chance that a war of some description did take place here.

The Hittites – who ruled much of what is now Turkey in 1250 BC – had plenty of reasons to take on rival Greeks landing on Turkey's western shore. Bristling tensions between Greeks and people living in Asia Minor continued almost until the present day.

In 1923, after the Greco-Turkish War, the Convention Concerning the Exchange of Greek and Turkish Populations was signed in Lausanne. A huge swap took place. In the 'Catastrophe', the western Turkish coast, colonised by Greeks for more than two thousand years, was returned to the days before the Greeks attacked Troy: 356,000 Muslims in Greece headed to the newly formed Republic of Turkey; 1.5 million Greeks, living in Asia Minor, fled to Greece.

There are some garbled Hittite references on chunks of clay to foreign tribes, possibly Greeks, living near Troy at the time of the legendary war. There's even a letter from a Hittite ruler in modern Turkey to a king of Ahhiyawa – might this be Achaea, an early name for Greece?

And there seem to have been pre-Homeric scuffles between west and east, between proto-Greeks and proto-Trojans. In the thirteenth century BC, there are references to the Hittites being attacked by the Attarsyas – Greeks, maybe?

There are other Hittite references to Mycenean meddling on the Trojan coast. In one Hittite cuneiform tablet of around 1260 BC, there's a reference to an unfaithful princess, living in a foreign court after a diplomatic marriage alliance. The infidelity led to two kingdoms, the Amurru and the Ugarit, going to war. Might this be Helen?

The figure of the meddlesome beauty is – along with the Trojan horse – the most memorable thing about *The Iliad*; the original scarlet woman, the pin-up girl for all misogynists. *Dux femina facti*, Virgil said of Aeneas's mistress, Dido, in *The Aeneid* – 'It was a woman's fault.' If you're looking for trouble, *cherchez la femme*.

Homer was also weirdly spot-on about Mycenean objects. Again and again, Homer referred to Mycenean things – including boar's tusk helmets – which didn't exist in his day. His history, too, was largely correct. According to Homer, Menelaus went to Egypt and 'saw Ethiopians in their native haunts' – just at the moment Greeks and Old Kingdom Egyptians were mixing. 'Ethiopian' was Greek for 'burnt faces', the term for anyone from below the Sahara Desert.

The relationship between Greece and Egypt was strong during the Mycenean period – strikingly so in early Greek sculpture, where the stiff arms, wigs and left feet thrust forwards are so reminiscent of the earlier, Egyptian civilisation.

That most Egyptian of animals, the sphinx, is a Greek word – possibly from *sphingo*, 'I squeeze' – derived from the lionesses who squeeze their victims to death. Sphincter has the same origin. Or perhaps 'sphinx' is a Greek version of the Egyptian *shesepankh*, meaning a 'living image', referring to the statue of the sphinx.

Sphinxes regularly cropped up in Greek mythology, chief among them the one who set Oedipus the riddle: 'Which creature has one voice and yet becomes four-footed and two-footed and three-footed?' Oedipus got the riddle right – 'Man, who crawls on all fours as a baby, then walks on two feet as an adult, and then uses a walking stick in old age' – and so he escaped strangulation, or *sphinxis*, to give it its Greek name.

The close relationship between Greece and Egypt meant hieroglyphics were deciphered in 1822, thanks to the Rosetta Stone – subject of the best-selling postcard in the British Museum. The stone – a crushingly dull decree about tax breaks – was inscribed in 196 BC under Ptolemy V. Discovered in the town of Rosetta, it originally stood in the temple at Sais, on the Nile Delta, 40 miles away.

Because the same text was inscribed in Greek, Demotic Egyptian and hieroglyphs, the French linguist Jean-François Champollion could crack the code. His brilliant leap was to work out that hieroglyphics were a mixture of phonetic symbols – like our letters – and logograms, where pictures represented words.

All in all, I tend to think something approximating to *The Iliad* did happen – if much embellished and altered over the centuries. The alternative – a perfectly feasible one – is that it was all dreamt up by an early genius. But could he have invented quite such a complex combination of real-life places, and heartfelt tragedy, without some basis in truth?

You can see why Schliemann and I so desperately wanted it to be Priam's Troy. *The Iliad* and *The Odyssey* have that sort of elemental, passionate effect on their devoted readers. Both epics speak so powerfully and truthfully about war, death, loss, travel, return and love, that they create a complete mental landscape.

The temptation to believe it all really existed is irresistible – and Schliemann's discovery of real cities that correspond in so many ways with the myths remain the greatest proof that it might all have happened.

The Iliad and *The Odyssey* have haunted the Western mind for more than two millennia. The earliest surviving works of European literature, they were peerlessly influential in the classical, Renaissance and modern worlds – in art, literature and thought.

Up to the present day, too – Homer Simpson, the most famous cartoon character on the planet, is named after the author of *The Iliad*. The father of the creator of *The Simpsons*, Matt Groening, was named Homer because his mother was an obsessive reader. Groening's uncle was called Victor Hugo.

'I can't separate the name Homer from *The Iliad* and *The Odyssey* and from Odysseus, even though Homer is the teller of the tale,' Groening said in a 2012 interview. 'I think of it as a very heroic name, in that Homer, even though he is getting kicked in the butt by life, is his own small hero.'

The Greek Homer is prized for the pure originality of the first known poems. But perhaps he was influenced by previous epics. Who knows what tantalising books, by hundreds of classical writers, have been lost to us? Of the many poems written by the fourth-century BC Greek poet Menander, only one work survives complete today. There are references in ancient texts to lost epics predating *The Iliad* and *The Odyssey*; stories about Heracles, Theseus and the Argonauts. *The Iliad* and *The Odyssey* themselves refer to earlier poems. The bards mentioned in Homer had to sing compositions by somebody.

But, in the absence of any predecessors, both epics appear uncorrupted, apparently free of the impressions of what went before. They had such a strong effect on later ancient Greek literature that they must have been the most influential of all the early epics, however many of them there were.

The Trojan War was also the launching pad for the concept of modern Greece. Ancient Greece wasn't a single, integrated country, one dazzling civilisation. The Greek city states were independent of – and often hundreds of miles from – each other. There were varying, loose-knit confederations of those states that, together, constituted a general idea of Greece. The first time that general idea cropped up was in *The Iliad*.

Thucydides said, 'We have no record of any action taken by Hellas [Greece] as a whole before the Trojan War ... Homer keeps the name "Hellenic" for the followers of Achilles who came from Phthioti [in central Greece] and were in fact the original Hellenes.'

Long after *The Iliad* and *The Odyssey* were written, the Greeks still thought of themselves as a group of separate city states. The earliest surviving inscription grouping the Greeks together as Hellenes is as late as 480 BC – celebrating the victory of a Greek alliance over the Persians at Salamis.

The Greeks didn't call themselves Greeks, either. That was an invention by the Romans, who named them Graeci, after the Graeci tribe from Epirus in northern Greece, or Graecia, as the Romans called it. 'Achaeans' was the collective, Mycenean name for the Greeks. In the Dark Age that followed, the collective group of loosely connected cities was known as Hellas – as the Greeks still call their country.

Modern Greece is an extremely recent creation. The Dodecanese Islands, swiped by Italy from the Ottoman Empire in 1912, were not given to Greece until as late as 1947. Mussolini was particularly keen on using Rhodes, one of the Dodecanese, as a jumping-off point for invading the Near East.

The thousand or so ancient Greek city states weren't just independent of each other. They were often at each other's throats, and rarely capable of working in each other's interests. In the fifth and fourth centuries BC, Athens was at war, for three years out of every four, with one or other of its rival city states. In the Persian Wars of 490–479 BC, more Greek city states fought for the Persians than for the Greeks. Only 31 *poleis* – the plural of *polis*, a city state – stood against Persia.

In January 2014, Rory Stewart, Conservative MP for Penrith, proposed that Britain should become a Greek-style group of '1,000 little city states, [to] give power right down to all the bright, energetic people everywhere who just feel superfluous'. A nice idea – but even Britain's modern unity, however fractured it feels to Scottish, Welsh and Irish nationalists, is much greater than that of ancient Greece.

As Plato put it, the Greeks were scattered like ants or frogs around the great big pond of the Mediterranean. Even Homer referred to the Greeks as a swarm of bees, attacking together, but as separate entities. Many of those city states barely understood each other. 'Solecism' – a spoken or written mistake – was derived from the Athenian colony of Soli, in Cilicia, modern Turkey. The Athenians thought the Soli natives spoke particularly incomprehensibly.

Those *poleis* were tiny, too – with around five thousand people in each one, living in the city or the neighbouring fields. At its height in the fifth century BC, the biggest city state, Athens, had 430,000 inhabitants, but only around 60,000 were citizens.

Aristotle suggested every citizen should know each other personally, and that a city should be small enough for everyone to hear the voice of a single herald. Plato thought the perfect state had 5,040 people – the mystical Pythagorean number you got from multiplying 1 x 2 x 3 x 4 x 5 x 6 x 7.

Wherever I went on my odyssey – from Mycenae, to Sparta, to Pylos, to Athens – the ancient cities always struck me as tiny. How extraordinary that these little settlements produced so much, as Saki said in his 1911 short story, *The Jesting of Arlington Stringham*: 'It was during the debate on the Foreign Office vote that Stringham made his great remark that "the people of Crete unfortunately make more history than they can consume locally." '

I felt Arlington Stringham's words particularly strongly in 2008 on a press trip to the Byzantine sites of Greece, ahead of a Royal Academy show on the subject. One hot afternoon, on the way from Athens to Delphi, we stopped at a petrol station at a crossroads on the outskirts of Thebes. As I bought a chocolate bar from the kiosk, the man behind the till told me this was the crossroads where Oedipus killed his father.

I stopped and stared through the plate-glass window, as the petrol pump attendant filled up our minibus. Heavy trucks careered across the crossroads, leaving a trail of red dust. Low-rise, concrete flats and shops were sprinkled at random spots along the road. There wasn't a single sign – no stall selling Oedipus-related tourist tat; no Oedipus Complex shopping centre. And yet this was the spot that spawned not just one of the great Greek myths, but also a psychological condition – even if Dr Freud wasn't quite right in his analysis.

The thing about the Oedipus story is that Oedipus didn't know he was killing his father or marrying his mother. He was brought up in Corinth by adoptive parents he thought were the real thing. The moment he heard the prediction of the Delphic oracle about what he would do to his parents, he fled to Thebes, only to meet, unwittingly, his real father and mother, with disastrous consequences.

For a few seconds before climbing back on the bus with the other hacks, I felt unaccountably moved by this distinctly unlovely place.

The Greeks like to show off about how they are directly descended from the first great civilisation – and the jury's out on that one. But, like the Italians, they don't get too excited about their ancient sites – there's just too much of it about. Imagine the fuss we'd kick up over the Oedipus Crossroads if it were in Godalming or New York. Here, they took it all for granted. The myth was part of the place – it didn't need to be exaggerated, shouted from the rooftops, or celebrated in neon signs attached to associated shopping outlets.

Arlington Stringham's words apply to the Mediterranean as a whole. It's a strikingly small sea – particularly when you think about how much has happened there. You can fit more than 42 Mediterraneans into the Atlantic Ocean – and yet the smaller sea is crammed with vastly more history than the bigger one.

Those hundreds of Greek city states weren't pooled until 338 BC, when Philip II of Macedon, father of Alexander the Great, conquered them all and bundled them together in a political federation. Philip II started on his land grab thanks to a typically cryptic bit of advice from the Sibyl at Delphi. In 359 BC, she told him, 'With silver spears you may conquer the world.' Philip II promptly took over Greece's silver mines and set about extending his vast empire.

Whether Philip II and Alexander were themselves Greek is another matter. In what is now the Former Yugoslav Republic of Macedonia, they claim Alexander as their own, not least at Alexander the Great Airport in the capital, Skopje. They also claim Alexander was a Slav – highly unlikely. The Greeks have a better claim to him, even if one of their justifications – that his ancestors competed in the Olympic Games – is a bit thin.

Whatever the truth of their bloodline, Philip II and Alexander did a lot to stretch the boundaries of the Hellenic world. After uniting the Greek city states, Philip II expanded into Persia before he was assassinated in 336 BC.

He was killed by his angry bodyguard at the wedding of his daughter, Cleopatra – no, not that one. Philip II had to leave it to his son, Alexander the Great, to take his empire further east, travelling to Afghanistan, Tashkent, Kashmir and Karachi.

A dozen cities were named after Alexander, including Kandahar in Afghanistan – Alexander called the city Alexander-in-Arachosia. Also in Afghanistan, the Kalash tribe are said to be his descendants, with their blue eyes, and their blond and red hair.

That's a rather more likely story than the rumours currently leaking out of Amphipolis – the site in northern Greece where a major tomb from the age of Alexander is being excavated. At one point in 2014, an excited reporter claimed a body with red hair and blue eyes – matching Alexander's description – had been discovered. All very thrilling, until a seasoned archaeologist said the eyeballs – which are largely water – are among the first parts of the body to decompose.

At its height in 326 BC, Alexander the Great's empire stretched from the Adriatic to India. Thus the peerless piece of sports commentary by the late Sid Waddell, the Voice of Darts, on Eric Bristow winning the World Darts Championship, 1984: 'When Alexander of Macedonia was 33, he cried salt tears because there were no more worlds to conquer … Bristow's only 27.'

Waddell, a history scholar at St John's, Cambridge, made a minor slip. Alexander was, in fact, 32 when he died in Babylon in 323 BC, possibly from poisoning, possibly from malaria, possibly after a massive drinking bout. In one account of his last days, Alexander, a renowned *philokothonistes*, or booze-fiend, downed a 12-pint drinking cup in one – enough to kill anyone.

After his death, however it happened, Greece, so recently united, began its long decline and eventual eclipse by Rome.

A detail from Heinrich Schliemann's mausoleum in Athens's main cemetery, the Proto Nekrotafion. In a soot-blackened pith helmet, Schliemann reads The Iliad to his wife, Sophia - 30 years his junior - while his workers excavate Troy.

Stephen Collins in the Guardian, July 26, 2014.

7

In the Wake of Odysseus

So *The Iliad*, as well as marking the beginning of the story of Greece, could be based on fact. But *The Odyssey*?

Even that old romantic Boris Johnson is more sceptical.

'The sort of journeys described in *The Odyssey* must have happened, even though the Odyssey itself didn't,' he told me with some certainty.

What precisely was I doing, then, following in the footsteps of a fictional character? In my desperation to get away from one failed romance, was I just getting tangled up in another lost cause? As I headed south from Troy towards Lesbos, Boris's words kept on niggling away at the back of my mind: did Odysseus – and his journey – exist?

Once you're in the romantic camp, it's easy to think the principal Homer sites all have their real-life architectural counterparts: that the three-storey building found on the island of Ithaca in the summer of 2010, complete with pottery fragments from the Homeric period, was Odysseus's palace.

Could this really be where Odysseus returned to save his wife Penelope from her wicked suitors, after his 20-year exile? The short, unromantic answer is probably no – even if I would think differently when I finally made it to Odysseus's palace at the end of my journey. As Fielding Gray says of *The Odyssey* in the Simon Raven novel, *Come Like Shadows*, 'It's all balls about historical locations. The whole thing's a legend … where it's not a fairytale.'

What's more, the creatures Odysseus meets on his journey are mythical and intentionally fantastic – like the Cyclops, the one-eyed giant who traps him in his island cave, the sweet-voiced Sirens, and the six-headed Scylla, who I later tracked down to the toe of Italy's boot. So why should his stopping-off points have their real incarnations?

There are so many imponderables that, if you are a brutal, unromantic realist, you can very easily prove to yourself that none of it ever happened. So, yes, maybe, the Trojan War did happen. But is Boris right – is the next step, to say *The Odyssey* happened, just too conjectural?

I'm not so sure. If there was a war between Trojan locals and invading Greeks, then those Greeks had to get home somehow, and one of them might well have got lost. Certainly, there are references to other ancient stories of Greeks returning from Troy. Five and a half lines, and a few critical references, survive of a lost epic called the *Nostoi – The Returns*, i.e. returns of the Greeks from Troy (as in nostalgia).

Like *The Odyssey*, the *Nostoi* tells of the trials and tribulations of various returning Greeks: Diomedes and Nestor, who get back home without incident; Menelaus, caught in a storm, loses much of his fleet and is delayed in Egypt for several years; Agamemnon is killed by Clytemnestra, his wife. The only one left to make it home is Odysseus.

There are fifth-century BC references to other ancient epics about the war: the *Cypria*, which described the build-up to the war; the *Little Iliad*, which continues Homer's account of the war; and the *Telegonia*, which takes Odysseus from his homecoming to Ithaca up to his death.

Even the story of Jason and the Argonauts – a hero leading his gang from Greece in his quest for the Golden Fleece of a mystical ram – was, if not quite a *nostos*, a quest around the sea. Written in the third century BC by Apollonius of Rhodes, Jason's story had many of the same elements as *The Iliad* and *The Odyssey* – bloody bouts of mortal combat; the death and burial of great friends; long lists of great, mythical travellers. Jason, like Odysseus, also met the alluring witch Circe and the Sirens. He drowned out their hypnotic music by getting one of the Argonauts, Orpheus, to play an even more beautiful tune on his lyre.

I'm not the first to try to nail down Odysseus's real-life route and work out who Homer really was. There was a group of ancient activists, the euhemerists, who thought there was some truth to the Greek myths. They're named after Euhemerus, the fourth-century BC Greek from Sicily who maintained you could strip the magic from the myths and reveal the historical facts beneath.

As early as the fifth century BC, Thucydides and Herodotus were identifying the Land of the Lotus-Eaters, where Odysseus's men become fantastically lazy after they eat the intoxicating lotus plant. Herodotus and Thucydides nailed the lotus-eating land to a spot in Libya – now thought to be the island of Djerba, just off the Tunisian coast.

Djerba is today best known as the 1977 setting for the mystical moonscape in *Star Wars*. Obi-Wan Kenobi's little white house by the sea is now used for storage by local fishermen. A few miles north, Tosche Station – a sort of *Star Wars* petrol station, where Luke Skywalker powers up his moon buggies on Tattooine – is really a Muslim shrine.

I'm afraid that, of all the places Odysseus was supposed to have visited on his route, I avoided Tunisia. It was apparently perfectly safe. But at the time of writing, ISIS were running roughshod over neighbouring Libya. Odysseus would have been ashamed of my cowardice – and it would have made for great publicity – but I didn't want to end up in an orange jumpsuit, with my head being chopped off. The jihadist attack on Tunis's Bardo Museum in March 2015, which killed 22, tragically confirmed my worries.

By the fourth century BC, Homeric geographers were particularly thick on the ground. In the Socratic dialogues (*dialogos* – 'conversation'), Plato had a pompous character, Ion, who made his living as a Homer expert. 'I speak better and have more to say about Homer than any other man,' says the insufferable Ion.

It wasn't just *The Odyssey* that produced these geographical sleuths. Ancient scholars also identified the sites of the 12 Tasks of Hercules. The Nemean lion, the Lernaen hydra, the Ceryneian hind, the Erymanthian boar, the Augean stables and the Stymphalian birds were all in the Peloponnese. The bull was in Crete; the mares of Diomedes in northern Greece; the belt of Hippolyta in northern Turkey; the cattle of Geryon off the south coast of Spain; and the apples of Hesperides in north Africa. Cerberus's home in the underworld was identified in lots of different spots around the Mediterranean. I sided with the critics who placed Odysseus's underworld in Gibraltar.

Historians have tried to locate the site of Colchis, home to Jason's Golden Fleece, ever since Pliny the Elder in the first century AD. In 2014, scholars at the Ilia State University of Georgia revealed evidence of the Golden Fleece in what they claimed was Colchis, in north-west Georgia. Still today, locals in the Georgian mountains of Svaneti prospect for gold by lining the bed of sandy streams with sheep fleeces to trap golden particles. Among artefacts found by the scholars was a bronze bird with a ram's head, dating from the sixth to the first century BC, when Colchis is said to have flourished.

Despite these thrilling real-life clues, the search for the real foundations of Greek mythology remains pretty speculative. Perhaps these investigations just show a collective human desire for myths to be true. But, so often, there's such a strong geographical foundation to them that it's tempting to believe some real-life incident sparked off the stories.

Odysseus's route is apocryphal (*apokrupto* – 'to put out of sight'). But that route has been argued about for so long – at least 2,500 years – that a hardened, very much visible route has been hammered out. The route I followed is the one with most followers – although many will disagree with it.

It helps that plenty of place names in *The Odyssey* still exist, not least Corfu and Ithaca. Still, even that hasn't stopped some historians arguing the crazy case that today's Ithaca isn't ancient Ithaca. There are some named Homeric places that don't survive today; others that are given no name at all. In these places, the really creative Odysseans – who like to think *The Odyssey* did happen in real, recognisable places – stitch together Homeric geographical descriptions and graft them on to real-life places that apparently fit the bill.

It helps that Homer is lavish with local description. Even when he doesn't give a real place name – and often when he does – he gives lots of extraneous geographical detail. Like at that moment when the naked Odysseus is washed up, with that lovely full head of hyacinth-like hair, on the shores of Corfu, and taken to the house of the beautiful princess, Nausicaa. She gives him extremely precise local directions to her palace, like she's a local telling him the way to the pub.

'You'll find a handsome grove of Athene near the road,' Nausicaa says. 'There's a spring in it and it's surrounded by a meadow. There's my father's estate and his flourishing vineyard.'

I took the same drive from Ermones Beach – through fertile, spring-fed meadows – to the supposed site of that estate, Palaiokastritsa. It's now a busy little holiday town on Corfu's west coast, wrapped around a charming series of small bays. Between one pair of bays, a handsome monastery, now packed with tourists, sits on top of a steep promontory – an ideal spot for King Alcinous's palace.

As so often on my trip, a real-life place matched the description in *The Odyssey*. But, as so often, the description was vague enough that it could have applied to a thousand other spots. That ambiguity leaves a gap for every Mediterranean taverna owner, from Gibraltar to Croatia, to claim a connection with Odysseus.

Every time I approached a supposed Homeric site on my odyssey, the hoteliers and restaurateurs had got there first: whether it was the Maga Circe ('the Witch Circe') Hotel in Lazio, 50 miles south of Rome; Le Due Sirene ('the two Sirens') Casa Vacanza near Positano; or the hamlet of Scilla, on the Italian mainland opposite Sicily, wrapped around the rock on which the sea monster perched, grabbing several of Odysseus's shipmates.

The Odyssey is such an all-powerful story that, even way beyond the Mediterranean, people have fitted the book's topography on to their own. Just as people in the West Country insist Jesus visited Glastonbury on a tin-trading mission with his uncle, Joseph of Arimathea, the world and its wife claim Odysseus as their own.

Finnish writers insist *The Odyssey* took place in Finland. A Chicago patent lawyer, Henriette Mertz, has tracked Charybdis down to a whirlpool in Newfoundland, in the Bay of Fundy. There's a North Yorkshire version of the Cyclops story, where Polyphemus is a miller called Jack, who's stopped from going to the gypsy fair in Topcliffe, near Thirsk.

The Odyssey is an infinitely adaptable idea. There are 273 books in the London Library with 'Odyssey' in the title: from *Mormon Odyssey – the Story of Ida Hunt Udall, Plural Wife* (1992) to *Boudicca's Odyssey in Early Modern England* (2014).

Odysseus doesn't have to have visited a place for that place to adopt the story for itself. *The Odyssey* is so flexible that it lends itself to anywhere – not least Dublin. James Joyce divided his novel *Ulysses* into Homeric chapters: from Calypso to Scylla and Charybdis. Those chapters correspond to different bits of Dublin, all visited on the annual Bloomsday walk on 16 June – in memory of the day in 1904 when the novel is set.

The connections between ancient Greece and early twentieth-century Dublin are pretty tenuous. James Joyce became attached to the myth as a child, when he read Charles Lamb's children's book, *Adventures of Ulysses*. That explains his preference for the Latin form, Ulysses, over the Greek, Odysseus. A schoolboy essay he wrote on 'My Favourite Hero' was devoted to Ulysses, not the Greek original.

I wonder if Joyce didn't also choose the legend of Odysseus/Ulysses for the fabled, high-minded difficulty of Classics. If you want to write an impenetrable book – at one point, *Ulysses* goes on for 25 pages without a full stop – how better to advertise your mind-blowing brilliance than to base it on the most famous character in classical mythology?

It helped that the stories in *The Odyssey* are so famous that Joyce could make indirect references to them and you still get the connection. So, in the original Nausicaa story, Odysseus is caught unawares by the naked princess. In Joyce's 'Nausicaa' episode, Bloom masturbates furiously as Gerty MacDowell flashes her underwear at him on Sandymount Strand.

In 'Penelope', the last episode in *Ulysses*, Bloom is back at home, in bed with Molly Bloom. The last words of the book are Molly's memory of his marriage proposal: 'he asked me would I yes to say yes my mountain flower and first I put my arms around him yes and drew him down to me so he could feel my breasts all perfume yes and his heart was going like mad and yes I said yes I will Yes.' The parallels with Odysseus's return to Ithaca are clear enough.

The euhemerists kept on trying to track down Odysseus's original route under the Roman Empire. In the first century AD, the Greek historian Plutarch placed Calypso's island five days' north of the British mainland – in the Faroe Islands, perhaps. Some British patriots claim Odysseus even touched down on British soil, when he visited Hades in Book 11 of *The Odyssey*. He went there to seek the oracle of the wise man, Teiresias – as well as to see his dead mother, Agamemnon, Ajax, Patroclus and Achilles.

Odysseus watches clean-heeled Achilles, marching away with long steps over a meadow thick with asphodel – the flower of the underworld which I kept on seeing on my journey; in profusion on Ithaca, particularly. Odysseus also got to witness some of the greatest hits of Greek mythology in the underworld:

Tityos, helpless as a vulture pecks away at his liver; Sisyphus, forever rolling a boulder up a hill, only for it to roll back down to the bottom again; and Tantalus, incapable of drinking from the lake of water at his chin that vanishes whenever he bends to drink it, unable to eat the figs and juicy apples dangling from trees that disappear at his reach.

In among all these character sketches, Homer said the entrance to Hades was home to 'The fogbound Cimmerians who live in the City of Eternal Mist'. Here, 'The bright sun never shines down with his rays, neither by climbing the starry heavens nor turning back again towards earth, but instead dreadful Night looms over a wretched people.'

Where else could that be but gloomy old Britain, say British *Odyssey* nuts? Failing that, what about the only British outpost in the Mediterranean – Gibraltar, which stakes a claim to being Hades, and the westernmost extent of Odysseus's travels?

The two sides of the Strait of Gibraltar have long been compared to the Pillars of Hercules. The idea was that Hercules smashed through a great mountain connecting Africa with Europe. In so doing, he left behind the Rock of Gibraltar on the European side; on the African side, he left behind either the Moroccan peak of Jebel Musa or Monte Hacho, in the Spanish colony of Ceuta. Beyond the Pillars of Hercules, said Euripides, 'lies the end of voyaging and the ruler of the ocean no longer permits mariners to travel on the purple sea'.

Not quite true – the Phoenicians, and probably the Minoans and Myceneans, too, travelled beyond Gibraltar into the Atlantic. Still, the myth lives on – and a modern bronze monument, marking Gibraltar's Pillar of Hercules, has been arbitrarily placed, on the site of an old British gun emplacement, high up on the Rock of Gibraltar.

Nearby, St Michael's Cave – a vast, underground cavern, bristling with stalactites, high on the Rock of Gibraltar – is supposedly Odysseus's underworld. Other euhemerists preferred to place the entrance to Hades at Lake Avernus, about five miles west of Naples.

The truth of it is that Odysseus's original itinerary is a highly movable feast. While I was travelling the Odyssean trail on that cruise ship in the autumn of 2014, an intellectual farmer from Hampshire produced an utterly credible argument that the whole *Odyssey*, apart from the final destination of Ithaca, took place on the western coast of Turkey. Thirty miles north of Izmir, there are even rocks on the coast, shaped like flutes; when the right wind blows, they are said to whistle the seductive melodies sung by the Sirens.

It certainly isn't difficult to find ancient settlements around the Mediterranean that approximate to the rough dates of the Trojan War. The Mediterranean – in particular the waters along the coast – was the principal travelling route of the ancient world, connecting the cities of Greece and, later, the Roman Empire. So those shores are jam-packed with ruined buildings – and contemporary household goods – stretching back thousands of years.

Want to find a modern counterpart for Charybdis, the whirlpool that threatened to swallow up Odysseus's boat? Well, you'll track down a near approximation somewhere in the million square miles of the Mediterranean. Want an ancient palace that might have been Menelaus's? Somewhere in the rough ruins of Mycenae, you're bound to find something pretty close to Homer's hazy, poetic description.

Serious historians have even argued that the island of Santorini – the remnants of an ancient volcano, much of it now under the sea – was once the lost land of Atlantis, held up by Plato as an island near Gibraltar, and a great rival to Athens in 10,000 BC. One scholar, Professor Hans Goedicke, has placed the exact date of the Santorini eruption at 1477 BC – the date of the parting of the Red Sea to let the Israelites through, according to a pharaoh's inscription during the reign of Tutmosis III. Did the same eruption and subsequent tsunami end the Minoan civilisation and appear in the Bible? Unlikely, but not impossible.

As a university friend once said to me of the joys of ancient history, 'It's just far enough ago that you can make stuff up. And near enough that you know certain things did definitely happen.'

That's why Robert Graves could make up the fictional lost autobiography of Claudius in *I, Claudius* and *Claudius the God*. Claudius's life was pretty well documented but not so exhaustively that you can't make up a few juicy extra details.

Greece's history is full of gaps, as is its literature. Aeschylus, Euripides and Sophocles wrote around 300 plays, of which only 33 survive. Another 150 playwrights are known of in fifth-century Greece – not a single one of their plays survives. Lucretius's poem *On the Nature of Things*, about the theories of Epicurus, only survives thanks to a single ancient copy. The temptation is to fill the gaps with supposition, as people often do with anonymous Greek sculpture. Again and again on my travels, I saw statues labelled with the words, 'possibly the work of Pheidias', greatest of the Greek sculptors. He must have been very quick with his chisel if he did them all.

New statues and documents are emerging all the time – some of them from the greatest rubbish heap in history, found by the British papyrologists Bernard Grenfell and Arthur Surridge. From 1897 to 1907, their dig in ancient Oxyrhynchus – 'City of the Sharp-Nosed Fish', now el-Behnesa, a village 100 miles south of Cairo – produced half a million papyrus documents that survived thanks to the hot, dry sand. There are still thousands of Oxyrhynchus papyri yet to be translated, written in a mixture of Greek, Coptic and Demotic Egyptian, and, occasionally, Latin.

In 2014, a new seventh-century BC poem by Sappho, on a third-century AD papyrus, was discovered by Dr Dirk Obbink, a papyrologist at Oxford University. The new fragment was found to fit perfectly with an old, tattered papyrus. This papyrus had been ripped and repaired in ancient times – a replacement papyrus strip, used to mask the tear all those centuries ago, survives on the newly discovered fragment.

Papyrus – as in 'paper' – sounds pretty flimsy: made out of the stems of Egyptian reeds, criss-crossing in vertical and horizontal strips, to form scrolls up to 22 feet long. And, indeed, papyrus was superseded in the first century BC by more substantial Roman codex books: parchment and vellum sheets held together by leather straps. The word 'parchment' was derived from the ancient city of Pergamum – where they first developed the skill of writing on both sides of the page. Still, that flimsy papyrus can survive thousands of years. What a thrilling thought that more documents may emerge, telling the truth about Homer and *The Odyssey*.

Just like us euhemerists – who believe in that truth – there were ancient sceptics, too. In the late third century BC, the Greek geographer Eratosthenes said, 'You will find the scene of Odysseus's wanderings when you find the cobbler who sewed up the bag of winds.'

Eratosthenes was referring to the bag of winds Aeolus, ruler of the winds, gave to Odysseus to guide him to Ithaca – only for Odysseus's shipmates to rip open the bag, thinking it full of gold and silver. Just as he's approaching Ithaca, Odysseus is blown right back by the escaped winds to Sicily and then on to Corsica.

I never found the cobbler who sewed up Aeolus's bag – but I did find his kingdom, the Aeolian Islands, off the coast of Sicily. And I like to think I crossed Odysseus's path from time to time, as I headed across the Mediterranean on a cruise ship – with my parents.

THE GATE OF LIONS AT MYKENÆ.

The earliest coat of arms in the world – the 13th century BC Lion Gate at Mycenae. The lions flank an early Doric column. (1890 drawing)

Going aboard the Corinthian with my parents, Julia and Ferdy Mount.

8

Sex Life in Ancient Greece

Some readers will remember *Sorry!*, the comedy starring Ronnie Corbett as tragicomic Timothy Lumsden, living at home with his parents in his forties. I can't recall any holiday specials where Lumsden went on a Mediterranean cruise with them – as I did with my parents in September 2014.

At 43, I was distressed to learn that I was older than Lumsden. He was meant to be 41 in the first three series, 42 and 48 in subsequent series. Corbett himself was, more gratifyingly, 50 when he first played the character in 1981, 57 when the programme came to an end in 1988.

Odysseus had to sail the seven seas for a decade to find his way back to his family. It wasn't so difficult for me – my parents were four cabins along from me on the Ariadne Deck, on the same cruise ship now taking us towards the island of Lesbos, 50 miles south of Troy.

The *Corinthian* was slightly more luxurious than Odysseus's unnamed, black-hulled ship. As the cruise brochure puts it, 'This private yacht-like ship accommodates up to 100 guests in 50 suites which are spread over five decks. Each suite affords ocean views and measures from 215 square feet to 285 square feet. There is also a sitting area or separate living room area, twin or queen-size beds, spacious closet and air conditioning. Every suite is also furnished with satellite television, DVD/CD player, telephone, mini-refrigerator which is replenished with complimentary water, marble-appointed bathroom with fine toiletries and teak flooring, plush terry robes and slippers.'

Unlimited free wine and soft drinks with dinner, too. Even the Sirens would have had a hard job luring me away – particularly since I didn't have to pay the £8,995 for three weeks in a Category E Deluxe Suite, with windows, on the Ariadne Deck. I was even being paid £100 a day, plus expenses, as a guest lecturer, to give talks on 'The story of *The Iliad* and the ruins of the city of Troy', 'What have the ancient Greeks ever done for us?' and 'Following in Odysseus's footsteps 3,000 years on'.

We weren't quite following in his footsteps. I'd sent Odysseus's original itinerary to the cruise director in Belgravia. He'd then combined the ancient route with ports that could accommodate the *Corinthian* – along with some of the greatest hits of ancient Greece, such as Delphi and Ephesus, which Odysseus never visited.

He never went to our next stop, Lesbos, but it deserved its place on the itinerary as the birthplace of Sappho, the seventh-century BC poet and original lesbian. Sappho was so celebrated in the ancient world that Greeks referred to her as 'the poetess'; and to Homer as 'the poet'. She was even described as the tenth muse, alongside the other nine: Calliope (epic poetry); Clio (history); Erato (lyric poetry); Cithara (the lyre); Euterpe (song and elegiac poetry); Aulos (the flute); Melpomene (tragedy); Polyhymnia (hymns); Terpsichore (dance); Thalia (comedy); and Urania (astronomy).

The muses live on in our museums – from *mouseion*, Greek for 'the temple of the Muses' – and in music, derived from *mousike*, 'the art of the muse'. The muses' birthplace was Pieria, in Macedonia, northern Greece. Thus the Alexander Pope couplet:

A little learning is a dangerous thing.
Drink deep, or taste not the Pierian spring.

Sappho was prominent enough to lend the name of her birthplace to lesbianism – even if her poems rarely describe the physical act, and are often written to men as well as women. In classical Greek, the verb 'lesbiazein' — 'to behave like a citizen of Lesbos' — meant 'to perform fellatio,' which Lesbos inhabitants were thought to be very good at. What's more, Sappho was married and seems to have had a daughter called Cleis.

Still, she was probably a little more outrageous than the character portrayed by nineteenth-century British scholars. Because Sappho ran a school on Lesbos, she was characterised by the Victorians as a stern schoolma'am, rather than the rampant lesbian she's presented as in our free and easy times.

There's long been an awkward collision between ancient Greek homosexuality and the prudish but Classics-worshipping British public school. A century ago, Lytton Strachey wrote,

> How odd the fate of pretty boys!
> Who, if they dare to taste the joys
> That so enchanted Classic minds,
> Get whipped upon their neat behinds.
> Yet should they fail to construe well
> The lines that of those raptures tell
> It's very odd you must confess –
> Their neat behinds get whipped no less.

The easiest way to avoid the awkward collision was to censor any sexual reference, gay or otherwise, in lessons. When Lawrence Durrell was at St Lawrence's School, Canterbury, in the 1920s, his Greek teacher brandished a photograph of a naked Venus de Milo, thumped his fist on his desk and barked, 'What do you think they were trying to do? Make us tingle with lust? Certainly not! They were asking themselves what beauty is, and whether it lies in proportion.'

These days, schools are much more relaxed about the classical approach to sex; particularly the Greek approach, even more easy-going than the Roman one. The late Kingsley Amis liked to put on a face he called 'Sex Life in Ancient Rome' – a debauched grin, eyes closed in bliss, in imitation of a satyr's mask he'd seen on the cover of a Classics book. His Sex-Life-in-Ancient-Greece face would have been far more debauched.

That pre-war censorship of sexual references in Classics had long gone by the time I was at Westminster School in the 1980s. Gone were the days when Sappho's lesbianism was glossed over – quite the opposite in fact. Homosexuality was positively celebrated. One master at Westminster said the only sexual sin was exclusivity – although, in his own personal life, he seemed to stick pretty exclusively to the male half of the human race.

The same master, now long dead, was fond of pointing out how heavily edited a popular wedding reading from Plato's *Symposium* was. A symposium was originally a sort of drunken party; from *sun* – 'together' – and *posis* – 'drink'. The word was only later reinvented by European classicists to mean an academic conference. In the passage, Plato said we are all conceived as paired souls who are separated at birth; and we spend the rest of our lives trying to find our beloved, long-lost soul partner.

What no wedding reading – well, no heterosexual one – ever includes is the passage that said the ideal union of souls is between two men. The definition of platonic love has changed quite a bit. Nor does any wedding reading refer to Plato's words about humans originally having their genitals on their backs. Us poor humans were eternally frustrated by our awkwardly placed genitals until Zeus generously moved them to the front.

There's an echo of a conversation between Christopher Hitchens and Martin Amis, who thought women would be more attractive if their breasts were on the same side of the body as their bottoms. A long debate followed: would it be best to have all that equipment gathered on the back of the body or the front?

We were brought up to speed on all this by our Classics teacher, as we were on the Greek word for an Athenian punishment for adulterers: *hraphanidooh* – 'I thrust a radish up the fundament.' All in all, we became strangely well informed about gay life in Greece. And not just at Westminster. *Greek Homosexuality* by Kenneth Dover was, I am reliably informed by an Old Etonian friend, the most borrowed book in Eton's library in the 1980s.

The attitude to homosexuality in Athens was even more open. Socrates cheerfully admitted he lost the power to philosophise when he glanced down a beautiful youth's tunic. He also said having a libido was like being chained to a madman. Even – especially – in Sparta, the idea was that older men should instruct younger men about life, and then hop into bed with them.

In Thira, on the modern party island of Santorini, a series of sacred, sexual games – *gymnopaidiai*, from *gumnos*, 'naked', and *paizdo*, 'I play' – took place in the burning August sun. Naked adolescent boys danced and fought on an exposed rock terrace next to the sea, as older men looked on. One frank inscription in the rock reads, 'Amotion and Kripon fucked here.'

Even more graphic graffiti was unveiled in July 2014 on the island of Astypalaia, 30 miles east of Santorini. Dr Andreas Vlachopoulos stumbled on two enormous fifth-century BC phalluses, alongside the name 'Dion' scored into the dolomite limestone of the Bay of Vathy, in the north-west of the island. A sixth-century BC inscription read, 'Nikasitimos mounted Timiona here.'

'This graffiti is not just among the earliest ever discovered,' Dr Vlachopoulos told the *Guardian*. 'By using the verb in the past continuous [tense], it clearly says that these two men were making love over a long period of time, emphasising the sexual act in a way that is highly unusual in erotic artwork.' How many and varied are the uses of Greek grammar.

Ancient writers weren't prudish about heterosexual sex, either. *The Odyssey* is crammed with sex, particularly in those trysts with Circe and Calypso, in Odysseus's naked dealings with Nausicaa, and in his yearning to hear the bewitching Sirens. Greek heterosexuality did crop up at school, too – even if Etonians didn't read about it much. It was in the sixth form that I learnt how the Greeks used rudimentary condoms, fashioned from pigs' bladders.

We're much more gauche about sex now than the Greeks were, 2,500 years ago. When I visited the museum on Apollo's holy island of Delos in 2014, it was pretty empty. A handful of tourists marched through rooms containing some of the greatest Greek sculpture on earth. Among the statues were the crouching, roaring Delos lions – set up in 600 BC in honour of Apollo by the islanders of Naxos. The tourists raced past the lions and gathered round a small display cabinet in a remote corner of the museum. There, they posed, giggling, in front of a stone frieze of a pair of jousting, winged penises, each with its own tail – with each tail made out of two penises. This pair of penises had a charming inscription below: *Touto soi kai touto emoi* – 'This for you, and this for me.'

The ancient Greeks wouldn't have giggled in titillated excitement at jousting penises. They would have taken them in their stride, utterly relaxed as they were about sex, and thoroughly, unembarrassedly keen on it.

Greek women, too, had a cheerful, open approach to sex – like the women in Aristophanes's *Lysistrata*, who go on the first ever sex strike, to bully their husbands to stop fighting in the Peloponnesian War. For much of the play, the desperate men hobble around the stage with outsized erections. The women are equally desperate. They mourn the shortage of dildoes, even the inadequate 'eight-finger-width' ones; that is, around five inches long. There are still sex strikes going on today: in the Ukraine in 2014, Ukrainian girls set up the campaign 'Ne Dai Russkomu' – 'Don't Give it to a Russian'.

For all the sexual openness, the Greek world was hardly a feminist society. There was no such thing as rape, except as an act of criminal damage on the property of the husband, father or guardian of the violated woman. You could be fined for rape, but only as a property crime.

The punishment for adultery was even more extreme, because the family was considered sacrosanct. Thanks to the Draconian punishment code – set up by Draco, the hardline Athenian lawmaker in the seventh century BC – you could kill an adulterer on the spot if you were responsible for the violated woman.

Women couldn't attend the Assembly, restricted to male citizens over 18, let alone hold office. They couldn't own property, either, or conduct legal business. They lived only through men: every woman was the legal ward of her nearest male relation. In the unlikely event that a woman inherited property, she held it on behalf of her son. And only women were thought to suffer from hysteria, a condition supposedly induced by a wandering womb; *hustera* is Greek for 'womb'.

Even marriage didn't provide many benefits. Married women were banned from entering the Olympic stadium – although one boxer's mother, Callipateira, also his trainer, disguised herself as a man to get in. Even though she was caught out, she was spared punishment as a reward for maternal devotion. Baron Pierre de Coubertin wasn't much more enlightened in 1896, when he founded the modern Olympiad. Women's athletics, he said, would be 'Impractical. Uninteresting. Unaesthetic. Incorrect.'

Greek mythology hardly buttressed the female cause. Pandora – the first woman, built out of clay by the blacksmith god, Hephaestus – may have had a flattering name, meaning 'all the gifts'. But her purpose, as laid out in Zeus's assembly instructions to Hephaestus, was to have a bitch's mind, to lie and to ruin man. She duly did exactly that by opening her box, containing all the evils of the world – leaving only hope behind, as scant consolation to the human race.

The divisions between men and women were absolute, even in art. In Minoan paintings at Knossos, men were painted red, the women painted white. Aristotle argued in *Politics* that, by nature, men are superior to women. Men, he said, were born to rule women. I'm afraid Homer wasn't much better. *The Odyssey* provided the earliest surviving example of a man telling a woman to shut up. It's right at the beginning of the epic, when Penelope comes downstairs from her bedroom to tell the local bard to stop singing. You can see why it was a sensitive issue: the bard was playing a melancholy tune about how tricky it was for the Greeks to get home from Troy.

'Mother,' Telemachus says, 'go back to your room, and do your work on the loom and spindle, and tell your maids to do their work. Speech will be the business of men, all men, and of me most of all; mine is the power in this household.'

The word Telemachus uses for 'speech' is *muthos* – not our 'myth', but in its meaning as authoritative, public, male speech; as opposed to the silly, private chit-chat of the ladies.

Back at Westminster School in the late 1980s, I was certainly keen on the idea of sex – but only as an abstract quality. Those little gobbets of sexual excitement in the Classics were entirely literary – there was no physical reflection of them in my monkish school life. By the time I left Westminster in 1988, I had been studying Latin for nine years, Greek for eight. And still there hadn't been any Bacchic, wine-fuelled sex rituals for me, just a million prepositions and a thousand optatives.

I could have told you exactly when you should use the subjunctive in a conditional clause. Stick me on the coast of Corfu, naked, with an enthusiastic Greek princess and a beach ball, and I was lost. While my friends spent their school holidays snogging girls, I was writing Greek inscriptions on an abandoned slate, to hang in a ruined outbuilding in Venn Cottages, my parents' holiday home in Pembrokeshire.

How pleased I was with my adaptation of a Sophocles line from *Antigone*, *Polla ta deina kouden anthropou deinoteron pelei* – 'There are many formidable things in the world, but there is nothing more formidable than mankind.' The Sophocles quotation is famous for asserting the power of man over the gods. My version substituted 'Venn Cottages' for 'mankind'. Not the kind of thing that gets the girls.

On my last holiday before starting at university, I went with my family to a villa in Tuscany belonging to a rich Italian bachelor friend of a friend of my parents'. Also there was my sister's best friend – Lucy, a 16-year-old with a saturnine wit, great big brown pools for eyes and the kind of interplanetary confidence possessed only by cool teenagers.

In a bid to impress her, I tried to swim the full length of the villa's swimming pool underwater. To garner maximum power, I compressed my legs against the wall of the shallow end, took a deep breath, and launched myself – straight into the floor of the shallow end. I surfaced with an open rectangle of a gash, an inch long, running down the bridge of my nose, streaming blood.

It didn't stop there. Both Lucy and I got out of the pool with water trapped in our ears. I'd seen on TV that the cure was a forward roll – which I proceeded to execute in the rich Italian bachelor's sitting room. I did the forward roll in the narrow gap between a pair of brocaded armchairs and a glass coffee table, sprinkled with small porcelain animals – bears, boars, sea lions.

My head and torso folded over in a neat straight line in the gap between the table and armchairs. But my legs came turning over at a strange angle to my hips, crashing down on the glass top of the table. The bears, boars and sea lions were shaken out of place, but remained standing. A single loathsome glass frog leapt off the table, and broke into three bright green chunks on the hard, tiled floor.

My mother nobly wrapped the smashed frog in a day-old copy of the *Telegraph* and put it in the bin. The next day, the Italian bachelor's ancient, devoted maid marched over to us as we ate lunch in the vine-shaded pergola. *Cos'è questo?* she said, unwrapping a crumpled *Telegraph* obituaries page to reveal the shattered frog. Mum should have camouflaged it inside *La Nazione*.

That day, my sister took a photo of me, lying low on the sofa in the sitting room, the rectangular scab hardening on my nose. I'm doing my holiday reading – Book 24 of *The Iliad*, the last book, which tells the sad story of Priam retrieving the body of his oldest son, Hector, from Achilles. I'm looking a bit sad, too. Not because of poor old Priam, or because of my now healing injury; more a little shamefaced at my doomed attempts to impress Lucy.

And so I'd taken refuge from real life, as I always did – and still do – in a book. Not, though, without a little pulse of smugness. In the photograph, I'm pointing my index finger to the words on the cover, 'Iliad – Book 24', a not-so-subtle reference to my cleverness at reading Homer in Greek. At the age of only 17! I may be rubbish with girls – but look what an intergalactic brain I possess!

That book of *The Iliad* had a commentary by Colin MacLeod – in my sister's photo, you can see his name on the cover, partly obscured by my pointing finger. MacLeod was the brilliant Christ Church Classics don who won a scholarship to Balliol at the age of 16 – only to kill himself in 1981 at the age of 38. My Greek master at school, who'd been taught by him at Oxford, said he did it because he'd divined the essential bleakness of the human condition through his deep understanding of the works of Thucydides.

Even then, that struck me as an over-dramatic response to the searing brilliance of the Classics – and, for all my neurosis, not something I was in danger of doing. But, still, perhaps like Colin MacLeod, I had over-developed my intellect at the expense of an under-developed, closed, arid heart. After I fell in love for the first time, at the late age of 32, my girlfriend burst out laughing when I told her the last time I'd felt so emotionally confused: on the day I changed from Classics to Ancient and Modern History at Oxford when I was 19.

It didn't help that, like MacLeod, I left school at 16, thanks to an acceleration system at Westminster School where you jumped a year if you passed an exam in your first year. So I'd done my A-Levels – and my Oxford S-Levels and Cambridge Step exams – before I'd snogged a girl.

I managed, just, to do that on my last evening at the school at Westminster's Election Dinner. The dinner is an ancient event – held in the school's medieval dining hall – to celebrate the election of boys to Oxford and Cambridge. After dinner, as the occasion demanded, I recited an epigram in ancient Greek – with a topical joke incorporated.

Mike Gatting, the England cricket captain, had just been exposed for an alleged affair with a barmaid. Among my lines were the Greek words, ... *gar tin skandalon* ... Put the wrong emphasis on it, and it can be made to sound like 'Gatting scandal'. The idea of the epigrams was that the Greek meaning would be different, but related. My epigram, translated, meant: 'For it is a trap.' I didn't think it was very funny, either.

Another guest at the dinner was Enoch Powell, who had lost his Ulster Unionist seat in South Down a year before. Powell made up a Greek epigram on the spot, unlike us pupils, who'd been honing them for months under close supervision.

I shouldn't have been surprised. Powell was an exceptional Greek scholar before the war. At Trinity College, Cambridge – where he was a devotee of

A. E. Housman's lectures – he was asked to translate an English passage into Greek in a three-hour exam. In only an hour and a half, he did two translations, one in the style of Thucydides, one in the style of Plato. After a double, starred first, Powell became Professor of Greek at Sydney University at 25; he was disappointed not to match Friedrich Nietzsche's appointment as a professor at 24. In 1938, at 26, Powell published an edition of Thucydides's *Historiae* and *A Lexicon to Herodotus*.

A short while after Enoch Powell recited his impromptu epigram, a charitable girl in the year below took me by the hand and led me to a scholar's empty bedroom in College, the house for Westminster scholars. There she kindly subjected me to an extremely innocent spell of kissing that wouldn't have shocked Lawrence Durrell's Greek teacher in Canterbury 60 years earlier.

An evening with a kind girl from the year below didn't do much to change my innate squareness. A year later, I took a gap-year trip with three school friends to Ios, supreme party island of the Cyclades. On our first night, one school friend stayed up all night, drank a bottle of ouzo, snogged a large-breasted peroxide blonde from Chesterfield and was sick all down his light pink shirt. That same night, I hiked with two other friends across the island and slept rough on the mosquito-ridden beach where Homer was supposedly born. Who'd had the better time?

Even in Homer's time, Ios was the quintessential party island. Aristotle said, 'Homer was born from a spirit, a daimon, who danced along with the Muses.' Homer's mother, a party girl, supposedly became pregnant with the poet after sleeping with the daimon. I should have followed Homer's mother's example and got into the party spirit. But, as always, I went for the dull, worthy option, the escape from real life.

The pattern continues today. Greece remains a wild, easy-going place; I remain the ruin-loving dork. In Philip Larkin's phrase, I remain 'randy for antique' – putting the old before the new, the young and the sensuous.

Still, being a ruin-loving dork doesn't mean your heart has altogether died. How it throbbed at the prospect of the next stop. My parents had now disembarked from the *Corinthian*, so Timothy Lumsden would be back on his own when the ship docked in Chios, the island with the best claim to being Homer's birthplace.

Misspent youth – The 17-year-old author reading Homer with a nose injury, self-inflicted in a swimming pool while trying to impress a girl.

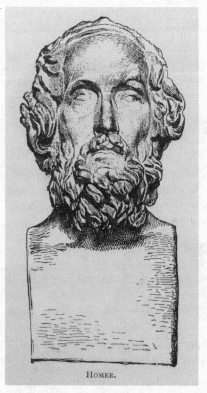

HOMER.

A blind Homer (1890 drawing)

9

Homer – the Early Years

In Alan Bennett's *The History Boys*, Hector, the inspirational gay teacher with the Trojan hero's name, talks about the power of great books: when a writer stretches his hand out from the pages and you reach out to take it in recognition.

Homer's is the oldest, grizzliest hand of all. Again and again, he stretches it out, and you think, 'Yes, that's what the sea looks like; that's how a deep sleep feels; that's the horror of loneliness.'

The Iliad and *The Odyssey* are full of domestic details you recognise around the Mediterranean today: goats cooked in their own fat, washed down with strong, rough, local wine; lamb roasted on spits, inspiration for the kebab. In *The Iliad*, Book 9, Achilles and Patroclus prepare magnificent kebabs of pork, mutton and goat for Odysseus. Speared on skewers, the kebabs are cooked, as they turn, on glowing coals. Sprinkled with salt, they're then wrapped in bread.

And Chios is just as its most famous son, Homer, described it: craggy, or *palipoessa*. *Palipoessa* is a classic Homeric epithet – a description used over and over again, of the same people and places. His epithets for Greek islands are often pretty austere – not least craggy Chios and rugged Ithaca, Odysseus's home island. The overwhelming look of Chios is the Greek look: beautiful, but infertile, scrub; part rock, part grass scorched to premature hay.

Chios, in all its craggy, inhospitable beauty, is Greece in miniature; a reminder that the country, as a whole, was never built for political or economic dominance. Eighty per cent of Greece is mountains. There are no great rivers and few open plains. Until 600 BC, Athens, and its surrounding city state of Attica, was pretty much a third-rate power. And then, 2,500 years ago, a slice of Mediterranean coast smaller than Gloucestershire – with a population as big as Bristol's – bloomed into the most sophisticated civilisation the world had ever seen.

In a strange accident of history, the Greeks had the eastern Mediterranean pretty much to themselves and made unequalled political and artistic advances on the back of it. To make those achievements more remarkable, the Athenian golden age barely lasted a century – while its Roman successor hung on for half a millennium. Over the course of that brief century, the human mind was changed, changed for good and changed to a more considerable degree than under 500 years of Roman rule. That Roman cultural cringe towards the Greeks is infinitely understandable.

Like most things to do with Homer, the evidence he was born on Chios is a little scanty. He certainly mentioned the island several times in *The Odyssey*. In sixth-century BC Chios, a group of bards – the Homeridae, or Sons of Homer – claimed to have been Homer's descendants, who'd been handed down his poems in manuscript. One of these Homeridae supposedly composed a poem, the *Homeric Hymn to Delian Apollo*, in 522 BC, addressed to the maidens in the choir:

> 'Whom think ye, girls, is the sweetest singer that comes here, and in whom
> do you most delight?' Then answer, each and all, with one voice: 'He is
> a blind man, and dwells in rocky Chios; his lays are ever more supreme.'

In the ancient Greek dialect spoken on Delos, the word *homer* is thought to have meant 'blind', supporting the myth that Homer couldn't see – his eyes are almost always blank in ancient statues of him.

That's still pretty limited evidence. But it's enough for Chios to claim Homer for its own. As the *Corinthian* docked in Chios Town, we were met by the usual tide of place names that follow in Odysseus's wake. Just across the tarmac apron of the harbour from my cabin window stood the Mansion Omeros Rooms, a rundown mini-tower block of bedsits for rent.

A little further north, up the eastern coast of the island, I drove my hire car to the fringes of the town. In the suburb of Vrontados, I parked in fancifully named Omeroupoli – 'Homer's City'. There, I sat on Homer's Seat – a two-foot-tall cube of stone which perches on top of a colossal boulder, known as the Teacher's Rock – and stared out to sea. This is where the great man is supposed to have sat dispensing wisdom to local children.

Volissos, on the other side of the island, is celebrated as Homer's actual birthplace. After a long, sunset drive, switchbacking around the crags of Chios, I searched through the town – but there was no Homer's Bar or Trojan Horse Restaurant. This was the only time in my travels I came to a famous Homeric spot and found no commercial exploitation of it.

The presence of apocryphal evidence – like Homer's Seat in Omeroupoli – is hardly more useful than the complete absence of any at Volissos. Still, the evidence on Chios is earlier than the evidence in other potential birthplaces. That is its own evidence. If Homer really did come from your home town, the chances are you'd find earlier, more substantial evidence there than elsewhere.

On Turkey's western coast, Smyrna – now the Turkish city of Izmir – is the other major candidate for Homer's birthplace, thanks to a ninth-century AD manuscript staking a claim.

Smyrna had lots of Greek residents until the Greco-Turkish War of 1919–22, when the Greeks fled west. Still, today, there's an Athenian suburb called Nea Smyrna – New Smyrna, settled by exiles from old Smyrna. Other Athenian suburbs include Nea Ionia and Nea Philadelphia – a once-Greek settlement, now a Turkish town, Alaşehir, 80 miles east of Izmir. Literally meaning 'brotherly love', this Philadelphia is the precursor to the American city.

Now that Smyrna is Izmir, in modern Turkey, the Turks are particularly keen on its Homer claim. The map I got in Ephesus – 100 miles east of Chios, near the Turkish coast – stated, as a matter of fact, that Homer was born in Izmir. Other claimants to Homer's birthplace include Ios, Egypt, Ithaca, Thessaly, the Argolid, Pylos, Athens and Colophon, a little south of Smyrna.

There is no definitive answer. But that stretch of coast around Chios and Izmir – only 50 miles apart – has the strongest claim. It's close enough to Troy; and it's also in pole position for odysseys to the Cyclades, Crete, the Peloponnese and Ithaca. The meltemi – that prevailing northerly wind – opens up much of the ancient Greek world to any clever Chiot, sitting on his cubic rock and staring out to sea.

Chios and Smyrna were at the crossroads of the different dialects of ancient Greece: Doric, spoken in Crete and the southern Peloponnese; Aeolic in what is now north-western Turkey; and Ionic, spoken in the Cyclades and Attica. A dialect of Ionic – Attic – spread from Athens through the Greek-speaking world in the Hellenistic period and became what we now call ancient Greek.

Ionic was also spoken on Chios. And – important evidence for those who claim Chios as Homer's birthplace – Homeric Greek was largely Ionic.

One of Homer's many astonishing gifts was his deft combination of those dialects. Alexander Pope – who wrote best-selling translations of *The Iliad* and *The Odyssey* in 1720 and 1726 – said Homer wrote 'Ionic, which has a peculiar sweetness, from its never using contractions, and from its custom of resolving the diphthongs into two syllables, so as to make the words open themselves with a more spreading and sonorous fluency. With this he mingled the Attic contractions, the broader Doric, and the feebler Aeolic.'

No wonder so many parts of ancient Greece can claim this linguistic genius for their own. No wonder, too, that some scholars insist such a multi-faceted man must have really been several different people. This knotty mystery over Homer's identity – known as the Homeric Question – has been hanging around for centuries. Even in antiquity, there were *chorizontes* – 'separators' – who thought there was more than one Homer. In recent years, the authorship theories have grown even more complex.

These scholars can't bear the simple, pleasing beauty of a single genius – of unknown pedigree, from a remote corner of Greece – being the fount of Western European literature. And so they invent over-complicated new explanations. The same pattern happened – and is still happening – with Shakespeare. Snobbish critics can't conceive of a glover's son, a Midlands grammar-school boy, being capable of such genius – and so they insist he must be the Earl of Oxford, Christopher Marlowe or Francis Bacon.

I'm with Lawrence of Arabia. He concluded that Homer was just an exceptionally early one-off, gifted, as people very occasionally are, with a mysterious genius. Lawrence translated *The Odyssey* from 1928 to 1931, while serving with the RAF. Wherever he served – first in a mud-brick fort in Afghanistan, then in a flying-boat station at Cattewater in Plymouth – he took his Homer, and toiled away on his translation. He never got any closer to cracking who the real Homer was.

'He is baffling,' Lawrence said. 'Not simple, in education; not primitive, socially. Rather a William Morris of his day, I fancy.'

Modern scholars are equally baffled. There are no contemporary documents about Homer's life. Those scholars still don't know who Homer was, exactly when the epics were written down for the first time, or where he was born.

Or whether he was a she. This is no modern feminist interpretation. Samuel Butler, author of *Erewhon*, was so impressed by Homer's female characters that he was convinced she was a woman – however unlikely it was that a woman could be a travelling bard in ancient Greece.

The idea that two different people wrote *The Iliad* and *The Odyssey* seems unlikely, too. Not only are the epics written in too similar a style, but they also dovetail too neatly. *The Odyssey*, in a series of flashbacks, filled in the gaps about the Trojan horse and the death of Achilles, neither of which were mentioned in *The Iliad*.

If there were two Homers, it gets even more complicated – because one borrowed from the other. Some lines in *The Odyssey* are near identical to others in *The Iliad*.

One suggestion is that Homer's works passed from generation to generation via a precarious oral tradition – with poets reciting the epics in public for centuries before they were written down. It would have been quite a feat: there are 15,693 lines in *The Iliad*, 12,110 in *The Odyssey*. It helped that, like all early Greek literature, it was poetry, with its own memorable rhythm. The first prose, now lost, was supposedly written by Pherecydes of Syros in 550 BC; the earliest surviving Greek prose is Herodotus's work of the mid-fifth century BC.

They must have had longer attention spans in ancient Greece, too. It takes around 20 hours to recite the whole of *The Odyssey*; a task made only slightly easier by the fact that more than half of the poem's lines are in direct speech. Reciting *The Odyssey* would have been like playing a very long part in a play. There are only 4,042 lines in *Hamlet*, and Hamlet only has to speak 1,438 of them. Still, it's not impossible. Oral cultures may seem strange in the written culture of the West. But, across the world, writing cultures are the exception. There are 3,000 languages spoken today; only 78 of them have a body of written works.

In his *Barrack-Room Ballads*, Rudyard Kipling certainly thought Homer was a bard, singing copied songs rather than writing them down.

When 'Omer smote 'is bloomin' lyre,
He'd 'eard men sing by land an' sea;

An' what he thought 'e might require,
E went an' took – the same as me!

The market-girls an' fishermen,
The shepherds an' the sailors, too,
They 'eard old songs turn up again,
But kep' it quiet – same as you!

They knew 'e stole; 'e knew they knowed.
They didn't tell, nor make a fuss,
But winked at 'Omer down the road,
An' 'e winked back – the same as us!'

If Homer did smite his bloomin' lyre, rather than write with his bloomin' pen, he wasn't the only one. For all the sophistication of its written literature, ancient Greece remained a largely oral culture into the fifth and fourth centuries BC. Socrates never wrote a single surviving word. All we know of him we know thanks to his pupil, Plato, who took down his master's dictation. Aristotle's works largely survived through his pupils' lecture notes.

It wasn't just bards and philosophers who memorised great tracts of literature. Plutarch said the Athenians, captured in Syracuse, Sicily, in 413 BC, only stayed alive because of their impressive skill at reciting screeds of Euripides from memory.

One Homeric scholar, Milman Parry, a former chicken farmer from Oakland, California, travelled to Dubrovnik in 1933 to get to the bottom of the Homeric Question. Parry interviewed Slav bards who were still reciting thousands of lines of poetry from memory, including recently composed epics. One was about the 1914 assassination of Archduke Franz Ferdinand. Other oral traditions continued until recently in Albania, Armenia and Ireland – where the last prose epic bard died in the 1940s.

When Heinrich Schliemann visited Ithaca in 1868, he came across six different versions of *The Odyssey* recited by locals. One of them, a scholarly miller called Asprogerakas, spent hours regaling Schliemann with his interpretation of *The Odyssey*, paraphrased by him and his ancestors.

Before Parry could come to a certain conclusion about Homeric composition, he accidentally killed himself at the age of only 33. Visiting his mother-in-law in Los Angeles, and unpacking a suitcase in his hotel room, he was killed when a revolver mixed up with his clothes went off.

Just before he died, however, Parry did come to one conclusion: *The Iliad* and *The Odyssey* were much more uniform in their phrasing than the Slav epics he'd studied. Either a single composer wrote the Homeric epics, Parry thought; or there was a single, closed, professional group of bards, all given identical training.

If there was such an oral tradition, then no wonder these bards needed regularly repeated tropes and epithets to keep the poetry pouring forth, without the singers drying up at any moment. Nearly a third of all Homeric lines are repeated or contain repeated phrases and epithets. That repetition has encapsulated the legendary view of ancient Greece, with its wine-dark sea and rosy-fingered dawn. 'Lucky dawn,' as my late Greek master liked to say, repeatedly.

Thirty-seven of the leading gods and heroes of *The Iliad* and *The Odyssey* have their own epithets. Odysseus is called *polytlas dios* – 'much-enduring, divine' – 38 times. Even Odysseus's name had its own in-built epithet. It might be related to *odune*, 'pain'; there are also echoes of *odysato*, 'to be hated'. The name of his son, Telemachus, stranded on Ithaca during the Trojan War, meant 'far from battle'. Oedipus meant 'swollen foot' – from the legend that his feet were impaled with a spike as a baby.

The myths of Pro-metheus ('Fore-sight') and Epi-metheus ('Hind-sight') were behind the Pandora story. Prometheus told Epimetheus not to accept gifts from the gods. Ignoring him, Epimetheus, persuaded by Hermes, married lovely Pandora, who brought with her the jar crammed with the world's evils, and madly opened it. She could have done with more Prometheus.

Those epithets were rigidly applied even when they made little sense – like the ship that's still 'swift' after it's been turned into stone or the skies that are 'starry' at midday. That fits with the idea that epithets were little memory-joggers and gap-fillers for the bard, or bards, who first created and sang *The Iliad* and *The Odyssey*.

Two of these bards – professional singers called Demodocus and Phemius – turn up in *The Odyssey*. Demodocus told the story of the Trojan War to King Alcinous's court on Corfu, and reduced Odysseus to tears. Homer said Demodocus was the minstrel loved by the Muse above all men. This minstrel also happened to be blind – reinforcing the idea that Homer couldn't see.

In *The Iliad*, Book 2, Homer narrated as if he himself was a bard:

I couldn't speak of, or name, the massed ranks of Greek soldiers at Troy,
Not even if I had ten tongues and ten mouths besides,
A voice that didn't break, and the heart within me were bronze.

Both *The Iliad* and *The Odyssey* open with pleas to a muse and a goddess, as if a bard is praying for help with the huge recital. *The Iliad* begins, 'Sing, goddess, of the anger of Peleus's son, Achilles, and its devastation, which inflicted a thousand pains on the Greeks.' And *The Odyssey* starts with the lines, 'Tell me, muse, about the man of many skills, who wandered many ways after he had sacked Troy's sacred citadel.'

The jury is still out over when Homer lived. Some critics think he must have been around close to the time of the Trojan War. That would explain his peculiar gift for describing Mycenean civilisation. A few have even placed Homer as early as the eighteenth century BC. Herodotus said Homer lived 400 years before his own time — i.e. around 850 BC. Others think Homer was so sophisticated that he must have come along later. '*The Iliad* and *The Odyssey* must have been written in the sixth century BC', Boris Johnson once told me. 'They're much too perfect.'

However many Homers there were – and whenever they were around – the majority opinion, at present, is that *The Iliad* was written in around 750 BC, *The Odyssey* in 735 BC. Homer's tentacles spread across the Greek world soon after. Homeric scenes started appearing on vases from around 700 BC. Around the same time, Greeks began to associate mandrake – the poisonous plant – with Circe and the drugs she used to send Odysseus's crew to sleep.

The Odyssey brand was beginning its extremely slow journey towards the domination of world literature.

Odysseus and the Sirens, from an Athenian storage jar of around 480 BC. The Sirens looked, and sang, like birds. Some place the Sirens on the Galli Islands – or the Sirenuse – off Positano. Others put them at Phocaea, 30 miles north of Izmir. When the wind blows over the flute-shaped rocks on the islands there, you hear the Sirens sing once more.

The Abduction of Helen – probably by Zanobi Strozzi, c.1450. Paris carries Helen from the Temple of Apollo and Artemis on the island of Cythera. At this stage, she's Helen of Sparta – she's still married to King Menelaus of Sparta.
The scene is set in around 1200 BC, but those Corinthian pilasters on the temple weren't invented until the late fifth-century BC.

10

How Homer Conquered the World

In the National Gallery, there's a charming, anonymous picture of *The Abduction of Helen*, probably painted by Zanobi Strozzi in around 1450. Charming but inaccurate – the Greek islands are painted a strange, muddy mixture of brown and grey; Helen is whipped away from an elegant classical temple, built in a style far later than any Homeric building.

Florence was only 300 miles north of Magna Graecia and the ancient Greek temples of Paestum – but, still, the understanding of the Greek world, and Homer, was minimal in the mid-fifteenth century. There wasn't a widespread understanding of Homer – and ancient Greek – among educated Europeans until the seventeenth century. In the sixteenth century, the most read classical author in Europe was Tertullian, a near-forgotten, early Christian Roman writer.

Petrarch, the fourteenth-century Italian poet, revered ancient Greece. He kissed his Homer manuscript regularly – but couldn't actually read it. In 1369, he asked Leonato Pilato, a Greek-speaking Calabrian, to translate *The Iliad* and *The Odyssey*, and to teach him Greek – but he never got very far.

The idea of Homer as the wellspring of Western European literature didn't bed in until printed editions and translations were widely available. The first printed edition of Homer appeared in Florence in 1488, published by a Greek. Seven editions were printed in Europe in the sixteenth century – and so the epics began their widespread dissemination across the Continent.

Us British were late on the scene. George Chapman's *The Whole Works of Homer* – the first English translation of the complete works – wasn't published until 1616. Keats – unable to read Homer in the original Greek – filled his poems with Greek references, from 'On Seeing the Elgin Marbles' to 'Ode on a Grecian Urn'. It's the Roman idea all over again – Greek was the highest calling, even if you couldn't actually speak it. No wonder Keats was so thrilled by Chapman's translation; he had no other way to appreciate Homer.

'On First Looking into Chapman's Homer'

Much have I travell'd in the realms of gold,
And many goodly states and kingdoms seen;
Round many western islands have I been
Which bards in fealty to Apollo hold.
Oft of one wide expanse had I been told
That deep-browed Homer ruled as his demesne;
Yet did I never breathe its pure serene
Till I heard Chapman speak out loud and bold:
Then felt I like some watcher of the skies
When a new planet swims into his ken;
Or like stout Cortez when with eagle eyes
He star'd at the Pacific – and all his men
Look'd at each other with a wild surmise –
Silent, upon a peak in Darien.

For all Chapman's brilliance, his translation had its longueurs, not least in his ham-fisted attempts to capture Homeric compound nouns: 'the white-and-red-mix'd-fingerd Dame' and 'the King, Good-at-a-martiall-shout'.

Funnily enough, earlier books about Troy had appeared in English before *The Iliad* and *The Odyssey* were first translated. In 1473, the first book printed in the English language – and the first book printed by William Caxton – was *The Recuyell of the Historyes of Troye*, a French courtly romance about the Trojan War. A copy was sold by the Duke of Northumberland in 2014 for £1.25 million.

It didn't help that Greece, under Ottoman rule from the mid-fifteenth century, was cut off from Christendom for several centuries. In 1465, Giuliano da Sangallo, one of Lorenzo de' Medici's favourite architects, could only make a very rough copy of a drawing of the Parthenon, done in situ by an antiquarian called Ciriaco d'Ancona. Sangallo couldn't make the shortish trip to Greece from Florence; he even adapted his picture of the Parthenon to fit with antique temples in Italy and southern France.

Only in the eighteenth century were accurate pictures of the Acropolis available across Western Europe. No wonder Renaissance pictures of *The Iliad* and *The Odyssey* were a bit hazy on the details.

Homer didn't become widely celebrated in Britain until the eighteenth century, either. By 1723, he was famous enough for the Duke of Buckingham to write this piece of doggerel:

Read Homer once, and you can read no more;
For all books else appear so mean, so poor,
Verse will seem prose: but still persist to read,
And Homer will be all the books you need.

One hundred and fifty years later, Homer's position at the top of European literature was firmly entrenched. The Victorian constitutional historian Walter Bagehot wrote that a man who has never read Homer is 'like a man who has never seen the sea. There is a great object of which he is unaware.'

Homer's literary supremacy is now taken as read. Goethe wondered, if Europe had taken Homer as its religious set text, and not the Bible, how different the world would have been. In many ways, Europe did take Homer as its secular set text – as the foundation stone of its literature.

For all that later influence, the early survival of the epic poems was touch and go. How different European literature would be if *The Iliad* and *The Odyssey* had been swallowed up by the sands of time – like the vast majority of classical literature.

The Iliad and *The Odyssey* weren't found in a fixed form until the mid-sixth century BC. At the Panathenaic Games, from the sixth century BC onwards, there was a Homeric recitation competition, an ancient sort of school speech.

In ancient Greece, Homer was revered by the fifth century BC at least – the story of Troy was given a prominent slot on the north side of the outer metopes of the Parthenon in 447 BC. Perhaps the works had been around for centuries before they became embedded in Greek culture. A time lag between ancient writer and his first published works wasn't unusual. Aesop was supposedly around in the sixth century BC; his first collection of fables didn't appear until 300 BC.

The earliest surviving papyri of *The Odyssey* date from the third century BC. In the third and second centuries BC, the varying texts floating around Greece were standardised at the Library of Alexandria. The Alexandria Library in the third century BC was one of those rare collisions of time and place – when the human mind took a great leap forwards.

In the early third century BC, the original librarian at Alexandria, Zeonodotus, first catalogued books alphabetically. Later that century, two other librarians at Alexandria, Aristophanes of Byzantium and his sidekick, Aristarchus of Samothrace, were the first to use asterisks – Greek for 'little star' – to highlight lines that were repeated in both *The Iliad* and *The Odyssey*.

In the third century AD, the Christian theologian Origen started using asterisks to denote missing bits in manuscripts of the Greek Old Testament. That's why your computer turns your password into asterisks when you log on to your online banking.

Aristophanes of Byzantium, head librarian at Alexandria, didn't just help invent the asterisk. He was the Father of Punctuation. He used a dot floating in mid-air to divide shorter passages, or *kommas*, as they were called – thus our word, 'comma'. A dot at the bottom of a line divided longer passages, or colons – thus our colon. For strong divisions between passages, he placed a dot at the top of a line, to produce the longest pause, or *periodos*, as in the American period, or the British full stop.

By the first century BC, *The Odyssey* was an established greatest hit in the Roman poetic repertoire. In the ode 'These Italian Hills', Horace wrote:

No one will harm you here; in my
Creative hideaway you'll sing
Of Ulysses, the temptress Circe
And his wife, Penelope.

Horace was responsible for the expression 'Even Homer nods' – to show that the greatest minds occasionally mess up. The expression came from a line in Horace's *Ars Poetica* in around 18 BC – *Indignor quandoque bonus dormitat Homerus* ('I get irritated when the great Homer dozes'). The expression 'Homer nods' was first used by Dryden in 1677, and copied by Pope in 1709.

By the time Dryden and Pope were around, Homer was a pan-European hit. Before then, there had been something of a lull in Homer's reputation – nearly a thousand-year lull.

The earliest complete manuscript of *The Odyssey*, from the tenth century AD, is in Michelangelo's Laurentian Library in Florence. The earliest complete *Iliad* is a mid-tenth-century vellum manuscript in Venice's Biblioteca Marciana. Soon after that, other manuscripts start appearing – until Gutenberg's printing revolution, 500 years later, started spreading Homer across Europe.

Whoever Homer – or the Homers – was or were, he, she or they set the template for the Greek literature that followed; the Latin literature that followed that; the Renaissance literature that followed that …

In the preface to his *Iliad* translation, Alexander Pope said it was near impossible not to be influenced by Homer's greatness.

'If Homer has funeral games for Patroclus, Virgil has the same for Anchises', Pope wrote, 'If Ulysses visits the shades, the Aeneas of Virgil is sent after him. If he be detained from his return by the allurements of Calypso, so is Aeneas by Dido.'

The Odyssey became the archetypal going home story, and the archetypal journey. Again and again, over the last 2,800 years, it spawned imitations, from Joyce's *Ulysses* – and Tennyson's – to the Coen Brothers' film *O Brother, Where Art Thou?*. However the epics were composed, they show exceptional literary confidence in their composer.

In *The Iliad*, Homer was so confident in his narrative technique that he cherry-picked only a few incidents from the ten years of the war. Most of the action of the book concentrates on only a few days at Troy – he doesn't even mention the fall of the city and its aftermath in *The Iliad*. He began the first book without even saying where the action is taking place.

Homer showed the same narrative control in *The Odyssey*. Odysseus doesn't appear until four books in, after 2,222 lines. For a sixth of the action, *The Odyssey* is

Hamlet without the prince. Odysseus even used a flashback – the earliest surviving instance in literature – when he told the story of his previous journey at King Alcinous's court.

Homeric epic is particularly sophisticated in a world of such terrifyingly short lives. Most men in ancient Greece were fathers by the age of 12, grandfathers by 24, and dead at 35. Hardly long enough to come to a considered opinion of the world, let alone write two eternal epics.

The quality of Homeric prose is astonishing, too, given it was composed at such an early stage in the life cycle of ancient Greek. The Greek alphabet, adapted from Phoenician, was probably settled by around 800 BC, less than a century before Homer was around. That alphabet – ancestor to our own alphabet and the Russian Cyrillic alphabet – was very different to Phoenician. There are no 'ch-', 'ph-' or 'ps-' symbols in Phoenician, and no vowels either. Phoenician had 25 letters, Greek 24.

Among the different versions of the early Greek alphabet, the western, Chalcidian version morphed into the Italic and then the Latin alphabet. The eastern, Ionic version became the familiar ancient Greek alphabet. The new Greek alphabet used signs for sounds rather than the Phoenician signs for syllables. That allowed Greek to become a much more flexible writing tool.

Eighth-century BC Greek writing – as *The Odyssey* probably is – should by rights be a little primitive, if the alphabet had only just settled into place. The earliest surviving bit of Greek poetry, from around 740–720 BC, is hardly sophisticated. It's on a pottery goblet, known as Nestor's Cup – after Nestor's gold-rimmed silver bowl, mentioned in Book 11 of *The Iliad*. The goblet was found in Ischia, in the Gulf of Naples – the first part of Italy to be colonised by Greeks, from Euboea, in 770 BC.

It was inscribed with these lines, two of them Homeric hexameters: 'Nestor had a certain cup, good to drink from. But whoever drinks from this cup will immediately be seized with desire for Aphrodite of the beautiful crown.' Compare the simplicity of the bawdy inscription on Nestor's Cup with the lyrical qualities of Homeric prose, and the gulf yawns.

There's another hint that Homer, for all his sophistication, wrote at this extremely early moment in the development of Greek. His avant-garde works are packed with *hapax legomena* – Greek for 'words that are only used once'. Some of these hapax legomena are derived from Linear B – the language that preceded Greek. Others are so obscure that no one can translate them with certainty; another reason why the epics remain eternally fluid, eternally open to interpretation, like Shakespeare and the Bible.

There are 868 recorded *hapax legomena* in *The Odyssey*, 1,097 in *The Iliad*. They include 'Hectoriden' – 'Hector's son' – used of Astyanax, a baby in *The Iliad*. It's significant that he's called Hectoriden just before he's murdered: because he is Hectoriden, he's bound to seek revenge, and so must be killed before he kills.

Homer didn't just use a new alphabet, then. He used rare – if not necessarily new – words to describe the ancient world for the first, or earliest surviving, time.

How staggering that this new language largely survives on the Athenian Metro today; that until 2001, when Greece adopted the euro, Greeks were still spending the ancient currency, the drachma – Greek for 'a handful'.

Celtic – spoken in the shadow of Stonehenge in 1800 BC – would be unrecognisable to English-speakers today; Latin has made a pretty big leap to Italian. But the most influential language of them all has survived nearly 3,000 years of linguistic buffeting. If you can read ancient Greek, you can read modern Greek – and bridge the millennia.

There have been small changes of meaning along the way. Philip II of Macedon, Alexander the Great's father, standardised *koine* – 'common' – Greek in the fourth century BC. This was the Attic or Athenian dialect, used for the New Testament four hundred or so years later. Modern Greek is called *dimotiki* – meaning 'the language of the people', as in *demos*, 'people'. Connections between modern and ancient Greek were even closer in *katharevousa* – the pure, official form of Greek, as opposed to *dimotiki*.

Katharevousa was invented by a revolutionary leader, Adamantios Korais, in the nineteenth century, combining a mixture of *dimotiki* and ancient Greek. The language flourished until 1976, when *dimotiki* was made the official national language. *Katharevousa* is still spoken by older, grander Greeks and remains the official language of the Greek Orthodox Church.

Greek is the original Western European language: the one in which so many thoughts, actions and idioms were first captured with direct, unadulterated force, imitative of nothing – or at least very little – of what came before.

Ancient Greek grew out of Linear B, used from around 1450 to 1200 BC across Greece – in Knossos, Pylos, Mycenae, Tiryns and Thebes. Linear B was first translated in 1952 by the British scholar Michael Ventris, at the age of 29, only four years before his death in a car crash on the A1.

An architect, Ventris had never been to university. He was helped by the classical and Japanese scholar John Chadwick, who honed his skills at Bletchley Park during the war, decoding messages sent by the Japanese navy. Linear A, an earlier Cretan language from around 1700–1450 BC, is yet to be unravelled.

Ventris cracked the code one evening, in the middle of a dinner party. He leapt to his feet, saying, 'I know it, I know it.' He had suddenly realised that some repeated words on Linear B tablets might be place names – and, even better, the same names later used by the Greeks. By trying different variants, he worked out references to *konoso* – Knossos. He then moved on to other places in Crete: *aminiso*, or Amnisos, and *turiso*, or Tulissos.

Linear B, Ventris calculated, was an abbreviated type of archaic Greek, as far removed from classical Greek as Anglo-Saxon is from Shakespeare's English. Several English words go all the way back to Linear B – including 'tripod', from the Linear B *tiripode*. Like us, Linear B also used a decimal system.

It was in Linear B, too, that the Greek gods first appeared, most prominently Zeus, Athena and Hermes. By the time Homer got to writing about the gods, he had formed a complete, coherent, influential picture of their existence: what they represent, their hierarchies, their celestial life on Mount Olympus and their relationships with mortals and priests.

Herodotus said Homer 'first fixed for the Greeks the genealogy of the gods and their titles, divided among them their honours and functions, and defined their images'. Quite an achievement, given the 600 Greek gods and their incestuous family tree – the royal families of Europe had nothing on them. The gods were so omnipresent in the ancient world that there was no Greek word for religion. Religion was so infused into everything, so part of everyday life and conversation, that it wasn't thought of as its own separate entity.

Even if Homer's picture of the Greek myths was fully formed and internally coherent, that's not to say it was set in stone. As Greek literature developed in the wake of *The Iliad* and *The Odyssey*, the myths were mangled for dramatic effect. In earlier versions of the Medea story, the inhabitants of Corinth murdered Medea's children. Euripides made the story more shocking, by having Medea kill them herself. What literary confidence to play with ancient mythology to make good copy; like Shakespeare taking the medieval story of King Lear, and deciding to kill off Cordelia and Lear to sex up the tragedy.

Today, those myths remain extremely protean – as in the Homeric sea god, Proteus, capable of changing into a leopard, lion, pig, tree or stretch of water. Even if we're familiar with the original story of, say, Theseus and the Minotaur, we're perfectly happy for that original story to be warped out of all recognition in cartoons, comic books and films.

The 2010 science fiction film *Clash of the Titans* had little in common with the 1981 film of the same name, let alone the original Greek story of Perseus and Andromeda. The connections between the 2004 film *Troy*, starring Brad Pitt and Orlando Bloom, and *The Iliad* are tenuous.

But we don't mind this butchery of Homer, the way we do a bad film adaptation of our favourite Charles Dickens or Evelyn Waugh novel. For all their genius, Dickens and Waugh are still specific to their time and place – any fiddling around with the details offends and throws the whole production out of whack. With epics like *The Iliad* and *The Odyssey* – and with ancient myth – the characters and stories have become so elemental that they take on a life of their own. They can be pillaged and cannibalised in little chunks for their individual symbolic value.

You can pick and choose iconic elements – Heracles's strength, Odysseus's search for home, Helen's beauty – and transfer them to the modern age, without having to import the whole story and all its baggage. The apparently eternal power of Homeric epic survives constant reinvention. The same is true of that other protean epic – the Bible, rooted in ancient Greek foundations.

A clay tablet, in Linear B script, from the Mycenean palace of Pylos. It gives details of the distribution of hides – from pigs, cows and deer – to cobblers and saddle-makers. The clay was baked hard, and preserved, by a fire that destroyed the palace in about 1200 BC.

A sign in the Ephesus souvenir market. It explains why the fish was a symbol for early Christians. The Greek for fish is ichthus, the acronym for the words, 'Iesous Christos Theou Uios Soter' – 'Jesus Christ, Son of God, Saviour'.

11

It was All Greek to Jesus

During the First World War, a pacifist teacher once appeared at a military service tribunal.

'I want to turn the other cheek,' the teacher said, 'if you don't mind me translating from the Greek of the New Testament.'

'Greek?' the blustering Colonel Blimp of a tribunal chairman replied. 'You don't mean to tell me that Jesus spoke Greek. He was British to the backbone.'

Jesus may not have spoken English but he was certainly quite a linguist.

In May 2014, Pope Francis had a good-natured disagreement about Jesus's language skills with Benjamin Netanyahu, the Israeli prime minister.

'Jesus was here, in this land,' Netanyahu said at their meeting in Jerusalem. 'He spoke Hebrew.'

'Aramaic,' said the pope, laughing. 'He spoke Aramaic, but he knew Hebrew.'

They were both right. Jesus's first language was Aramaic – still spoken in rare spots in the Middle East, including Maaloula, near Damascus, the town sadly battered in the Syrian civil war in September 2013. Until then, Melkite Greek Catholic and Orthodox Christians had lived happily alongside Sunni Muslims for centuries.

In Nazareth, Jesus spoke Aramaic's Galilean dialect, the language used in Mel Gibson's film *The Passion of the Christ*. Sadly, Mel's 'Theological Consulting and Aramaic/Latin Translator', Dr William J. Fulco, a Jesuit priest, got his Latin wrong: a man from Judaea is wrongly addressed as 'Judaeus' in the nominative, not 'Judaee' in the vocative.

Jesus's last words on the cross were in Aramaic: 'Eli Eli lama sabachthani', translated in Psalm 22 as 'My God, my God, why have you forsaken me?'

During his life, Jesus answered to the Aramaic name, Yeshu'a – Jesus is an anglicised version of the Greek translation of Yeshu'a, as is Joshua. It was only after he died that Jesus was given the Greek honorific title, 'Christos', meaning 'the anointed one', with Christian its associated adjective. Hebrew for 'the anointed one' is Maschiach – Messiah in its English translation. The first recorded use of the word 'Christian' was years after his death, hundreds of miles north of Jerusalem, in Antioch, now Antakya in southern Turkey.

Jesus also read Hebrew from the Bible, at the synagogue in Luke 4:16. At one point, he chatted with a Syrophoenician woman, who would have spoken Phoenician. And he was familiar with the greatest language of them all: Greek. Jesus and his disciples used the third-century BC Septuagint, the Greek translation of the Hebrew Bible. Septuagint is derived from *septuaginta*, Latin for 70 – the number of Hebrew scholars who worked on the translation.

Jews in the diaspora, including Jesus, mainly spoke Greek. Greek also laid the foundation of lots of English biblical words: angel is from the Greek *angelo*, 'I announce'.

We think of the New Testament as a story of the Holy Land – of a Jewish Jesus in a Middle Eastern country controlled by Latin-speaking Romans. But the New Testament – the most beautiful book he'd ever read, said Oscar Wilde – was written in Greek, even if it was composed under Roman rule. Greek was spoken by most of the senior administrators of the Roman Empire.

There are three primordial roots to Western European thought – classical, New Testament and Old Testament – and ancient Greece is at the heart of the first two. Even the Old Testament was largely read in Greek, after the success of popular translations from Hebrew in the third and second centuries BC.

Through understanding ancient Greece, you don't just understand the ancient classical world; you appreciate the roots of Christianity.

In a talk to the English Speaking Union in Houston, Texas, on 9 September 1977, Margaret Thatcher, then Leader of the Opposition, echoed the point. The 'common heritage' of British and American ideas depended, she said, on Christian values, which in turn 'rest on Hebrew and Hellenic foundations'.

The Jewish diaspora in the ancient world was considerable – there were 50,000 Jews in Rome – and many of them were Hellenised and classically educated. Those Jewish and Hellenic foundations often overlapped; not least on Pilate's epitaph on Christ's cross – 'Jesus of Nazareth, the King of the Jews', written in Hebrew, Greek and Latin. The foundations overlap, too, at the *seder*, the Passover meal. The seder, with its question and answer sessions, accompanied by wine, is very like a Platonic Symposium – and old-fashioned Oxbridge tutorials.

Synagogue is a Greek word, from *synagogeus*, 'a place of assembly'. In several places in Greece – such as the island of Thasos in the northern Aegean – there are still buildings called Hebraiokastro, or 'Jews' Castle'. These were named by modern Greeks on the understanding that the only significant civilisation that could be earlier than their own ancient predecessor must be biblical.

Renaissance artists often mixed up the two worlds, cheerfully placing classical buildings in Old Testament scenes. In Poussin's *Finding of Moses*, in the National Gallery, the baby looks like he was born in Augustan Rome, going on the pure classical temples all around him – not in Pharaoh's Egypt 1,500 or so years earlier.

Whichever language Jesus chose to speak in, his words in the New Testament were originally written in Greek – including lines now more familiar in Latin. *Noli me tangere* – 'Don't touch me!' – Jesus famously said to Mary Magdalene when she recognised him after the resurrection. In fact, in John 20:17, he said, *Me mou haptou*. A better translation is something like 'Stop clinging to me.'

Greek, too, was the native language of Roman citizens like St Paul, from Cilicia in south-east Turkey. Paul's Greek letters and speeches disseminated Christianity across great Greek-speaking stretches of the Roman Empire, including Ephesus, where the *Corinthian* was now docked – well, it was docked at the nearby port of Kuşadasi.

Ephesus was at the heart of early, Greek-speaking Christianity. The Gospel of St John was written at Ephesus in around AD 90. Ephesus was also home to one of the seven crucial churches named by Jesus in the Book of Revelation – revealed to John of Patmos, in a cave on the island of Patmos. Jesus asked John to write his revelations on a scroll and send it to seven major churches: in Ephesus, Smyrna, Pergamos, Thyatira, Sardis, Philadelphia and Laodicea. These were all Greek-speaking towns, with large Christian populations, gathered together in a loose cluster in western Turkey.

In AD 52, Paul came to Ephesus, preaching in the synagogue for three months. His evangelism was so successful that, according to Acts 19:10, 'All they which dwelt in Asia heard the word of the Lord Jesus, both Jews and Greeks.' It was at Ephesus that Paul wrote, in 1 Corinthians 15, 'O death, where is thy sting? O grave, where is thy victory?' It was also at Ephesus that Paul wrote the most popular of church readings, 1 Corinthians 13:

> When I was a child, I spake as a child, I understood as a child, I thought as a child: but when I became a man, I put away childish things. For now we see through a glass, darkly; but then face to face: now I know in part; but then shall I know even as also I am known. And now abideth faith, hope, love, these three; but the greatest of these is love.

It was at Ephesus, too, that Paul got into a tremendous row with an early group of souvenir sellers, the silversmiths who sold little statues of Artemis in the Temple of Artemis. Artemis, and her Roman equivalent, Diana, had been worshipped in the temple since at least the eighth century BC.

'Great is Diana of the Ephesians,' the silversmiths cried when Paul tried to persuade them of the virtues of Jesus. The silversmiths weren't just worried about blasphemy. They were also extremely angry at the loss of trade threatened by Paul's new religion, particularly at the possible destruction of the Temple of Artemis, one of the Seven Wonders of the World. They were quite right to be worried – the temple was eventually destroyed in AD 401.

All the other Greek wonders of the world fared no better. The statue of Zeus at Olympia was destroyed in the fifth century AD. The Colossus of Rhodes, a 100-foot statue of the sun god, Helios, was toppled by an earthquake in 226 BC. There's a suggestion that they're going to rebuild the Colossus, which stood for only 54 years before it was destroyed. There are plans, too, to rebuild the lighthouse at Alexandria – built in 280 BC and also damaged by three earthquakes between 956 AD and 1323 AD. The Mausoleum at Halicarnassus – Bodrum, a little further south down the coast from Ephesus – is now a sad pile of scattered column drums, unvisited by the sun-seekers who descend on the Turkish coast. I had the shattered mausoleum to myself for several hours on the day I visited a few years ago.

When it was built in the fourth century BC, it was a mighty memorial to the Persian king Mausolus; thus our word, 'mausoleum'. A series of earthquakes – along with the Knights of St John of Rhodes, who looted the mausoleum to build their castle at Bodrum – left little behind. The best bits of the mausoleum are now in London, at the British Museum.

And the best reconstruction is five minutes' walk from the British Museum – in the church of St George's, Bloomsbury, built by Nicholas Hawksmoor in 1730. On the great, stepped ziggurat that forms the tower, Hawksmoor replaced poor old Mausolus with a statue of George I. Around the base of the pyramid, the lion and the unicorn of the royal coat of arms skulk on the steps in defence of their monarch.

When I visited the Mausoleum at Bodrum, I sat on one of those toppled column drums and read Callimachus's poem to Heraclitus, a third-century BC poet from Halicarnassus; not the fifth-century BC pre-Socratic philosopher of the same name, who said you never step in the same river twice.

The poet Heraclitus was a friend of another poet, Callimachus of Cyrene. Callimachus came up with the wise words '*mega biblion, mega kakon*' – 'big book, big evil'. When Heraclitus died, in around 260 BC, Callimachus wrote a short epitaph for him. The melancholy translation of that poem, by William Johnson Cory, a Victorian Classics teacher at Eton, is still celebrated.

At Eton, Cory promoted the joys of Greek love. He was eventually asked to leave, after sending the boys love letters. He liked to rub his whiskers along their cheeks, while they recited poems of love and wine in Anacreontic metre – the rhythm used by the sixth-century BC poet, Anacreon.

Here is Cory's translation of Callimachus. 'Carian' referred to Caria, the ancient name for the region of south-western Anatolia, whose capital was Halicarnassus.

They told me, Heraclitus, they told me you were dead;
They brought me bitter news to hear and bitter tears to shed;
I wept, as I remembered, how often you and I
Had tired the sun with talking, and sent him down the sky.
And now that thou art lying, my dear old Carian guest,
A handful of grey ashes, long, long ago at rest,
Still are thy pleasant voices, thy nightingales, awake;
For Death, he taketh all away, but them he cannot take.

Back at Ephesus, the Greek and Roman ruins still dominated the town that later became one of the great Christian cities of the Roman Empire. In AD 431, the Third Ecumenical Council was held at the Church of Mary. Ephesus was supposedly the Virgin Mary's last home; her little house is a short walk from the heart of the ancient town.

At the council, convened by Emperor Theodosius II, the divinity of Christ was first proclaimed. On the same occasion, the Virgin Mary was officially declared *theotokos*, Greek for 'Mother of God', as in the Hail Mary – 'Holy Mary, Mother of God, pray for us sinners now and at the hour of our death.'

If all that wasn't enough business for this spectacularly efficient church meeting, the council also confirmed the wording of the Nicene Creed – originally set out in AD 325 at the Greek town of Nicaea, modern Iznik on Turkey's Black Sea coast.

Discussion over the Nicene Creed led to the Arian controversy of the fourth century AD. Supporters of the theologian Arius argued that God the Son and God the Father were *homoiousios* – similar. Their opponents said the two were *homoousios* – the same; that's where we get 'homosexuality' from, meaning sex with someone of the same gender.

The two arguments depended on the addition of a single 'i' or, as the Greeks called it, an *iota*. Thus the phrase, 'an iota of difference', to signify the tiniest of distinctions.

At the time of the council, Ephesus had long been part of the Roman Empire, but the Ephesians still spoke a mixture of Latin, Phrygian, Lydian, Old Anatolian and Greek.

Still, today, Greek dominates the private inscriptions on Ephesus's houses, statues and temples. One marble column I walked past on the Sacred Way had the jolly line, '*Agathe tuche*' – 'Good luck'. *Agathos*, 'good', is where we get the name Agatha – literally 'good girl'. *Agathos* also meant 'brave' – the equation between bravery and goodness in ancient Greece wasn't accidental.

Latin is much rarer at Ephesus, largely confined to official imperial buildings; the reverse of modern Britain where we almost always favour Latin over Greek inscriptions. The only regular exception I've come across is in Georgian pump rooms. On spa buildings you often get the same line from Pindar, the lyric Greek poet – '*Ariston men udor*'; 'Water is best'.

In Ephesus, Latin was used on the most prominent Roman building of all, the gate of Mazeus and Mithridates, built by two freed slaves in AD 40, in honour of the Emperor Augustus. The inscription on the gate reads, 'Mazeus and Mithridates dedicate this to the son of the divine Julius Caesar, to the greatest priest, Augustus, who was consul 12 times, and tribune 20 times; and to Livia, the wife of Augustus; and to Marcus Agrippa who was consul three times, and tribune six times; and to Julia, daughter of Caesar Augustus.' So, formal, high-falutin' inscriptions were written in Latin; easy-going, good luck messages were in Greek.

Early Christians were largely Greek-speaking, too. To advertise their faith, Christian martyrs in ancient Rome scored the walls of the catacombs on the Via Appia with a fish symbol. The Greek for fish is *ichthus*, the acronym for the words *Iesous Christos Theou Uios Soter* – 'Jesus Christ, Son of God, Saviour'. Another widespread acronym for Jesus – IHS – is also derived from the Greek: they are the first three letters of Jesus's name in Greek, *IHSOUS*.

When Christianity reached these shores centuries later, it was still wrapped in Greek clothes. At a Roman villa in Chedworth, Gloucestershire, built in the fourth century AD, the surviving coping stone around a basin is inscribed with the symbols X and P – *Chi* and *Rho*, the first two Greek letters of Christ's name.

For centuries more, Greek remained the language of the intellectual Christian. In September 2014, Cambridge University Library bought a rare book, the *Codex Zacynthius*, from the British and Foreign Bible Society for £1.1m. Discovered on the Greek island of Zacynthos, it was brought to England in 1821. The vellum of the codex was first written on in the sixth or seventh century, with the Greek text of Luke 1:1–11:33. The rarity of the codex was increased by the fact that it is a palimpsest: a manuscript where the words have been scraped off and written over, from *palin* ('again') and *psao* ('I scrape'). This codex was partly scraped away and written over in the thirteenth century with the text of an *Evangeliarium*, a book of passages from the Four Gospels. Six hundred years after the codex was first inscribed, the *Evangeliarium* was written in the same language – ancient Greek, still the language of the Church.

The idea of godlessness, too, was first framed by the Greeks. Eat your heart out, Richard Dawkins. Atheism comes from the Greek *atheos*, meaning 'godless'. There were several forms of atheism in ancient Greece. The Epicureans argued that there was no way to prove the gods' existence. And Socrates was sentenced to death in 399 BC for a sort of atheism. He was charged with 'refusing to recognise the gods recognised by the state, and introducing other, new divinities [and] corrupting the young'.

During his trial, Socrates made his *apologia* – Greek for 'defence speech', rather than apology – later written up by Plato. Jurors voted for his conviction, and the death penalty, in the traditional fashion: dropping pebbles (*psephos* in Greek, as in psephology) into an urn set aside for guilty votes.

Greek continued to frame the terms of religious discussion in Europe over the next two millennia. William Tyndale's 1526 first English translation from the Greek of the New Testament echoes down the ages today. When Islamic extremists murdered the soldier Lee Rigby in Woolwich in May 2013, one of them screamed, 'An eye for an eye, a tooth for a tooth.' They were unwittingly echoing Tyndale's 1526 translation from the Greek of Matthew 5:38.

Bob Dylan borrowed from Tyndale's Greek translation in 'The Times They Are a-Changin': 'And the first one now will later be last, for the times they are a-changin'. Tyndale's translation of Matthew 20:16 read, 'So the last shall be first, and the first last: for many be called, but few chosen.'

Back in Ephesus, Paul got away with all his limbs intact, and the souvenir sellers continued to do a roaring trade in silver knick-knacks. Things haven't changed much now at the site. I was with 50 passengers from the *Corinthian* cruise ship I was lecturing on – and we were swamped by thousands of tourists. The huge theatre, where the riot over St Paul kicked off, was overrun with tourists, too. The souvenir sellers were there in abundance, although they've now decamped to a vast, roofed area just beyond the exit from the site.

Not for the first time, I felt a surge of envy for Freya Stark, who wandered this western Turkish coast in 1952. She visited 55 ruins in Asia Minor and in only one spot – Pergamum, 100 miles north of Ephesus – did she meet a single tourist; and it was a single tourist. Funnily enough, when I drove to Pergamum, it was completely empty. All is not lost to the post-war boom in tourism. There were still plenty of empty spots on my journey, just as there were in Homer's time.

Tourists work on a hierarchy system when it comes to sites. At Knossos, King Minos's palace in northern Crete, the tour buses filled up the car park by ten-thirty a.m. An hour's drive to the south, Phaistos – another extraordinary Minoan site – there was one bus. A couple of miles east, at the Greco-Roman site of Gortys, there were fewer than a dozen tourists. The only noise was the clink of goats' bells as I looked at the Gortys legal code, inscribed on a curving wall behind the Odeon.

This fifth-century BC Greek law code was written in *boustrophedon* – 'cow turning round' style. One line reads normally, left to right; the next reads right to left, like a cow turning at the end of a plough-line in a field. You can see the logic. The eye doesn't have to zip back to the beginning of the next line before starting again. But it does mean you have to develop the ability to read backwards. The fashion for *boustrophedon* never caught on.

Tracing *The Odyssey* back to its original Mediterranean roots had its Elysian, deserted beauties like Gortys – and its distinctly ropy, overcrowded backwaters. My pain was caused more by a destroyed romance than destroyed landscapes. So I was loath to join the growing band of travel writers who despair of what's happening to the world. Paul Theroux couldn't complete his latest Africa trip because he so hated the modernisation of the place. By the time of his death in 2011, the late Paddy Leigh Fermor could only mourn for what had happened to the Europe he tramped through in the 1930s.

The Mediterranean, it's true, has been much damaged and inundated with tourists. When Byron visited the Temple of Poseidon at Sunium near Athens two centuries ago, he wrote, 'Sunium's marbled steep, where nothing save the waves and I may hear our mutual murmurs sweep.' Byron clearly wasn't there in high season, when the tourist buses drop in at Sunium on the way to nearby Athens Airport.

Still, plenty of Homeric spots around the Mediterranean are unchanged. Particularly in winter. When I returned to Sunium between Christmas and New Year in 2014, my friend Ned and I had Byron's marbled steep to ourselves – apart from a handsome pair of chukar partridges, puffing out their black, brown, buff and grey feathers as they sheltered from the freezing rain in the lee of the Doric pillars of the temple. Gods were worshipped according to local geography: Zeus was revered on the mountain peaks, and Poseidon by the sea – as he was here at Sunium.

The two worlds – the empty, Homeric one and the modern, touristy one – can live happily side by side. Gibraltar – Hades in *The Odyssey* – now overlooks the busy shipping lane that leads out to the Atlantic. On a freezing January day, I gazed down from the Rock of Gibraltar at the bay, crammed with 30 oil tankers and a single transporter ship carrying two gin palaces on its back. But the Rock itself was an empty wilderness, thick with lemon and olive trees, stone pines, cacti and its own unique plants: Gibraltar Campion, Gibraltar Saxifrage and Gibraltar Candytuft. Yellow-legged gulls hovered in mid-air, yards from the staircase I stood on, cut into the sheer limestone face of the cliff. Over and over again, I didn't need much poetic, or journalistic, licence to imagine myself back on the wine-dark sea, heading home to Penelope, as Homer plucked his lyre in the background.

One evening, as the *Corinthian* hugged the coast near Athens, I glanced at the map and saw we were passing the site of the Battle of Salamis in 480 BC, the great Athenian victory over the Persians, the auld enemy. It was cocktail hour in the bar – and the passengers were getting stuck into their Campari sodas as Eddie, the resident pianist, played 'Candle in the Wind'.

I took matters into my own hands, and commandeered the microphone to tell the passengers the historic news. Eddie stopped playing Elton John. The chit-chat – at lively, second-drink level – stopped. Everyone turned to the windows or walked out on deck to see Salamis, framed in the purple and orange Ready Brek glow of the setting sun, as the sea turned an electric, luminous blue.

At those moments, I remembered Tennyson's *Ulysses*. The poem pictured an ageing Odysseus on Ithaca, yearning to set sail again:

'Tis not too late to seek a newer world.
Push off, and sitting well in order smite
The sounding furrows; for my purpose holds
To sail beyond the sunset, and the baths
Of all the western stars, until I die.
It may be that the gulfs will wash us down:
It may be we shall touch the Happy Isles,
And see the great Achilles, whom we knew.
Though much is taken, much abides.

That last line was quoted by M, as played by Judi Dench in the 2012 Bond film *Skyfall*, to signify how Britain, MI6 and the forces of good will prevail. The same still applies to Homer's world – much has been taken, but an awful lot abides. A little less abided in my next stop – Mykonos, night-clubbing capital of the Greek islands.

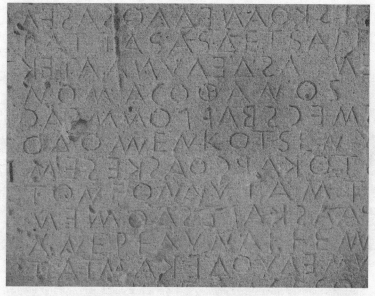

The fifth century BC legal code at Gortys, on Crete. It is written in boustrophedon – or 'cow turning round' style, like a cow turning round at the end of a plough-line in a field. Here, the top line is back to front. The next line reads normally.

The Gortys code dealt with adultery, divorce, property, marriage, adoption and rape. Rape was punished with fines on a sliding scale depending on status. A free man who raped a slave was given a small fine; a slave who raped a free man got the heaviest fine.

SUNIUM.

'Sunium's marbled steep, where nothing save the waves and I may hear our mutual murmurs sweep.' Temples of Poseidon – like the one at Sunium – were by the sea. Byron liked the Sunium temple so much that he carved his name into one of the columns. (1890 drawing)

12

Mykonos – the Party's Over

According to legend, the rocky island of Mykonos was created by Heracles on the day he hurled a pile of boulders at evil giants who were trying to topple the gods. Today, Mykonos is more the natural home of the god of wine and crazed dancing, Dionysus – the most popular figure in ancient art.

Since the 1970s, Chora, the main town on Mykonos, has tripled in size to deal with the tourist invasion. Those tourists largely come for the nightlife. Nightclubs in town and along the coast come alive at midnight and stay open until six in the morning. Over the last 40 years, Mykonos has grown particularly popular with gay tourists – although hotels are keen to stress they are 'straight-friendly'.

I made my way to Mykonos in 2014 on a press trip for the *Daily Mail* – I was no longer on board the *Corinthian*. Mykonos nightlife wasn't my thing – nor was Mykonos day life: I didn't go on the 'Special Gay Cruise', advertised on the noticeboard in my pretty whitewashed *pension* on the quiet fringes of Mykonos Town.

'We depart for an even more isolated and peaceful private beach for swimming and relaxing', the notice read. 'One bottle of sparkling wine, a chicken stick with sesame, Myconian traditional sweets. 20 euros.'

Instead, I got up early and took a ferry to Delos, Apollo's sacred island, 20 minutes from Mykonos harbour. Tiny little Delos was the most sacred island in ancient Greece, birthplace of the twins Apollo and Artemis, born under a palm tree. Odysseus referred to the holy palm tree when he met Nausicaa on that beach on Corfu. He went to Delos, he said, full of 'evil sorrows', and there he saw, by Apollo's altar, 'the stalk of a young palm tree shooting up'. It is holy Delos

Keats referred to in 'On First Looking into Chapman's Homer', when he wrote, 'Round many western islands have I been which bards in fealty to Apollo hold.'

I made my way through Chora at half past nine in the morning, while the clubbers made sweet love to each other, or slept off their hangovers. The town was returned, for a brief moment, to its inhabitants: the widows in black tending to potted geraniums and bougainvillea; the elderly men who look after the tiny Byzantine chapels scattered through the town.

Chora is a maze of twisting streets – designed, some say, to confuse raiding pirates; others say it's to deflect the lethal winds that come whipping in off the Aegean. Like most Greek seaside towns, its buildings are painted white to deflect the sun. It is a town shaped by heat and wind – the two forces that have dictated Greece's recent fortunes – a place for ship-owners and sun-seeking tourists. Despite the economic crisis, Greece still has one of the biggest shipping fleets in the world, and remains in the top ten tourism destinations.

Wind shapes the taste of Greek wine, too: the vines on the nearby island of Santorini are kept close to the ground, to dodge the lethal wind. On the superheated, near waterless island, the vines only survive thanks to the volcanic earth, so porous that it sucks up bucket-loads of morning dew.

Delos was the beating heart of the Greek religious world: the Cyclades Islands take their name from the rough circle (*kuklos* – 'circle') they circumscribe around Delos. The Cyclades were said to revolve around Delos in a permanent *choreia*, or dance. For such a tiny island – less than one and a half square miles – holy Delos punched way above its weight. It gave its name to the Delian League, the federation of islands founded by the Greeks to take on the Persian Empire during the wars from 499–449 BC. 'Delian' because Delos was home to the naval alliance's treasury.

I had the Delos ferry largely to myself – most of the tourists on Mykonos were still recovering from the *choreias* and special gay cruises of the day before. Delos itself was almost completely empty. No one is allowed to live on the tiny island because it's so littered with exceptional ruins, dating from the Romans back to the seventh century BC. A lot survives, even though the ruins were used as a quarry by the Venetians, the Turks and their neighbours on Tinos and Mykonos.

That sort of sacrilege wasn't uncommon. The temple on Naxos – where Ariadne saw Theseus fleeing over the horizon on the way back from tackling the Minotaur – was used to build the Venetian castle in the neighbouring town. Until the 1960s, the ancient site of Delphi – home to the oracle of the Greek world, and one of the most precious spots in classical history – was known to locals as 'the quarry'.

Empty Delos had a desolate desert island feel. I couldn't shake off the memory of the horrors inflicted on Delos in 426 BC, when Athens was ravaged by plague. The Athenian leadership ordered the purification of Delos, on the suggestion of the Delphic oracle – Pythia, the drug-crazed Sibyl of Delphi. Pythia was said to get high from chewing laurel leaves and inhaling ethylene from the stream flowing under the oracle building; not the best candidate for head of the Athenian government policy unit.

Heraclitus, the sixth-century BC philosopher, said of the god of the oracle, 'He neither speaks nor hides: he uses signs.' The tricky thing was interpreting them, as Croesus, King of Lydia, found to his cost. According to Herodotus, Croesus asked the oracle what his chances were against Cyrus, King of the Persians.

'You will destroy a great empire,' replied the oracle. A delighted Croesus asked if his reign would be long.

'When a mule is king of Persia, run for your life,' said the cryptic oracle.

Croesus, beaten by Cyrus, promptly took it up with the oracle.

'You should have asked which empire,' the oracle said, adding, 'Oh, and you're the mule in question because you're the son of a noble Mede mother, and a common Persian father.'

Purification of Delos meant exhuming all but the most sacred burials and transporting the bodies to the neighbouring island of Rheneia. The Athenians ordered that no one should give birth or die on Delos; anyone close to giving birth or dying had to go to Rheneia. The Greek historian Strabo said it was illegal even to keep a dog on Delos. It got worse. Four years later, the Athenians ordered all remaining Delians to leave the island because their impurity meant they were unworthy of the holy island.

Because there's no central Greek religious book, it's often said there was no dogma. But that didn't stop there being pretty violent cruelty in the name of religion. For all the avant-garde sophistication of the fifth-century Athenians, they could plumb grotesque depths of primitive violence.

In 416 BC, they ordered the island of Melos, a Spartan colony 60 miles south-west of Delos, to surrender. When the Melians refused, the Athenians besieged the island, killed all men of fighting age and sold the women and children into slavery. When the islanders of Samos rebelled, Pericles crucified the ringleaders and branded their skins with symbols of defeat.

It was only by a whisker in 427 BC that the Athenians didn't slaughter all the male adults in Mytilene on Lesbos, where the *Corinthian* had docked. They also planned to sell all the women and children as slaves. That was the initial decision the Assembly made after Mytilene rebelled against Athenian control.

A trireme was sent to carry out the Assembly's orders, just before another debate was held, overturning the decision. In a heroic mercy dash, a second trireme headed out, a day after the first, to rescind the orders. The second set of sailors rowed the 187 nautical miles at top speed, sleeping in shifts, fuelled by barley-meal mixed with wine and oil. They got there just as the execution order was being read out to the poor Mytileneans. They still killed the thousand islanders they thought responsible for the rebellion.

Today, the desolation of Delos has its compensations. I could stare alone at the Delian lions – ignored by the other tourists, huddled around that pair of jousting stone cocks. The windless island was silent. Every now and then, the still grass – burnt the colour of straw by the unrelenting sun – rustled at the staccato movements of the big dragon lizards of Delos, with their oversized, bobbing heads. These were introduced from Africa by the ancient Greeks because Delos was supposedly the birthplace of Apollo Sauroctonos – the 'lizard-slayer'.

It was time to head home to my hotel; the long day in that intense sun, trawling through the spreading acres of ruins, had left me exhausted. As the last boat of the day chugged east, away from Delos, the evening light drenched the fields of Mykonos ahead of me. I could make out drifts of soft-blue cornflowers and blood-red poppies, wrapped around the granite boulders Heracles flung at those evil giants. Like us, the Greeks associated poppies with military deaths: ever since Priam's son Gorgythion died in *The Iliad*, where Homer described his head drooping like a garden poppy.

For a moment, I was back in ancient Greece. Straight in front of me, ahead of the prow, the nightclubs of Chora – yet to pump up the thumping volume for the evening – felt three thousand years away. They wouldn't stay quiet for long.

Further east, on the horizon, lay the island of Ikaria – named after Icarus, the boy who flew too close to the sun and plummeted into the sea as the wax in his wings melted. These days, Ikaria inhabitants live much longer than poor Icarus. The island is celebrated for its exceptional life expectancy – a decade longer than in America and the rest of Europe, with one in three Ikarians living into their nineties.

The secret is thought to lie in a lifestyle insulated from bloated twenty-first-century habits. Unlike Mykonos, Ikaria is low on tourists and nightclubs. Scientists put Ikarian longevity down to a traditional Greek life: afternoon naps, strong family links, a vigorous sex life and a healthy diet – beans, herb tea, greens, potatoes, goat's milk and limited meat and refined sugar.

Other theories ascribe the longevity to the survival of the fittest: 20 per cent of the population died in the war. After the war, lots of Communists – including Mikis Theodorakis, composer of the *Zorba the Greek* theme tune – were exiled to the island. A widely shared altruistic attitude is said to be a Communist legacy, and another reason for the high Ikarian life expectancy.

As I turned to look south, the fading sunlight carved the mountaintops of nearby Naxos into bright, sharp-edged rectangles. These were the quarries which produced – and continue to produce – the purest white marble in Greece, after the neighbouring island of Paros. The light was reflected back in perfect rectangles, where mammoth cubes of marble have been scooped out of the jagged, scrub-covered skyline of the island for more than 2,500 years.

The last time I'd been to Naxos was with my ex-girlfriend. This sunset reminder was too agonising. I turned my back on Naxos and stared west towards Delos. The island was shrinking in the twilight, lying low above the water, its bumps and troughs like the switchback profile of the Loch Ness monster.

I had a grilled, fresh sea bass in a fish restaurant near the harbour – recommended in McGilchrist's Greek Islands, a sort of mini-Blue Guide. And then I retired to my little *pension*, carefully selected for its quiet ambience from *Small Hotels in Greece*. Clever old me! Thanks to my nimble navigation of upmarket guidebooks I had successfully dodged the horrors of the clubbing capital of the Greek islands – on a Friday night, too, in peak season!

Until midnight, that is. That's when I was woken by the room vibrating to the heavy bass notes relayed from a nightclub. The next morning, I traced the club to a remote spot on the far side of a football pitch and a municipal rubbish dump, on the less scenic side of my *pension*. Despite the generous size of the football pitch, and the dump, it was like the speakers were in my room. They were blasting out hardcore dance music to a hardcore gay clientele; and to me, several hundred yards away, earplugs in, head beneath four pillows, windows and shutters closed, despite the summer heat. Still, I could feel the mattress thud-thud-thud along the full length of my body.

I turned on the bedside light and started reading my little green Loeb edition of Aeschylus's *Agamemnon*. James Loeb was the American banker who provided a lifeline to all Classics students in 1912, when he devised the Loeb Classical Library. In the green Greek books, and the red Latin ones, the ancient language is on the left-hand page, and the English on the right – the perfect crib. The old editions we used at school censored references to homosexuality, and relied on much-prized euphemisms. How we laughed in the Remove at 'life whiteness', the Loeb translation for sperm.

In the thudding hotel room, my little green Loeb provided some consolation; not least when it got to the lines quoted by Robert Kennedy in Indianapolis in 1968, on the evening of the death of Martin Luther King. When he heard the news, Kennedy was on the campaign trail, addressing a group of mostly black voters. 'My favourite poem, my … my favourite poet was Aeschylus,' Kennedy said. 'And he once wrote:

Even in our sleep, pain which cannot forget
falls drop by drop upon the heart,
until, in our own despair,
against our will,
comes wisdom
through the awful grace of God.

What we need in the United States is not division; what we need in the United States is not hatred; what we need in the United States is not violence and lawlessness, but is love, and wisdom, and compassion toward one another, and a feeling of justice toward those who still suffer within our country, whether they be white or whether they be black.'

Two months later, Kennedy was himself shot dead. The Aeschylus quotation – and Kennedy's improvised postscript – were engraved on his memorial in Arlington National Cemetery.

I was still reading Aeschylus at 5.30 a.m., as dawn cast its savage, slatted light through the shutters on to my bed, and Adele's 'Someone Like You' drifted across the football pitch and the rubbish dump. Adele's stirring song was a regular companion on my travels. I heard it again, near the end of my journey, in a Gibraltar restaurant. The video of the song was playing loudly in Jurys – a restaurant by the law courts in the city centre, decorated with posters of bewigged barristers – as I ate beef and Guinness pie, washed down with PG Tips tea. The song's lyrics – 'I heard that you're settled down, that you found a girl and you're married now' – were strangely apposite. Just before my trip to Gibraltar, my ex-girlfriend told me she'd moved in with someone who wasn't very like me – a distinguished lawyer.

If I'd been Odysseus or Agamemnon, there'd have been some great showdown. But, unlike in a Greek tragedy, no one sliced anyone else into little pieces and threw them in the Thames; no one butchered anyone in the bath. We wished each other future happiness and parted for good.

Back in Mykonos, the next day's British newspapers were coming online. I started reading them, praying, every time one thudding song faded out, that a new thud wouldn't begin. Apollo finally answered my prayers at 6 a.m.

An easier-going person would have gone to the nightclub and made a virtue of the noise that was driving this not-very-easy-going person nuts. He would have joined the dance in the dancing islands; perhaps even picked up one of the few heterosexual girls there. But not me. Why was I still a captive of my sexless Victorian education – and my Edwardian, euphemism-filled Loebs – seeking an ever-declining hit from nostalgia? Hadn't I learnt my lesson: that looking back has nothing on enjoying the present?

My contemporaries were all moving forwards; I was living my life in reverse gear, and moving away from society. At one unguarded moment with my ex-girlfriend, I'd said, 'I don't ask anything of anyone, on the understanding they don't ask anything of me.' Hardly a recipe for contentment. Hardly the motto of the providing male, ready to set up home with a wife. A friend of mine refers to men who are keen to marry as nesting birds, twig in beak. I fled the parental nest late, at 27. Fifteen years later, I was in no danger of building a fresh one.

If I had always been prematurely middle-aged, why couldn't I do the normal things associated with middle age? While my friends – who had lived their youthful, sex-packed lives to the full – were getting married and having children, I was reverting to the obsessive swotting of my childhood.

But where had being clever, reciting Greek verbs through my teenage years, got me exactly? Sitting, sleepless in a Mykonos hotel room, reading the *Daily Telegraph*, while more stupid men danced and had sex on the other side of the rubbish dump. Lazier, more original-minded people than me often did worse at school and university. But they're the ones now selling more books and winning more prizes. Having more sex, and dancing in more nightclubs, too.

Being able to read ancient Greek didn't help me much here in Mykonos, sleep-deprived and miserable. Later on my trip, on the Athens Metro train to the pretty suburb of Kifisia, I congratulated myself on being able to translate, '*Parakaloume kleinete ta parathura. O CHOROS CLIMATIZETAI*' – 'Please close the windows. THE CARRIAGE IS AIR CONDITIONED'. Interesting enough, I suppose – but was it really worth a decade of Greek at prep school, public school and university? Wouldn't that time spent learning the plural imperative of the verb 'to close' been better spent snogging the girls that remained resolutely unkissed throughout my teenage years?

Writing books, too – writing this book, taking this journey – becomes a refuge from real life; from people, from sex, from relationships. If you write, everything becomes second-hand, a chance to step back from involved, primary experience and see it from the detached, disinterested observer's point of view.

Was I the last civilised man in Britain – or its leading ponce? Was there a beating heart beneath this cold, pompous skin? Or was the pompous exterior the real thing? Was I frozen in the classroom, the permanent schoolboy, while others danced and shagged the night away in Mykonos's loudest nightclub? Either way, it was time to flee the party island for the marble island.

Landscape with Aeneas on Delos - Claude, 1672. Aeneas is second from right in the group of four, with his father, Anchises, second left, and his son, Ascanius, on the right. They are chatting to Anius, King of Delos and a priest of Apollo, the patron god of Delos. Anius points to the palm tree, under which the twins Apollo and Artemis were born.

Delos looked nothing like this during Aeneas's time, in around 1200 BC. Claude has based the Temple of Apollo, in the background, on the Pantheon in Rome, built in 126 AD.

THE VENUS OF MELOS (NOW IN THE LOUVRE).

The Venus de Milo – The statue was found on the island of Milos by a Greek peasant in 1820. It's made of marble from Paros, which has the finest stone in the Mediterranean. There is speculation that her missing arms were positioned to show Venus spinning thread – an occupation popular with off-duty Greek prostitutes. (1890 drawing)

13

Into the Marble Mountain

In 1989, on a gap-year trip between school and university, our little mixed band of nerds and sexual adventurers began our trip in Athens. We had left Westminster School the summer before. It was my first trip to Greece.

On our first morning, in a café in Syntagma Square, I got chatting to a friendly, supersized local wrapped in a ballooning T-shirt, working off a hangover with a Greek coffee. The square was packed with youths shouting unrecognisable slogans – so much for six years' study of ancient Greek.

I'd already been rather impressed by modern Athenian graffiti. Rather being concerned with football teams or sexual insults, like in England, it was about PASOK or Nea Democratia – the left- and right-wing parties that swapped power from 1974, after the collapse of the military junta, until Syriza's victory in 2015. More recently, on my odyssey, graffiti artists had plumped for Syriza, the radical left-wing party fighting the austerity package imposed by the troika: the European Commission, the European Central Bank and the International Monetary Fund.

Back in 1989, I imagined these youths were on some high-minded political march.

'What are they protesting about?' I asked.

'The new law on nightclubs,' my new friend said. 'It's outrageous – the government are saying you have to close at 5 a.m. Before, you could stay open all night.'

The law must have lapsed – or been rescinded – by the time I got to Mykonos 25 years later. But, still, I was immediately charmed by the Greeks on my first day there.

What a country! Where people manned the barricades because they were only allowed to drink until five in the morning. Coming from stuffy old Britain – where pubs had only started opening all day the year before, and still didn't open all day on Sundays – it was a breath of fresh air.

Today, after more than 30 years in the EU, Greece retains that fundamental impulse towards personal freedom. How thrilling it was to be waved through the barriers at the Acropolis Museum by the security guards, without having to put my bag through the metal detector.

That impulse towards freedom has mutated into anarchy since the economic crisis. Back in Syntagma Square in 2014 – two years after the riots against austerity measures – there were still anarchy signs on the walls opposite the parliament, the old royal palace. Great holes were gouged into the floor of the square, where paving stones had been ripped out and hurled at riot police.

You could see anarchy signs, too, in the quietest corners of the Cyclades. On my trip to Mykonos, I hired a scooter and made my way over the central hump of the island to the tiny town of Ano Mera, home to the Tourliani Monastery, the religious heart of Mykonos.

I'd gone to see the delicate, eighteenth-century domed church, crammed with icons. Its classical tower was built as late as the 1930s by marble-cutters from the neighbouring island of Tinos – you could be forgiven for thinking it was several centuries older. The proximity of the greatest marble on the planet – at nearby Paros and Naxos – had produced a tradition of skilled carvers in the Cyclades, going back to 3,300 BC. Copies of early Cycladic figures – with a touch of Modigliani to them – are still bestsellers on Greek souvenir stalls, alongside the busts of Homer and Plato.

In the outskirts of Ano Mera, on the way to the monastery, I came across a modern, four-storey office building, flanked by two-storey, traditional, Cycladic houses of white, plastered stone. The glass and steel of the deserted building was thick with dust – a casualty of the economic crisis. Beneath the banks of glazing, the wall had been freshly scrawled with an A-for-anarchy symbol. Beneath, in English, someone had sprayed the words, 'Class war by all means'.

It was an odd sentiment in an apparently classless island. The major social difference in the island was between tourists and locals – and the locals were delighted to cater to the tourists' wallets. There was an even smaller distinction among the locals: between goat farmers who'd remained goat farmers; and goat farmers who'd opened nightclubs and moped hire shops in Chora, the island's party town.

Still – alongside the sad riots and the graffiti – Greeks still have that admirable desire for personal freedom I'd seen at the nightclub protest in Syntagma Square in 1989. I saw it again when I got to the ancient marble quarries of Marathi, on the island of Paros. Parian marble was the best in ancient Greece – renowned for its smoothness and the little sparkles in the stone you still see today in the greatest statues of antiquity.

After a long drive across the island, and a long walk in the punishing midday heat, the ancient quarry was closed. A big sign over the chain-link fence warned, in Greek and English, 'Danger – do not enter.' A little further on, the gate in the fence was not only unlocked but dangling open. Long live the Greek spirit of anarchy!

Beyond the open gate, two parallel shafts led deep into the belly of the Marathi mountain. One is nineteenth-century; the other ancient. Thirty yards apart, they are indistinguishable. On the same scale, they are both perfect squares in cross-section, both arrow-straight, leading at a 20 degree angle from the horizontal down into the ground, following parallel seams of translucent, smooth-grained, white marble.

As I clambered down the ancient shaft, the high-80s heat dropped into the 60s. The marble walls of the shafts were flat and smooth – not much good for support as I leant against them in the rapidly fading light. Beneath my feet, the flat marble floor was littered, several feet thick, with off-cuts from the cubes of stone hewn by ancient masons, the stone that fills the galleries of the British Museum, the Louvre and the Met.

This perfect marble is still abundant. On the neighbouring island of Antiparos, an Anglo-Greek friend of mine was mocked by his Greek neighbours for fitting his bathrooms with the best marble in the world – it's considered a little naff there.

For all its even greater profusion in ancient Greece, you still had to get the marble from Paros to the four corners of the Greek world – and the cost was enormous. Until mechanisation in the nineteenth century, transport of building materials was more expensive than the materials themselves. In 1438, the cost of carting limestone 12 miles – from the quarry in Ham Hill, Somerset, to the Hospital of St John in Sherborne – was greater than the cost of the stone itself. Paros marble had to be shipped so far – and was prized so highly – that, on many statues, it was only used for the head. A cheaper, rougher stone was used for the body.

Now 50 yards into the flank of the mountain, I picked up a round chunk of stone, the size of the palm of my hand, from the marble litter at my feet. On one side, it was humped like a scallop shell, worn to a dirty, matte pink over the course of several thousand years lying in the faint light of the mine shaft. On the other side, it was flat and even, carved by a stone chisel several millennia ago. A thousand mini-starlets sparkled on the dressed, crystalline surface, even in the cool, faux-twilight – I could see the shrinking square of the entrance behind me, illuminated to eye-scorching levels by the midday sun.

Despite the faint light, I could also make out the translucence of my little chunk of the stone. In ancient Greece, the best marble was called *lychnites*, from *lychnos* – 'a lamp'. The stone was thought so translucent that you could make out the light of an oil lamp through a sheet of the marble.

For all its beauty and ease of chiselling, Parian marble was fragile. It could only be cut in small blocks, meaning the Parthenon's builders needed to source its 22,000 tons of marble from a nearer quarry – at Mount Pentelikon, 15 miles north-east of Athens.

Smaller quantities of Paros marble were transported over great distances. It was used for the Nike of Samothrace, or the Winged Victory. Now in the Louvre, the statue was found on Samothrace, in the northern Aegean, several hundred miles north of Paros. Parian marble was used for many of the statues at Delphi and for the Hermes and the Infant Dionysus by Praxiteles, said to be the greatest sculptor of all time. The fourth-century BC statue is at the museum in Olympia – again, hundreds of miles from Paros.

The small size of Parian marble blocks meant life-sized statues required multiple blocks. The surviving part of the armless Venus de Milo statue is made of two blocks of Parian marble. Venus de Milo, also in the Louvre, was found on the island of Milos – thus 'Milo' – by a Greek peasant in 1820; it was quickly scooped up by a passing French officer. In this case, the stone – thought to have been carved around 130–100 BC – didn't come so far. Paros is only 30 miles north-east of Milos.

If you look at the Venus de Milo closely, you can see the join between the two blocks, hidden by the top fold of her deliciously titillating skirt, slung at a slanting angle from just above her left hip to just below her right, like an ancient Greek rapper. The complete statue would have been sculpted from as many as seven Parian marble blocks: the two that survive, plus one for each arm, another for the right foot, another for the plinth and one for Venus's accompanying herm.

Herms were busts on top of stone blocks. Halfway down the block, the flat surface was adorned with a cock and balls; Hermes, the messenger god, was also a phallic god. He took his name from *herma*, meaning one of these blocks of stone, thought to have apotropaic power – the ability to ward off evil. Ludicrous as herms look to us, they were sacred to the Greeks.

In 415 BC, during the Peloponnesian War – just before the Athenians set sail to Syracuse, in Sicily – all the *hermai* in Athens had their erect penises chopped off. Both the writer Xenophon and Alcibiades, a leading general and politician, were accused of the deeply sacrilegious act. Greece was a much easier-going society than our supposedly free one: the scandal wasn't the erect willies – the scandal lay in vandalising the statues.

The Athenians were generally much more relaxed about nakedness than we are. They would have been amazed by the Charlie Hebdo massacre in Paris in 2015, and the row over depicting religious figures, fully clothed or otherwise. Zeus, Apollo and Poseidon were regularly sculpted in the nude.

Fifth-century Athens was a strange, unprecedented combination of artistic freedom and rigid artistic rules. There were strict ratios governing the relationship between the height of columns, their width and how far apart they were. On those statues, the length of the torso was in precise proportion to the length of the line running at right angles to it, from nipple to nipple. Still, the extraordinary thing was that you were allowed to see the nipples at all. Kenneth Clark said the nude 'is an art form invented by the Greeks ... just as opera is an art form invented in seventeenth-century Italy'.

Before the Greeks, there had been naked depictions of Assyrians – you can see them in the British Museum. But these were humiliated, naked victims of war, flayed and beheaded by the victors. Unlike the Assyrians, Persians and Egyptians before them, the Greeks made heroes of the naked form. Greeks thought the idealised human form, the uniform of righteousness and heroism, was the naked one. Greeks are often naked in battle scenes, unlike their enemies – particularly the Persians, who thought the nude body shameful.

Greeks didn't actually fight naked in battle, nor did they stroll naked down Athens High Street. But they did take their clothes off for athletic events, in the wrestling school and gymnasium. The original Greek gym was far from its modern exercise-obsessed incarnation; it was also an intellectual hothouse, where philosophers, like Socrates, debated and taught the young. The gymnasium got its name from *gymnos*, Greek for naked – the ideal state for running about and throwing things, they thought. One explanation is that, in the 720 BC Olympics, Orsippus of Megara's loincloth fell off in the 200 metres – and the habit stuck.

When they wrestled, they covered themselves with oil and sprinkled themselves with sand to get a better grip. The earth arena – from *harena*, Latin for 'sand', the preferred surface in Roman amphitheatres – was sprinkled with water. A kind of naked mud-wrestling ensued, while restful flute music played in the background. Nakedness had its pitfalls. Boys were told not to sit down in the gym for fear old men would get too excited by the impression their genitals left in the sand.

It was in the perfect naked form – like that of Myron's mid-fifth-century Discobolus, the disc-thrower – that man was in perfect balance. It was said of the Discobolus that more mathematical knowledge of balance and stress was needed than for any previous statue.

The body was celebrated in all its forms. Ancient vases depicted the black bodies of the Ethiopians, who fought for the Trojans under their king, Memnon, held up as the Ethiopian Hector.

But the Greeks were a little more concerned about the naked female form. Venus – or Aphrodite, to give her her proper Greek name – was the only Greek woman sculpted naked; thus Venus de Milo's half-naked look. Praxiteles's fourth-century BC Aphrodite of Cnidus – which now only survives in copies – showed her carefully placing her dress on a vase before going for a dip. It's the earliest known sophisticated nude sculpture of a woman. Parian marble was also used for the naked Venus de Medici, in the Uffizi. This Aphrodite is a terrible flirt: completely naked, she only half-hides her breasts and crotch, leaving a pretty racy view from all sides.

It's hard not to see an intensely sexual element to some of the more sensuous sculptures of women: not least the Nereids from the 390 BC monument in Xanthos, in modern Antalya, Turkey. These sea nymphs, now in the British Museum, appear to be sprinting into a headlong gale, their thin gowns plastered against their chests by the wind and rain – the first wet T-shirt competition.

In earlier Greek sculptures of men, the sexual element was even more graphic. The earliest known representation of a mythical figure – on show in the British Museum – is a three-inch-tall, mid-eighth-century BC statue of a naked Ajax.

Ajax, the strongest of the Greeks, is deeply depressed at losing Achilles's armour to Odysseus, after wily Odysseus is characteristically more eloquent in staking his claim to it. And so Ajax falls on his sword – a rather delicate operation since he also happens to have an enormous erection. On top of that, his whole body is shaped like an enormous erection, with his head moulded into the head of a penis.

No wonder it was kept in the British Museum's Secretum – the name for Cupboard 55, where all rude objects were kept from 1865. The Secretum wasn't opened up until the 1960s. It's only half a century ago that we caught up with the Greeks' avant-garde approach to naked beauty. 'Ithyphallic' (straight-phallus) figures like Ajax were common in Greece. To find one of the great Greek heroes of the Trojan War naked and excited at the moment of death shows how at ease the Greeks were with sex.

The convention on later classical Greek statues was to give them small, non-erect penises. This wasn't to console male citizens, but to show the virtues of self-control among the mighty gods – even that celestial love-rat, Zeus, and the acme ('highest point') of male strength, Heracles. Only ludicrous figures lacking self-control had big penises; like the actors in Greek comedies, who had huge willies dangling from their tunics. In the gym, large penises were so unfashionable that the Greeks tethered them to their waist with a leather thong rather than let them swing around.

When it came to naked statues, the Romans imitated the Greek originals –
that's why so many original Greek bronzes, later melted down, are only known
today thanks to Roman copies. The Greek ideal of the naked body was
celebrated during the Renaissance, too. Michelangelo based his naked Adam,
on the Sistine Chapel ceiling, on the Belvedere Torso, a twisting, contorted
fragment of a first-century BC copy of a second-century BC naked male. The
torso so influenced Michelangelo that it was once known as 'The School of
Michelangelo'.

Before the Elgin Marbles came to Britain in the early nineteenth century,
the Belvedere Torso was considered the ideal sculpture of the human form.
That it had such influence was particularly striking, given the absence of a
head. How brilliant, critics said – of the torso and of Michelangelo's work – to
portray emotion through stomach muscles alone.

That ideal of the perfect Greek body lives on today. From Bondi Beach to
Venice Beach, people yearn to emulate the Greek six-pack look. Adonis, the
Greek god of beauty, is revered now just as much as he was by Sappho, in one of
her heterosexual phases, in a poem of around 600 BC: 'Gentle Adonis is dying,
Cythera, what shall we do? Beat your breasts, girls, and tear your dresses.'

You could hardly call the fifth-century Greeks secular – the gods were
everywhere, in sculpted form, and in the popular subconscious. But this
cheerful willingness to strip their gods naked showed they didn't defer too
crazily to them. The naked anthropomorphism of the gods buttressed the most
celebrated line by the fifth-century BC philosopher Protagoras, also Pericles's
teacher: 'Man is the measure of all things: of things which are, that they are, and
of things which are not, that they are not.' The line appeared in Plato's *Protagoras*.

At around the same time, Sophocles made a similar point in *Antigone*,
in that quote I laboriously adapted and painted on to a battered slate in
Pembrokeshire: 'There are many formidable things in the world, but there is
nothing more formidable than mankind.' Socrates enlarged on the related idea
of self-knowledge. He only thought he was more intelligent than other men
because they thought they knew something; after much self-examination, he
knew he knew nothing.

'Know thyself' – '*Gnothi seauton*' – was originally said by the oracle at
Delphi. The words were inscribed over the entrance to Delphi's Temple of

Apollo; the accompanying inscription read, 'Nothing in excess'. The Delphic motto inspired Alexander Pope's early eighteenth-century *Essay on Man* – 'Know then thyself, presume not God to scan; The proper study of mankind is man.'

Socrates expanded on the idea in his line, 'The unexamined life is not worth living.' 'Isn't it obvious,' Socrates said, 'that people are successful when they know themselves, and failures when they do not? Those who know themselves know what suits them best, because they can distinguish between what they can and what they cannot do.' Not much room for the gods there.

Back on Paros, I clambered out of the ancient mining shaft and peered down into the nineteenth-century one. The quarry was specially reopened in 1821 to provide the marble for the gallery and statues flanking Napoleon's tomb in Les Invalides, Paris.

Parian marble is still prized. When Paddy Leigh Fermor built his house in the Mani in 1964, pride of place in the sitting room went to a marble slab from Paros, with a delicate, perforated, star-shaped pattern.

The marble also produces a surface of staggering warmth, softness and smoothness – the look of youthful human skin you see in the Venus de Milo. That ultra-smooth surface was created by aggressive polishing with emery. This abrasive, dark grey stone is serendipitously found in great quantities on the island of Naxos, only a few miles east of Paros. The Greek for emery was *smuris* – as in Smyrna, now Izmir, the principal ancient trading post for the stone.

Not only does that hardened, polished, outer layer of Parian marble look like a miraculous kind of stone skin. It also provided a steely protection for the softer stone beneath. On lots of statues in Athens, that protective layer of outer, hardened stone has often been worn away by pollution. When the outer layer decomposes, the softer stone below becomes a rough, blurred layer of powdered gypsum.

That was not the fate, thank God, of the *korai* – the maidens carved from Paros stone – on the Athenian Acropolis, my next destination.

TEMPLE OF THESEUS AND ACROPOLIS FROM
THE WEST.

Athens in 1890. You can see how the Parthenon lost most of its middle section in
1687, when a Venetian soldier fired a mortar at the temple, then a Turkish mosque
and a gunpowder store.
In the foreground, the Temple of Theseus - in fact the Temple of Hephaestus - was,
like the Parthenon, a Doric temple built in the mid-fifth century BC. It has survived
much better. (1890 drawing)

14

The Athenian Miracle

As I examined the battered Doric columns of the Parthenon, it was hard not to raise a cheer – at a discreet distance from any Greeks in the vicinity – for Lord Elgin. He whipped his marbles away from Athens in 1803, paying £75,000 for them before Athenian exhaust fumes could do their worst.

How extraordinary the Parthenon must have looked before it was bombed and eroded, and how striking, in its original greens, blues and reds. In the east pediment of the Parthenon, particularly dramatic blue stripes have been found in the Parthenogenesis ('birth from a virgin') scene – the birth of Athena from the head of her father, Zeus.

Using UV light and high-intensity lamps, a German archaeologist, Vinzenz Brinkmann, has recently discovered that the Parthenon, and most classical statues, were painted – as most medieval cathedrals were. The translucency of the hardened marble was intensified by the application of coloured wax which seeped into the stone.

For centuries, Renaissance experts and Renaissance sculptors based their theories of Greek aesthetics on pure, white statues. In fact, the colour on the ancient statues was washed away by the elements or eroded by centuries buried underground. Where fragments of faded colour survived in the deep folds of the drapery, experts dismissed it as dirt. The eighteenth-century German art historian Johann Winckelmann said of ancient sculpture, 'The whiter the body is, the more beautiful it is as well. Colour should have a minor part in the consideration of beauty because it is not [colour] but structure that constitutes its essence.'

Scholars should have paid closer attention to Greek literature. In Euripides's play *Helen of Troy*, Helen, the most beautiful woman in the world, said, 'If only I could shed my beauty and assume an uglier aspect. The way you would wipe colour off a statue.'

That's the worrying thing about the classical world. It was so long ago that it's hard to say anything too definitively. Best to stick to a few definite truths about the ancient world, rather than do too much guesswork. Better to be a hedgehog than a fox, in the words of Archilochus, the seventh-century BC poet from the marble island of Paros. Archilochus is best known for the idiom Isaiah Berlin was so fond of: 'The fox knows many things; the hedgehog knows one great thing.' Less well known is Archilochus's dirty poetry:

Many a sightless eel have you taken in …
And I used to explore your rugged glens
In my full-blooded youth.

Best to root your theories in the solid evidence – like the Parthenon, much ruined and much depleted, but still a definite chunk of a distant past.

After a three-hour ferry from Paros to Piraeus, I checked in at the Hotel Herodion at the foot of the Acropolis, and climbed up to the Parthenon. Greek for 'the virgin's apartment' – in honour of the goddess Athene – the Parthenon was built, under the control of the master-artist Pheidias, from 447 BC to 438 BC. It was an extraordinary and precise moment, when Greek politics, art and architecture clicked into place. Pericles called Athens the School of Greece; the artistic, as well as the political and intellectual, centre of the world.

In the sixth century BC, Greek sculpture was still pretty clunky. Primitive, stiff, chunky, largely symmetrical humans marched forwards like stone automatons, their arms locked to their sides, with a single leg making a formal step forwards. And then, within a century, they raced into the sublime, with anatomically accurate representations, full of human spirit and expression, turning on their heel, twisting their bodies in contrapposto, off-axis pose, as Michelangelo's David did, nearly two thousand years later.

The Elgin Marbles were in a class of their own; in Thucydides's words, a possession for all time. The folds of the Athenians' flowing, sleeved chitons – which a century before had been thickly carved into straight, blockish bands – came to wild, realistic, asymmetric life. The oozing, flowing, swerving, unpredictable lines of fifth-century BC drapery have been compared to liquid chocolate in their natural, liquid movement.

Literally liquid, in the case of the statue of Ilissos – lent by the British Museum to the Hermitage in St Petersburg amid much controversy in December 2014. Ilissos was named after a river that still flows through Athens, and his cloak is sculpted to look dripping wet. With his twisting, bent body, Ilissos could fit snugly into the corner of the western pediment of the Parthenon. What a change from that primitive, stiff, chunky Greek sculpture of a century before. When Ilissos turned up at the Hermitage, the Russian curators were staggered by his melted-chocolate brilliance.

'He has made our own ancient statues look dead,' one curator told Neil MacGregor, Director of the British Museum.

That chocolate melted even further in the fourth century BC, when Hellenistic statuary grew more mobile with the use of the running drill. Boring holes at unprecedented speed, the running drill undercut the marble and produced crisp, deep-shadowed drapery.

The fifth century BC marked the height, too, of Greek vase painting – a by-product of the Athenian tradition that every father had to teach his son a trade. On earlier, black-figure pottery from the seventh to fifth centuries BC, the figures were initially produced by adding clay shapes on to the vase. The details were then incised into the clay surface. The figures were highlighted in red and white colours, and the plain, clay background was painted black – which turned orange when fired. Thanks to a sophisticated firing process, the added–on clay figures turned black. And so you ended up with black figures on an orange background.

In around 520 BC, a new technique – red-figure pottery – emerged. The background was filled with glossy clay, which turned black on firing; while the figures turned red. The details were painted on – rather than being incised – leading to more vivid, realistic, sophisticated figures.

Painting, too, by all accounts, reached new heights. Although not a single Greek panel painting survives, several painters are celebrated – chiefly Apelles, thought to have lived in the fourth century BC when he supposedly painted a portrait of Alexander the Great.

Why was there this great clicking of the arts and politics, and why particularly in Athens? Some put it down to the dreary factor of high Greek unemployment, and the ultimate in Keynesian make-work schemes: the building of the Parthenon. Money helped, too. There was enough cash in the treasury to pay for an artistic revolution. Pericles had swiped the treasury from Delos and rehoused it in Athens.

Not long before, in 483 BC, the Athenians discovered a huge silver mine at nearby Laurium. Athenian prosperity was built on silver, in the same way that Cypriot prosperity was built on copper. The word 'copper' comes from the name Cyprus – Kupros in Greek. The periodic table symbol, Cu, for copper, is derived from *cuprum*, the Latinisation of the Greek place name.

Laurium – now the modern town of Lavrion – was revived as a mining centre in 1859, with the discovery of lead and zinc. Today, the nineteenth-century mining buildings are largely in ruins, their walls plastered with graffiti supporting Syriza. Still, in the hills above Lavrion, the rolling, stony ground is pitted with ancient little punctures – tiny caves, no bigger than the average kitchen, now scoured clean of all silver.

The high silver content of Athenian currency meant it was highly trusted. A particularly popular coin – minted in Athens in 480 BC – had Athena on one side, and her symbol, the owl, on the other. The owl was flanked by the first three letters of her name: an alpha, a theta and an epsilon. This silver tetradrachm – a four-drachma piece, known simply as an 'owl' – was the first widely traded international coin. It also pioneered the use of a head of a significant person on one side and a tail, or animal, on the other.

The Athenian cause was helped by two recent victories over the Persians, at Marathon in 490 BC and Salamis in 480 BC. The dominance of the Athenian fleet meant they could tax any ship they came across. Their naval force was much boosted in 493 BC, when the politician Themistocles moved the navy from grotty old Phaleron port, a few miles up the coast, to the new mega-harbour at Piraeus – still the main hopping-off point for backpackers en route to the islands.

So Athens was the richest city at the head of a loose-knit empire. And it had the money and confidence to commission art. Rich Athenians paid for the comic drama festival, the Lenaia, in January, and the tragedies and comedies of the Dionysia in April. Athens had the artists, too. Pheidias, the genius of Greek architecture, was available for hire as the master of works on the Acropolis. Pheidias, Myron and Polykleitos – the three greatest sculptors of the period – were trained in a workshop belonging to a single master. Pheidias and Myron even went to the same school in Argos together.

The Parthenon was built, too, just at the moment when Greek architecture had passed through its Doric, Ionic and Corinthian stages to a new peak of harmony. Inasmuch as anyone knows, the simple, plain, robust, Doric order was invented in around 700 BC; the Ionic order, with its volutes, like little girls' curls, on the capitals, in 600 BC; and the Corinthian, with its bristling thicket of acanthus leaves on the capital, in about 500 BC.

And so, when Pheidias plumped for old-fashioned Doric for the Parthenon, he did so after 250 years of gradual perfection of the Doric temple – with its *pronaos*, or porch, leading to a *cella*, or hall, containing the god's image.

The longevity of use of the orders is staggering. On the cover of this book, I'm leaning against an understated Ionic column – the little girls' curls have been minimised and it's almost Doric in its simplicity. That column – in Priene, 50 miles north of Bodrum on the western Turkish coast – was built in 130 BC, nearly 500 years after the first Ionic columns were erected.

My fogeyish Ionic column was originally part of a now-ruined, 380-foot-long sacred portico, wrapped inside an outer screen of Doric columns. This might have been a reflection of the Parthenon, which has Doric columns on the outside, topped with metopes – separate scenes, like a cartoon strip, divided by a triple strip of vertical stones, called triglyphs. The inner hall – the *cella* – of the Parthenon had a continuous frieze above the columns, a pattern usually found in Ionic temples.

The attachment to the old Ionic style is remarkable when you consider what was happening just down the coast in Xanthos, near Antalya. There, in 375 BC, a tomb was built for Payava, a Lycian aristocrat. On one side of the tomb, there's a Greek athlete; on the other side, there's a nobleman in full Persian dress. Most extraordinarily of all, this Greek tomb had an arched, pointed roof, like something out of thirteenth-century England. The Gothic arrived in south-east Turkey 1,500 years before it hit northern Europe.

Vitruvius, the first-century BC Roman architectural historian, had an intriguing explanation for the perfection of Greek architecture: the different orders reflected the innately harmonious qualities of humans. Doric mirrored the robust, no-nonsense strength of helmeted soldiers. The slim, Ionic columns, with those girls' curls, represented lissom, curly-haired maidens. As for the very idea of columns, Vitruvius claimed they took their shape from trees – thus the columns of the Parthenon tapering towards the top, their grooved flutes inspired by uneven bark.

Really? It all sounds a bit fantastical, coming up with outlandish theories to fit an inexplicable beauty. Look at the shallow fluting on the column I'm leaning against on the cover of this book – hardly looks like bark, does it?

What is true – a hedgehog fact, not lazy-fox speculation – is that the Greeks were the first to use *entasis*: the special effect that came of letting columns bulge ever so slightly outwards in the middle. Entasis was designed to counteract the ugliness produced by a straight-sided column. The eye plays a strange practical joke on the brain, and cons it into thinking the straight sides of the column actually dip inwards in the middle.

The entasis trick is even harder to pull off when you see that the columns of the Parthenon aren't carved from one single, long chunk of stone. They're made of a series of column drums, held almost imperceptibly together by mortice and tenon joints to form a single, swelling, column. The flutes were carved once the columns had been laid on top of each other, to make the joins even more imperceptible.

Entasis wasn't just used on the columns of the Parthenon but also on the stone platform on which they stand. On the 228-foot-long sides of the temple, the base rises in the middle by 4¼ inches from the level at either end. That's only a gradient of one in 300, but it's enough to hide a paperback, if you lay it at one end of the base and try to see it from the other end.

The Parthenon had a rough time of it over the years, not just from pollution and Lord Elgin. Its biggest blow came in 1687, under Turkish occupation. Athens was a Turkish city from 1458 until the kingdom of Greece was proclaimed in 1832.

In the 1460s, the Parthenon became a mosque – fragments of the building survive today. And then, in 1687, a Venetian soldier, besieging the Turkish occupiers, fired a tragically accurate mortar round, hitting a gunpowder magazine at the heart of the temple. Three hundred people were killed; the roof, of Parian marble tiles, collapsed, as did 60 per cent of the frieze sculptures. Six columns fell on the south side, eight on the north; only one column remained in the eastern porch.

But, still, enough of it remains; though much is taken, much abides. That evening, the hotel guests sipped their Mythos beers on the rooftop of the Herodion, and just sat and stared at the Parthenon. I had never seen people just look at a great work of art for so long.

Most of us race around great buildings and galleries – ten seconds for that picture, five seconds for that one. As the great tourist hordes drive through Venice, Florence, Paris and London, they chat, they look at their mobiles and examine the prices outside restaurants. But they barely look at the things they came to see, even when they are photographing them. The selfie is the apotheosis of your self over the object. I apologise for my ancient Greek selfie on the cover – my sainted ex-girlfriend had felt no great urge that day to drive for several hours to the ruins at Priene; thank God for the self-timer.

There are older buildings than the Parthenon – Stonehenge among them. But the Parthenon is the first piece in the jigsaw – a building whose Doric columns could easily be transported to a twentieth-century town hall without looking antiquated. A sort of perfection had been hit on. And, with all due respect to Stonehenge, you can see which one was built first.

The other reason – the greatest one – for the genius of the honey-yellow ruin staring down on us was democracy.

In 508 BC, 60 years before the Parthenon was begun, the first democratic reforms were introduced by Cleisthenes, Pericles's great-uncle. Cleisthenes was a leading member of the Alcmaeonids – the Athenian Kennedy family – who dominated politics from the seventh to the fifth century BC. Both Pericles and the leading politician, Alcibiades, were Alcmaeonids.

For 180 years, until Philip II of Macedon, Alexander the Great's father, took over the city in 322 BC, Athens was the first, and possibly the last, true democracy. It's no coincidence that those 180 years encompassed the golden years for Athenian literature, architecture, sculpture and all-round civilisation.

The basis of that democracy was simple enough. Political decisions were made by the *demos*, or the people, in the *ekklesia*, or assembly. The *ekklesia* was held every eight days on the Pnyx, the hill half a mile west of the Parthenon, with a carved stone speaker's platform. It comes from *puknos* – 'crowded'. In fact, there's rather a lot of space at the Pnyx. The crowded bit is thought to refer to the single entrance to the hill.

Democracy was the undercurrent to the Elgin Marbles. For all the gods and goddesses on the Parthenon frieze, there wasn't a single overbearing tyrant, king or pharaoh there.

The frieze is thought to show the Panathenaic procession: the festival where Athena's sacred robe, or *peplos*, was dedicated to the olive-wood statue of Athena Polias – Athena of the City – in a temple by the north façade of the Parthenon. Athena was the patron god of Athens; thus the name. The Greek for Athens was 'Athenae', the plural of Athene (Athena in the Attic dialect). So, strictly speaking, Athens is a plural, meaning 'Athenes'; perhaps because the city swallowed up lots of small villages, each called Athena.

If Poseidon had had his way, Athens would be called Poseidon – or Poseidons, perhaps. He staked his claim to the Acropolis by magically causing a stream of water to appear there; Athena countered with an olive tree, conjured out of nowhere. The gods declared her the winner, with the right to confer her name on the city.

At the centre of the Panathenaic procession – bang in the middle of the east façade, between Hera and Zeus on one side and Athena and Hephaistos on the other – there stands not a king, not a god, but a little girl. She's taking the sacred *peplos* from a figure thought to be the Archon Basileus – the King Magistrate, the chief religious official, but certainly not a king. The implication is clear: man, or, in this case, a little girl, is, as Plato said in the *Protagoras* not long after, the measure of all things.

Unless that man was a slave – and there were as many as a hundred thousand slaves in Athens, around 40 per cent of the population. That's about the same proportion as in the Deep South before the American Civil War – and few would claim that as an ideal society. Women, foreigners and non-citizens, slaves especially, were very much not part of the demos. Slaves were treated as sex objects to be abused at will, with their heads shaved, as you'll often see on Greek pottery. Even the most sophisticated democrats of them all took slave ownership for granted: Plato's will mentioned five slaves, Aristotle's more than fourteen.

It doesn't make things much better that the slaves were allowed to do sophisticated work. The accounts for building the Erechtheum, the temple next to the Parthenon, show that, of 86 builders used, 24 were citizens, 42 were metics (resident aliens) and 20 were slaves, who did much of the exceptional painting, woodwork and carving.

Metics, too, were treated pretty well: Pericles's mistress, Aspasia, was one, from the city of Miletus on the west coast of Turkey. He kissed her every evening when he got home from running the world's first democracy, and burst into tears when she was charged with running a high-end brothel. Slaves weren't treated quite so nicely.

The slave-built Erechtheum is famous not just for the caryatids – the pillars modelled on girls from Karyai in Laconia – but also for the earliest surviving use of the egg and dart motif. Slaves may well have come up with the motif – and on a much venerated, ancient building, too.

For all the sophisticated work of the Athenian slaves, you'd be hard-pressed to say ancient Greece was a world that belonged to the many, not the few. In *The Iliad*, there is a single prominent figure of lowly origins. Poor Thersites suggested giving up the Trojan siege early, only to be beaten up by Odysseus with a sceptre for being such a total oik.

Strictly speaking, Athens wasn't really a democracy in the modern sense of the word. The Greeks would have considered British government – with representatives who hold delegated, pooled power – a kind of mob rule.

The Greeks may have invented democracy but they thought of it utterly differently to us. The Greek word *demokratia* – 'control by the people' – was used by Plato and Aristotle to mean government by the poor, a regime they viewed as a kind of up-ended oligarchy or tyranny (a Lydian, not a Greek, word). They preferred to use *politeia* to describe the essential Greek idea of government by general consent.

Democracy was an urban idea, too. When Aristotle said, 'Man is a political animal', what he really meant was, 'Man is an animal whose characteristic it is to live in a city state.' The word 'political' comes from *polis*, Greek for city.

Despite the modern differences, the origins of democracy do lie in Athens: with the members of the council of 500 and the courts, all drawn from free Athenian males over the age of 30. It was an astonishingly fair system. The

500 members of the council were chosen by lot, with 50 from each of the ten tribes. They served for a year and could be re-elected only once, but not in successive years. The Assembly – of citizens over 18 – then voted on the council's proposals. Everyone, including Pericles, could only talk, at most, twice in an Assembly meeting.

The checks and balances on Athenian government were extreme. And the powers of the 10,000 Athenian citizens were much greater than those of citizens in modern democracies. The Athenians who passed the laws in the Assembly also acted as judges and jurors in the Athenian courts, without lawyers. The idea of the separation of powers would have seemed ridiculous. In the Athenian Assembly, any citizen could speak and propose anything before it was voted on. In the more primitive world of Spartan politics, the motion was carried by the person who shouted the loudest.

One of the things the Athenians repeatedly voted for was the continued election of Pericles, from 461 to 429 BC. For 32 years, he was voted in as *strategos*, or military leader (as in 'strategy'). In busts of Pericles, he was invariably shown wearing the *strategos*'s helmet – it also helped to hide his dolichocephalic, or long-headed, forehead.

No wonder Pericles is Boris Johnson's hero. When he said in 2014 that David Cameron would be prime minister for another 30 years – denying his own leadership ambitions – he was joking. He didn't think the idea of a politician ruling for 30 years was odd; more that it would be odd if David Cameron were in charge for so long, rather than some other unnamed politician. A bust of dolichocephalic Pericles sits in the Mayor's office in City Hall.

'I grew up in the Cold War and, in my childish imagination, Periclean Athens was America – free, democratic, exuberant, culturally rich,' says Boris. 'Russia – nasty, closed, repressive, militaristic – was obviously more like Sparta.'

Boris isn't the only one to model himself on the Athenian political model. Thucydides, the fifth-century BC political historian, is the hero of the American neoconservative movement. One of its members, Irving Kristol, called Thucydides's history of the Peloponnesian War 'the favourite neoconservative text on foreign affairs', thanks to its popularity with Professor Leo Strauss of Chicago and Professor Donald Kagan of Yale. The parallels between America and Athens – two dominant powers entangled in difficult overseas campaigns – aren't hard to spot.

The freedoms of democratic Athens were admittedly limited. Socrates was sentenced to death in 399 BC for taking free speech a bit far in Athenian eyes. Still, those limited freedoms were unprecedented. And it makes sense that a free city produced an explosion of untrammelled literature, art and philosophy.

Because of this relative freedom of speech, Athens had double the number of literary festivals of other cities. Euripides and Sophocles rushed to compete in the Dionysia, the Athenian theatrical festival. Repressive old Sparta had nothing on erudite Athens – Communist Russia against the enlightened West again.

Pericles was a Renaissance man *avant la lettre*. He inspired Thucydides, and commissioned the Parthenon and its sculptures. He also backed Herodotus and Sophocles – who served alongside him as Athens's *strategos*, after writing *Antigone*. Intellectual triumphs brought political ones in artistically sensitive Athens.

No wonder oratory flourished in the first home of relatively free speech. Athens was the birthplace of modern rhetoric – a subject rated above philosophy in the curriculum of the grand schools of Hellenistic and Roman Greece. Greek is still at the root of most rhetorical terms: oxymoron, anaphora, assonance and dozens more.

In many ways, Athenian democracy was more accountable than modern British democracy – thanks to the custom of ostracism, introduced by Cleisthenes. Every year, in the Assembly, any citizen could bid to kick out a politician by scoring their name on a chunk of broken vase – an *ostrakon*. A group of at least 6,000 citizens put their *ostraka* in a pile allocated to a particularly unpopular politician. The politician was kicked out of Athens – or ostracised – for ten years, with no further penalty. The great and the good were regularly ostracised, including Pericles's father and Themistocles, a prominent politician.

Ostracism may seem brutal now, but it was rather an effective, non-violent way of removing the leader of a potentially rebellious faction. How refreshing for the body politic to get rid of an Athenian David Mellor or Jeffrey Archer.

None of these democratic measures would have been tenable without the security brought by military supremacy. And the greatest of those military victories – in 490 BC, at a crucial time in the birth of democracy – was on the plain of Marathon.

An Ionic capital on the Erechtheum, the late fifth-century BC temple next to the Parthenon. Note the earliest surviving use of the egg and dart motif, used on four different levels here. Note, too, the single volute – the twirly-whirly bit, often compared to the curls in a girl's hair. The other one has been lost. You can also just make out the popular honeysuckle motif, right at the bottom of the picture.

PERICLES.

Pericles, with his dolichocephalic – 'long-headed' – fore-head, covered by his strategos's ('military leader') helmet. The inscription – 'Pericles Xanthippou Athenaios' – means 'Pericles the Athenian, son of Xanthippus'. Xanthippus was a rich general who married into the Alcmaeonids – the Athenian Kennedy family. Pericles's mother, Agariste, was the niece of the Alcmaeonid, Cleisthenes, who introduced democracy to Athens in 508 BC. (1890 drawing)

THE MOUND AT MARATHON.

'The mountains look on Marathon, and Marathon looks on the sea.' The Athenian burial mound on the plain of Marathon has barely changed since Byron wrote his lines; or since the Athenians beat the Persians in 490 BC. (1890 drawing)

15

A Marathon Effort

It should be easier to do an authentic marathon in Athens than anywhere else on earth.

The first marathon – run in 490 BC by the Athenian messenger Pheidippides – was a lot shorter than the official 26-and-a-bit miles it is today. It's just over 21 miles from the seaside plain of Marathon to the centre of Athens. That's the distance Pheidippides ran to proclaim the news that the Athenians had beaten the Persians in the crucial battle at Marathon. Pheidippides managed to get to the centre of Athens and announce the two words '*Chairete – nikomen*' – 'Hail – we've won' – before dropping dead.

The victory was so crucial that John Stuart Mill, the political philosopher, said Marathon was more important to nineteenth-century British politics than the Battle of Hastings. According to Mill's thinking, Marathon secured the golden age of Greece over the next half-century, the construction of the Parthenon, the consolidation of democracy, the liberal enlightenment of the West and the future of European civilisation.

Mill had a point. Booty from the battle filled the Athenian treasury at Delphi; and the victory laid the foundations for the triumph of Pericles's Greece half a century later. Today, the information board at the battlefield says how crucial the victory of 'young Greece' over the old Persian Empire was. Just like Tony Blair, ancient Greece was the future once.

Runners like Pheidippides were vital to the smooth administration of the far-flung corners of the ancient world. And not just in Greece: Herodotus said of the Persian couriers, 'Neither snow nor rain nor heat nor gloom of night stays these couriers from the swift completion of their appointed rounds.' The line is inscribed in enormous letters on the huge, classical post office on Eighth Avenue in Manhattan.

There's some question over whether Pheidippides ran the original marathon. In the first mention of his exploits, Herodotus, writing his *Histories* around 35 years after the battle, didn't refer to the run. Instead, he said, Pheidippides ran a much longer distance – around 150 miles – from Athens to Sparta and back, to ask the Spartans if they'd fight with the Athenians against the Persians. The earliest surviving writer to mention the Marathon run was Plutarch, more than 500 years after the battle.

These days, runners still do an annual 'Spartathlon' – that gruelling 150-mile return trip. In 1982, an RAF Wing Commander, John Foden, and four colleagues attempted it, with the winner, John Scholtens, finishing in 34 and a half hours.

At the first modern Olympics, in Athens in 1896, they settled on a distance of 25 miles. Baron de Coubertin was persuaded to include the race in the Olympics by a friend, Michel Jules Alfred Bréal, the founder of modern semantics. Coubertin was also much moved by Browning's poem 'Pheidippides', and its lines on his death:

'Rejoice, we conquer!' Like wine thro' clay,
Joy in his blood bursting his heart, he died – the bliss!

It was only at the 1908 London Olympics that the modern distance – 26 miles and 385 yards – was set, to accommodate Queen Alexandra. The queen wanted the marathon to start on the lawn at Windsor Castle, so the royal children could see it from their nursery. The distance from Windsor to the royal box at White City just happened to be 26 miles and 385 yards – confirmed as the standard marathon distance in 1921.

That explains why the winner of the 1908 marathon – the Italian, Dorando Pietri – had to be helped over the finishing line: he wasn't used to the longer distance. He was later disqualified for receiving assistance.

For the 2004 Athens Olympics, the original, ancient route was extended to the full standard length, from the town of Marathon, some way north of the battlefield, to the centre of Athens. My friend Ned joined me to follow the much shorter, original route. He was the same friend who'd swum the Hellespont with me; the difference being that he made it across, and I didn't.

I should have learnt my lesson from the Hellespont. Thanks to my inadequacy, we failed to complete the shorter course even though, unlike Pheidippides, we weren't wearing full armour. Unlike Pheidippides, we didn't drop dead when we got to Athens – although my feet were in agony, thanks to the thin leather soles of my Chelsea boots. Unlike Pheidippides, we took a cab for the last ten miles.

The humiliation got worse when I met Sir James Mellon – formerly our man in Ghana, Togo and Denmark – on the cruise I took in the footsteps of Odysseus. He'd run the marathon course – all 26 miles and 385 yards of it – in the boiling heat of the Athenian suburbs. In his sixties.

We began our walk – 21 miles north-east of Athens – by the great mound in the plain of Marathon, where the Athenian dead were buried. The mound was investigated by – who else? – Schliemann in 1884. On top of the mound, he found several arrowheads, made of obsidian – volcanic glass – which he thought much older than the Battle of Marathon. Other experts say they were used by the Ethiopian archers – 'the tallest and most beautiful of men', according to Herodotus, who said they fought at Marathon. Ethiopia is rich in obsidian.

Six years after Schliemann's dig, other archaeologists rootled through the mound and found decomposed bones, ash and *lekythoi*, one-handled vases from the early fifth century – i.e. dating from the battle.

The Persians planned another monument at Marathon that was never built. They rashly brought a chunk of that lovely Paros marble with them to the battlefield. Their plan was to build a memorial to their victory after the battle. Instead, the great Athenian sculptor Pheidias ended up carving a statue of Nemesis – the Greek goddess of divine retribution – out of the Persian block of stone.

Nemesis, a daughter of Nyx or Night, took her name from the verb *nemein*, 'to give what is due'. Even more sweetly, Nemesis – who punished those guilty of hubris, or arrogance before the gods – came from the sanctuary of

Rhamnous, only five miles north-east of Marathon. The Persians really should have examined their atlas more closely before lugging a huge chunk of stone all that way.

Thanks to the unexpected victory, the burial mound at Marathon has remained a place of pilgrimage ever since the battle – with Athenians still visiting under the Roman Empire. In the dead time between Christmas and New Year, when we visited, the site was empty – we had to scale the fence to get in. The peace was only disturbed by a Greek Orthodox priest, bicycling painfully slowly up a shallow incline in his bulky black vestments.

There was a little light birdsong, too. Even in December, early spring was creeping north through Attica. Crocuses and orchids were unfurling on the plain and on top of the mound. An orange grove on the other side of the fence was still thick with unpicked fruit. Sadly, there was no sign of any fennel; *marathon* is Greek for 'fennel field'.

Beyond the grove, the plain was criss-crossed with lines of cypress trees and thick-girthed olive trees. As Ned embraced one of them, a startled chaffinch flitted out of its branches. He determined the olive tree was eight and a half feet in circumference, half a millennium old. As we stood on top of the mound, we could confirm Byron's lines from *Don Juan*:

The mountains look on Marathon,
And Marathon looks on the sea;
And musing there an hour alone,
I dreamed that Greece might still be free.

The sun glinted off the sea. Those mountains – which shield bucolic Marathon from the spreading suburbs of Athens – were dusted with snow. As we tumbled down the squidgy earth of the steep-sided mound, we could have been back in 490 BC – but for a few small modern villages, as quiet as the grave we'd been standing on. If we stayed till nightfall, our guidebook assured us, we would hear the neighing of horses and the groaning of dying Persians.

Away from the city, we returned to the friendliness of old-fashioned Greece, even if there were no actual Greeks about. Alongside the main road to Athens, the fields were crammed with Brussels sprouts, harvested by dark-skinned

Armenians who hailed us cheerily. An Egyptian roadside fruit-seller gave us local oranges and tangerines for nothing.

We must have looked pretty odd. The kilometre posts of the 2004 Olympic Marathon course still pepper the main road from Marathon to Athens. But no one else was running – or walking – the route in midwinter. I don't see why not – it must have been agony in the summer for brave Sir James Mellon.

The fields and the roads were even emptier when we took our fatal decision not to follow the classic marathon route alongside the main road. The long, curving road hugs the coast before swooping into Athens south of the mountains. Why not cross the mountains, and make the route even shorter and more scenic?

Some scholars say that's what Pheidippides did – he must have known all the shortcuts of his native Attica. He certainly would have known them better than us – or, to be precise, me. I misread the map – and led us in a series of ever-decreasing circles around the foothills of Mount Pentelikon, the mountain that provided the stone for the Parthenon.

The first time we saw the mountain quarries glinting in the sun, it was quite a thrill. The wild, jagged lines of the hillside have been carved into neat rectangular voids, eating deeper and deeper into the flank of the mountain. Across the mountainside, 20-foot-long streaks of rusty orange iron oxide dribbled down the gleaming white, flat surfaces of the quarry; just as they did 2,500 years ago, when Pheidias turned that stone into the soft, golden, shallow relief of the Elgin Marbles. That lovely golden shade – which you can still see in the British Museum – was formed by the iron oxide.

The ancient Mount Pentelikon quarry was only opened in 490 BC, after the victory at Marathon. The new source of stone – along with the confidence and financial boost of victory – led to the building of a sort of pre-Parthenon on the Acropolis. That was smashed to pieces by the Persians in 480 BC – the other red-letter year for the Athenians. In the late summer of that year, the Spartans, fighting on the Athenian side, lost to the Persians at the heroic last stand of Thermopylae. Days later, though, the Athenians beat the Persians at the Battle of Salamis.

With further victories in 479 BC – over the Persian army at the Battle of Plataea, and the Persian navy at the Battle of Mycale on today's western coast of Turkey – the stage was set for the Athenian political and artistic triumphs of the later fifth century BC.

Down on the valley floor, in the shadow of Pentelikon, the fields were dotted with ten-foot-long, coffin-shaped chunks of marble – grooved with the drill lines that split the stone from the mountain.

Alongside a German cemetery for thousands of soldiers killed during the liberation of Athens in 1944, the gravel at our feet was made up of thousands of little rectangles of pure, white marble. I picked one of them up. The freshly cut sides were an even salt-white colour, sparkling with so many tiny, dazzling, gleaming points that they joined together in a continuous band, as if a snail had just trailed along the surface.

Flanking our path were big, rough off-cuts of the stone, crested by crinkly ridges of orange-brown iron oxide. Today, on the Elgin Marbles, you can see exactly the same consistency of rough stone where the marbles were smashed by the Venetian shell that hit the Parthenon in 1687. What a transformation – from that rough stone to the liquid flesh of the sculptures in the British Museum.

When we saw the same quarry for the third time – albeit at a different angle – the thrill began to evaporate. As had any cross-country advantage over the grim, but flat, motorway route. We tried to take a mountain path, clearly marked on the map. A friendly OAP – out for a walk with his cat – said the route was closed off by a landslide. He was the only person we saw in the mountains all day, even though we were only 15 miles, as the crow flies, from Athens.

The route he called *kalos* – 'beautiful' – retraced our footsteps back to the main road. Instead, we slid down the mountainside – a *kakos* route, or a bad one, our new friend cried after us. He whistled at us in vain, as we took an hour slip-sliding down the marble-strewn mountain, before crossing a dried-up riverbed and scrambling up the other side of the valley.

After several hours' unintentional close examination of the inner workings of Mount Pentelikon's quarries, we stumbled on the main road. This led through a pass in the mountains, down the other side of Mount Pentelikon, into Kifissia, an upmarket suburb of Athens.

The last time I'd been in Kifissia, a year earlier in 2013, I had dined with the former Greek minister for finance, Giorgos Papakonstantinou, and his wife, Jacoline Vinke, a travel writer. It was safer to eat at his house. He was barely able to go out in public in Athens since he'd become a scapegoat for the financial crisis – after a mysterious scandal that exposed the machinations of Greek politics at their most dastardly, Byzantine and tragicomic.

Educated at the LSE and New York University, Papakonstantinou was once the golden boy of PASOK – the Greek socialist party – first as press spokesman and then, in 2009, as finance minister. He'd been brought in to clear up the Augean Stables of the Greek economy – with its massive government debt, combined with grotesque levels of tax evasion.

He had the honesty to admit the deficit was much bigger than had previously been admitted: the seven billion euro deficit turned out to be more than 30 billion. So Papakonstantinou sorted out a 110 billion euro loan from the International Monetary Fund and the EU, and began to grapple with tax reform – or, in other words, tried to get Greeks to do something that isn't in their cultural lexicon: pay tax.

'Even I was amazed by how people cheated,' he said. 'We had the finance ministry's Christmas party at a hotel near the Acropolis. At the end, the manager came up to me and said, "You won't be wanting a receipt, will you?" I told him I was the finance minister and he said, "I know – you won't be wanting a receipt, will you?" Unbelievable.'

After PASOK fell in 2012, Papakonstantinou was golden boy no more. It was revealed that, in 2010, he'd asked Christine Lagarde, the former French finance minister, for the 'Lagarde list' – the names of 1,991 Greek potential tax evaders. Papakonstantinou told a parliamentary inquiry that he'd passed a CD, containing the list, to the Greek tax police, who promptly lost it. His successor as finance minister, Evangelos Venizelos, claims to have stumbled on a USB stick in his secretary's desk drawer, containing the list; with one crucial omission – the names of three of Papakonstantinou's relations.

The 64 billion euro question is – did Papakonstantinou remove the names of his relations before handing the list on to the tax authorities?

'Would I really be that stupid?' Papakonstantinou said, earnestly but not pleadingly, over dinner. He hadn't brought up the issue that had ruined his life – and that of his family. I had. I felt terrible as his other friends round the table dropped their small talk and listened to a story they knew so much better than I did.

His steady, low-key demeanour – and the fact he hadn't raised the issue with me, a journalist, who might in some tiny way have been useful to his cause – convinced me of his innocence. The courts didn't agree. In March 2015, he was cleared of causing damage to the state but was found guilty of a misdemeanour — doctoring a document. He was given a one-year suspended jail sentence. A light sentence, yes. But, if he is innocent, he is a figure out of Greek tragedy: the man who has to bear responsibility, unjustifiably, for the collapse of a whole country.

As I left, his wife, Jacoline Vinke, gave me a copy of her newly published book about small Greek hotels. It was the volume that directed me to the hotel by the nightclub in Mykonos; otherwise, it's been invaluable. 'Did you have a dazzling launch party for it?' I asked. 'It didn't really seem the time for one,' she said, extremely politely. Of course they couldn't have a launch party in Athens when Giorgos was abused every time he went for a walk in Kifissia. I was agonised by my faux pas.

Not as agonised as on my return to Kifissia a year later. By the time we stumbled into the outer fringes of Athens, it was seven in the evening, and we'd been walking for eight hours.

'The oldest man ever to do the Marathon did it in eight hours,' said Ned cheerfully. 'He was 100.'

The thin soles of my Chelsea boots each had a big hole beneath the balls of my feet. Water had seeped into my socks – first from the sodden mountain turf, now from the slick rain varnish of the Athens streets. I began to stumble at a depressingly slow pace down the hill into the city but could take no more.

After a kebab and chips in Kifissia – in traditional fashion, the chips were tucked into the pitta bread alongside the sliced lamb – we climbed into a taxi. It wasn't much consolation when I discovered that, in the first modern Olympic Marathon, in Athens in 1896, Spiridon Belokas, who'd come third, had been disqualified. It later emerged that he'd taken a horse and carriage for part of the way. A horseless carriage seemed no more honourable.

The Plato café, next to the site of Plato's Academy, the first university.

16

The Decline and Fall of Plato's Athens

The cab journey to central Athens – through the sea of unlovely white tower blocks that circle the ancient city – didn't lift my spirits much.

That expansion of Athens is a very recent thing. Despite occupation by multiple invaders, this extraordinary cradle of civilisation had barely shifted its boundaries until 150 years ago. Early nineteenth-century prints of Athens show a city wrapped around the foot of the hill topped by the Acropolis. Athens had declined to a little Turkish backwater of only about 1,300 houses. Its biggest buildings were its ancient ruins, not least the Temple of Olympian Zeus, the biggest temple in Greece.

Compare the progress of Londinium to modern London in 1,600 years and you see how little Athens developed in the 2,400 years between Periclean Athens and the nineteenth century. When Thomas De Quincey visited Greece in the nineteenth century, he said, 'What are the nuisances, special to Greece, which repel tourists from that country? They are three – robbers, fleas and dogs.'

Athens has mushroomed since it became capital of a newly independent Greece in 1834. But it has got uglier, particularly since the war, when those tower blocks self-seeded in every direction – except on the mercifully steep slopes of Mount Pentelikon we'd spent most of the day scrambling up and tumbling down. As we gingerly stepped through central Athens the next morning – my feet had recovered after deep immersion in my dwarf-sized bath in the Hotel Herodion – I could just about make out the ancient Greek skeleton at the heart of the modern, jerry-built city.

Beyond that ancient heart, central Athens largely remains the creation of the Bavarian architects of King Otho. Otho, the first king of Greece from 1832 until 1867, was the second son of King Ludwig I of Bavaria. Still, today, that Bavarian inheritance is loathed by some Greeks. When the Germans were demanding in February 2015 that Greece pay its debts, the elderly composer of the *Zorba the Greek* theme tune, Mikis Theodorakis, wrote a letter to the Syriza prime minister, Alexis Tsipras. He told him him to defy the German finance minister, Wolfgang Schäuble, and kick out the 'Bavarians'.

Theodorakis was still bristling at the Wittelsbach dynasty taking over Greece 180 years before, without Greek consent. In Theodorakis's view, the young country became bankrupt after the German monarchy destroyed Greek customary law and 'disfigured' a Byzantine nation. It was time, he said, for Greece to split from the Western enemies of the Hellenic Orthodox world, the Germans in particular. He didn't mince his words.

'How is it possible for us Greeks to accept Ms Merkel's threats and the Germans' intention to impose on us a new Gauleiter?' he wrote. 'This time wearing a tie.'

Today, 400 years of Turkish rule – before the German monarchy turned up – have left remarkably few modern marks on the city. Even the Roman agora is much more prominent than the Ottoman madrasah, built there in 1721.

Attica was annexed by the Ottoman Empire in 1456, and, soon after, Mehmed II ordered the Acropolis to be seized. Even the bit of central Greece that remained largely cut off from Turkish control was given a non-Greek name – Roumeli, 'the land of Rome' – during the years of Ottoman occupation. Most of the great sights of Greece were deserted over the centuries, as Greece was taken over not just by the Ottomans – but also the Romans, Normans and Venetians.

Again and again on my odyssey, the route to a temple or citadel – at Mycenae, Didyma, Miletus, Ephesus, Troy, Epidaurus and Delphi – was through wild, open country. At other places – like Corinth – later inhabitants built a modern town, way down the steep hillside from the remote, deserted, defensively-sited acropolis.

Athens, though, was different. Other great, ancient cities may have collapsed and disappeared under several millennia of accumulated dust. But Athens always survived. The old Mycenean palace which predated the Parthenon may have gone – Homer refers to a 'strong house of Erechtheus' on the north side of the Acropolis. But the Parthenon is still hemmed in by Mycenean defence walls.

Still, Athens lives on in much-reduced splendour. Like American cities in the 1970s, the city is being hollowed out. Since the crisis, the rich have moved out to the suburbs, leaving the city centre to rot. In the shadow of the Parthenon, not far from my upmarket hotel, handsome nineteenth-century mansions were collapsing, spilling their entrails on to the pavement, itself cracked by the sprawling roots of roadside trees. Sometimes this was thanks to the crisis; sometimes, thanks to generations-long disputes between shared family owners who refused to do the repairs.

Graffiti was plastered all over Athenian buildings, though not yet the ancient ones. At the foot of the Acropolis, elegant, nineteenth-century villas were covered with slogans defending Kostas Sakkas, a Greek anarchist. He had been jailed for participating in the Conspiracy of Cells of Fire, which had firebombed banks and luxury car dealers in Athens and Thessaloniki in 2008. 'Fuck the system,' read a graffito in green spray paint on the fine, streaked marble of a palazzo. 'Solidarity to the anarchist hunger striker, K. Sakkas.' Sakkas was released on bail in January 2014 – only to jump bail a month later.

At dinner that night, a former politician told me that parts of the city were now no-go areas for the police. The void has been filled by thuggish protectors from Golden Dawn, the increasingly popular far-right party. It was agonising to see a country in reverse. Still, Greece remained far ahead of how it looked when I first came to Syntagma Square in my gap year in 1989.

I don't want to romanticise those closing years of a rural, peasant civilisation – a *Zorba the Greek* world of widows in black, farmers on donkeys and bedrooms for an astonishingly small amount of drachmae. Poor but picturesque is all very well for the tourist – not so good for the man on the donkey with the pitiful handful of drachmae you've paid to steal his bed for the evening. Still, there was something deeply melancholy about a country falling back from a high point, especially when it feels like free fall.

Where did it all go wrong? The simple answer is Europe. By joining the eurozone, Greece was tied into a German-run international conglomerate it couldn't keep up with. It massaged its budget deficit to get into the euro with all sorts of dodges: moving its pension and defence expenses off the books; even removing expensive tomatoes from the consumer price index to cut inflation figures. And then, once Greece got into the eurozone in 2001, it kept its enormous deficit and debt concealed, until the whole thing exploded into the open in 2009 – thanks to Giorgos Papakonstantinou.

Forced to pay higher interest rates on borrowed money, Greece essentially went bankrupt, saved only by a 240 billion euro bailout from the troika. And then Syriza, the new far-left party dominating the government, asked the impossible: to stay in the euro, while cancelling that enormous debt and putting an end to the austerity measures demanded by the troika.

What caused this break between the world's greatest ancient civilisation and its melancholy, bankrupt descendant?

After the Roman conquest, Athens – for all its fashionability as a Grand Tour destination for Roman rich kids – fell into quiet decline for the next 1,500 years. By the late fourteenth century, the Duchy of Athens and Neopatras was being run by Sicilian general commissioners. Greece's star had fallen so low that the family of Nerio Acciaioli, the governor of Corinth, was considered by Gibbon to be 'plebeian in Florence, potent in Naples and sovereign in Greece'.

Four centuries of Turkish rule over Greece had its effects. By the late eighteenth century, the link between ancient and modern Greece was pretty tenuous. Walking through Athens then, the historian Edward Gibbon accused the Greeks of 'walking with supine indifference among the glorious ruins of antiquity'.

That changed with the Greek War of Independence from 1821 to 1829. It wasn't just Byron who made explicit the connections between ancient Greece and its new-found freedom. In 1821, at the beginning of the war, Athens and the Acropolis were claimed by a Greek called Odysseus, no less. Odysseus remains a popular name. The twentieth-century poet Odysseus Elytis, who won the 1979 Nobel Prize for Literature, was placed on the Greek €200 note in 2015.

Today, Greeks emphasise the link between modern and ancient Greece more than ever before. In the Grace Hotel on the volcanic island of Santorini, the maid left a little bejewelled card on our pillow every night, instead of a chocolate. Each one had a different ancient Greek quote. On the first night there with my ex-girlfriend a few years ago, the card read, 'Seek not good from without; seek it from within yourselves, or you will never find it' (Epictetus, Greek Stoic philosopher, *c*. AD 55–135). We never found it.

During the economic crisis, Greeks were particularly prone to looking back to an ancient golden age. In Athens in 2014, not long after the collapse, a witty graffiti artist wrote on a tram ticket booth, 'The 300 of Leonidas [the Spartan hero at the Battle of Thermopylae against the Persians in 480 BC] had balls and saved Greece. The 300 of the Parliament are pricks, and sold her out.'

The graffiti artist's history wasn't quite right. There were 301 Spartans, including Leonidas, and they actually lost, thanks to the treachery of a Greek traitor called Ephialtes – still today the Greek word for 'nightmare'. All the same, the Athenian navy did beat the Persians later, in 480 BC at the Battle of Salamis. Thermopylae was really a tale of heroic failure, as echoed in the battle's epitaph by the poet Simonides:

> Go tell the Spartans, passer-by,
> We followed orders. Here we lie.

The Athenian graffiti artist had a sort of point, then. The 301 at Thermopylae had been heroic failures. The more recent failure of Greece has been a hero-free zone.

Soon after the crisis, the *Daily Telegraph* interviewed Costas Mitropolous, a banker selling off government assets, such as land and mobile phone frequency bands, to reduce the national debt.

'Greece dropped out of the global economy's premier league after the death of Alexander the Great,' Mitropolous said. 'If you consider the Byzantine Empire as Greek, our economic role has declined ever since the eleventh century.'

That decline felt at its most acute when I hired a bike and pedalled out to the northern suburbs, to the site of Plato's old Academy, just outside the walls of ancient Athens. I biked first through Kerameikos, the area of Athens where the *kerameis*, or potters, worked from the seventh century BC. Ceramics gets its name from *keramos*, Greek for 'pottery clay', or, more precisely, from the Kerameikos. Kerameikos was also the site of the main Athenian cemetery, where Pericles gave his 431 BC funeral speech for the dead of the Peloponnesian War against Sparta.

The speech, said to have inspired Lincoln's Gettysburg Address in 1863, was recorded by Thucydides.

'We enjoy a form of government that does not emulate the institutions of our neighbours; indeed we ourselves are more often the model for others than their imitators,' said Pericles. 'Democracy is the name we give to it since we manage our affairs in the interests of the many, not the few.'

Tony Blair was never coy when it came to nicking other people's ideas.

I locked up my bike and strolled along the Sacred Way through the Kerameikos ancient graveyard. The graveyard and its museum were still crammed with finely carved reliefs and affecting epitaphs.

On one 430 BC tombstone in the museum, a woman dandled her grandson on her knee. Her headscarf, gown and the blanket wrapped around the child showed all the sophistication of late fifth-century BC carved drapery – that melted chocolate look, with the folds twisting and overlapping with delicate accuracy. Both the grandmother, called Ampharete, and the grandchild have died. The inscription reads, 'I hold here the beloved child of my daughter, which I held on my knees when we were alive and saw the light of the sun, and now, dead, I hold him dead.'

After ten minutes' leisurely biking, I passed the foot of Lykabettos hill, site of the Lyceum – where Plato's pupil, Aristotle, taught. Just as the Lyceum gave its name to British theatres, Odeon cinemas were derived from the *odeon*, the smaller kind of Greek theatre. Ditto the London Palladium – the Palladium, a cult statue of Pallas Athene, was said to protect Troy and was later taken to the future site of Rome by Aeneas.

I biked on to Plato's Academy. What a hallowed spot! Sacred to the goddess of wisdom, Athene; named after the Greek hero Akademos, who perhaps not so heroically abducted Helen before Paris did – but gave her up to her twin brothers, Castor and Pollux, rather than letting them destroy Athens.

Here, in around 388 BC, 40-year-old Plato turned up and set up a philosophy school, the Academia, borrowing the name from a neighbouring gymnasium. Greek gymnasia were open-air places, often outside the city walls – as I now was – with natural water sources and shelter in shaded groves. There's still a gym next door to the small park on the Academy site.

The Academy was the founding father of all universities, academies and high-minded institutions of the following 2,500 years. Here Plato continued the most impressive ever transfer of knowledge from teacher to pupil: Socrates taught Plato; Plato taught Aristotle in Athens; Aristotle taught a 13-year-old Alexander the Great. Quite a common room.

Plato wasn't his real name. He was called Aristocles; Plato was a nickname – from Platon, meaning 'broad', referring either to his waistline or his intellectual curiosity. Here, for 40 years, Plato taught until his death. Out of Plato's Academy grew Aristotle's philosophy school, known as the Peripatetics after the *peripatoi*, the colonnades where Aristotle liked to teach on the hoof.

The modern Western mind is still largely built around the ancient Greek skeleton constructed here nearly 2,500 years ago. Here, Plato fine-tuned his philosophy: the idea of an eternal, absolute deity that softened up the Western world for the acceptance of a universal religion. Here, he pondered his theory of forms: the objective essence of a thing – the form of absolute beauty, virtue or whatever it might be – without which it loses its identity.

Here were the original groves of Academe, once home to 12 sacred olive trees, legendary off-cuts of Athena's tree by the Parthenon. Still today, there is a sort of grove – a rectangular park flanked on all sides by decent enough six-storey tower blocks, a middle-class Athenian suburb.

I parked my bike by a stream – perhaps the Kephissos river that, according to the Greek historian Plutarch, was diverted in the sixth century BC and turned the area 'from a bare, dry and dusty spot into a well-watered grove, with shady walks and racecourses'. There isn't much room for racehorses these days in this tiny patch of green among the sprawling acres of Athenian concrete.

I ate my lunch – feta cheese and ham from a nearby Spar – in the shadow of the olive trees. Might these have been the same shadows that inspired Plato's visionary thought in *The Republic*? Humans, he suggested, were just deluded cavemen, watching shadows of a puppet show, flickering on the cave wall, and mistaking them for real life.

The park was empty but for a single dog-walker. There were no fences around it, and no charge to see the ruins of the most important academic site on earth. But oh, how low Plato's Academy has been brought. A low-walled *peribolos*, or courtyard, has been excavated, where schoolboys' writing slates have been found, bearing the thrilling names of Sophocles and Demosthenes. Nearby, there was an eighth-century *heroon*, or temple to a Greek hero, of mud bricks.

But no tourists come here. That should produce all the charm of the wilderness. But, instead, all is decay. The Academy was home only to dogs' messes and old Rizla packets. A few yards from the spot where Plato gave the first ever tutorial stands a crumbling, breeze-block wall, covered with years of accumulated graffiti. The only indications that Plato was ever here were a few faded signs by the *peribolos*, with brief captions. Just beyond the park is the Odos Plataion – Plato Street, its blue and white sign defaced by an indecipherable graffiti tag. Nearby, the Plato café had a big picture of the philosopher on its outside wall, proclaiming itself a 'Traditional Coffee-Snack Corner'. It was empty, too.

I sat on the Wall of Hipparchus – a three-foot-tall, sixth-century BC wall flanking the Academy – and brooded for a while, before mounting my bike and pedalling back towards the Herodion Hotel. Shelley must have felt much the same after he'd heard about the British Museum's acquisition of a big chunk of a statue of the pharaoh Ramesses II in 1817. Ramesses II's other name was Ozymandias.

Plato's Academy today – The author in the groves of academe.

The Roman walls of Sparta, plus graffiti. There were never any ancient Spartan walls – the Spartans thought they were so tough that they didn't need any.

17

Greek Tiger Mothers – the Spartan Guide to Bringing Up Baby

It's harder to find your way to the ancient acropolis of Mycenae today than three thousand or so years ago – when Agamemnon came home from the Trojan War to be murdered in the bath by his wife, Clytemnestra. When I drove to Mycenae from Athens, nobody stabbed me in the bath. But I did get lost, thanks to the economic crisis.

Agamemnon would have found his way home pretty easily – the creamy stone palace of Mycenae stands out for miles around, perched on its rocky outcrop in the middle of a plain. Much of the palace still survives, built on a mammoth scale – not least the Lion Gate, with its thirteenth-century BC pair of colossal lions, either side of a Doric pillar; the earliest coat of arms in the world.

I depended on road signs, though – and the main one to Mycenae had been obliterated by graffiti. I could see the palace on the hill, looming above me, but drove straight past the vandalised brown sign, pointing left to the palace.

Ireland has had a similar problem since its own financial crisis. A year later, driving out of Dublin – where I'd been tracking James Joyce's *Ulysses* – a road sign, raised high above the N3 to Cavan, had been covered with a scrawled black tag by an athletic graffiti artist.

On O'Connell Street, Graham Lemon's sweetshop also revealed how shabby the Celtic Tiger was getting. The shop appeared in the Laestrygonians chapter of *Ulysses*, with 'a sugarsticky girl shovelling scoopfuls of creams for a Christian Brother', instead of the human flesh preferred by the Laestrygonian cannibals. Graham Lemon's was now a Foot Locker and the old sign above the shop had lost most of its letters – 'E Confectioners HA L' the butchered sign now read.

Pulling in at a petrol station to ask the way to Mycenae didn't help – it had closed down. Greek roads, subsidised with EU billions, were in a much better state than they were a quarter of century ago – when I walked and drove along sandy tracks that are now immaculate blacktop highways. The problem is, those roads are practically empty these days. Driving around the Peloponnese was like touring a post-apocalyptic ghost town.

Once I got out of the sun-bleached concrete sprawl of Athens, the splendid motorway to Kalamata was eerily empty all day. Rocketing along at 80 mph, I could afford to stare for several seconds at the Corinth Canal below me, and the ancient acropolis of Corinth above, with little danger — there was no one to crash into. How ironic that the Peloponnese had been founded as a result of a mythical road accident at an early Olympic Games.

The ancient king of the Peloponnese, Pelops, won the chariot race by nobbling the chariot of his father-in-law, Oinomaus. Oinomaus was killed after the linchpins of his chariot wheels were replaced with wax. The wax melted, the wheels flew off and Oinomaus was thrown to his death. Pelops became king; and the island, or *nesos*, he ruled, became 'Pelops's island', or the Peloponnese.

These days, no one could afford the tolls at the unmanned booths that have cropped up every few miles on the empty road from Athens to the Peloponnese. Thank God, I was loaded down with a pocketful of euros to feed the automatic toll machines. No cars also meant no petrol stations. Pulling out of the defunct petrol station, I almost got mown down by a rare passing car. The trees and shrubs on the fringe of the forecourt had grown out of control, obscuring my view up and down the road.

For the previous 25 years I'd been coming to Greece, I'd suffered from cultural cringe – not just in deference to the superior ancient culture, but also to what looked like a superior way of life. I'd fallen for the enchanting dream, of going south and thinking everyone was spiritually better off – because they were browner, thinner, eating better food and working in surpassingly beautiful landscapes.

The bottom line, now – and then, too – was that, however lithe and healthy the Greeks still looked, they weren't being paid very much, if anything. Only now was the fallout of the crisis becoming tragically clear. Like a house that isn't maintained, everything looks fine for a while, then little things – the dirty windows, the unmown lawn – start to catch your eye. Soon the big things – the hole in the roof, the damp in the downstairs bathroom – start to kick in, with terrifying acceleration.

In the six years before my Mycenae trip, Greek GDP had shrunk by more than a quarter – a deeper, longer collapse than Europe's worst depressions in the 1930s. Unemployment was at 27 per cent, youth unemployment at 54 per cent. Pensions and wages had been cut by 35 per cent. Many of the effects of the depression wouldn't be apparent to an outsider like me; things like the collapse in primary healthcare and increased child mortality, homelessness and use of soup kitchens. But now the decline was beginning to bare its melancholy face for all to see.

The Greek countryside has been isolated from this decay for a while – dependent as it is on tourism and agriculture. Greek tourism hasn't just weathered the storm; it's already come out, triumphantly, on the other side. There was a collapse immediately after the crisis – from 17 million tourists in 2008 to 11 million in 2012 – but that figure has been climbing by more than ten per cent each year since.

I was told by the hotelier in my smart Mykonos hotel that not only were they fully booked for the summer of 2014; they were 110 per cent booked up. Even if there were any cancellations, the hotel would still run at capacity. If there were no cancellations, they would house excess guests in a nearby grand hotel at a discount.

For the first years of the collapse, the Greek countryside had also disguised the economic situation. Hard-bitten farmers reverted to the pattern of the previous 3,000 years, tending their olive trees and orange groves. Many of their children – who had gone off to make their fortunes in Athens – lost their jobs and returned to the family farm. To those farming families,

Greece's 30-year membership of the EU – an almighty splurge, followed by a drastic belt-tightening – was a brief blip in an unremitting story of rural self-sufficiency. For all the artistic and intellectual triumphs of ancient Greece, it had always been a pretty poor place, even in the ancient, golden days. Herodotus said, 'Greece and poverty were foster sisters.'

You could now see the signs of the new poverty, even in Arcadia, the ancient region beyond Mycenae: a wilderness of legendary beauty, celebrated by everyone from Virgil to Tom Stoppard. Arcadia was home to Pan, the goatish god of the wild, who gave his name to our own little boy god, Peter Pan. He inspired the word 'panic' – from the disturbing effect he produced on walking through herds of animals. His own name comes from *paon*, Greek for 'guardian of the flocks'. The wild, drunken, sex-mad centaurs – half-man, half-horse – also hailed from Arcadia.

Virgil made the really strong connection between Arcadia and rural bliss in his *Eclogues*, his first work, written in around 40 BC. The *Eclogues* were inspired by the *Bucolica* (Greek for 'care of cattle'), rural poems by Theocritus, the third-century BC poet. In the final, tenth Eclogue, Virgil wrote about an elegiac poet, Gaius Cornelius Gallus, dying of love in Arcadia, the wild heart of pastoral song. Virgil created the lingering vision of Arcadia as a sort of rural, blissful utopia: the word invented by Thomas More from the Greek *ou* – 'not' – and *topos* – 'place'; i.e. not a real place.

Poussin produced the most distinctive images of Arcadia in his two pictures of puzzled shepherds gathered round a tombstone in the middle of the Peloponnese. The stone's cryptic inscription reads, '*Et in Arcadia Ego*'. It wasn't just the shepherds who were puzzled. The meaning of the inscription has bemused scholars for centuries. The literal meaning was clear enough: 'Even I am in Arcadia' or 'I, too, am in Arcadia'. But who was the 'I'? The most popular answer was death, the implication being that even paradise has a sell-by date.

Not that Dr Johnson agreed when he saw Joshua Reynolds's 1769 portrait of Mrs Bouverie and Mrs Crewe, pondering the inscription.

'It's nonsensical – I am in Arcadia,' said Johnson.

Joshua Reynolds insisted the idea was simple enough, claiming George III got it in a moment the previous day.

'Ay, ay, death is even in Arcadia,' the king had said.

The interpretation of the line chopped and changed as it continued to capture the European imagination. Goethe called one chapter of his 1816 book, *Italian Journey*, 'Auch ich in Arkadien'; a more optimistic sentiment, meaning, 'Even I made it to Arcadia.'

Evelyn Waugh used both the jolly and gloomy meanings in *Brideshead Revisited*. 'Et in Arcadia Ego' is the title of the first chapter, when Charles Ryder finds himself in the supposed paradise of upper-class circles in Oxford. Ryder also has a skull from the School of Medicine, resting in a bowl of roses in his Hertford College rooms, inscribed on the forehead with the motto.

Guercino followed a similar theme in his picture of two Arcadian shepherds looking at a skull on a plinth, also inscribed with the motto. The ambiguity was helpful: even in the sunlit joy of post-war Oxford, death – or Sebastian's decline, at least – was in the air, scented with strawberries and Château Peyraguey.

Arcadia remains pretty Arcadian today. The empty motorway to Sparta may have been a pretty dramatic blot on the landscape – a thick, glossy, black strip slicing right through Arcadia. But, still, it was the only main road from Athens, which then split into three near Tripoli, Arcadia's capital. On either side of the motorway, ancient, Arcadian Greece survived largely intact: cypress and olive trees on the lush, green plain, skirted by mountains dotted with brown scrub, broken here and there to reveal white stone scars between.

Every now and then, a modest, red-roofed town did little to take the edge off the rural idyll look. From a distance, anyway. Move a little closer to the landscape – away from the distancing device of the E65 motorway from Corinth to Tripoli – and you could see how the gloom lingers on, even in Arcadia.

Away from the bright lights of the tourist hotspots, the rural infrastructure was now starting to fail: the charming railway round the Peloponnese didn't run at all. Not surprising, I suppose – in 2010, in the middle of the economic crisis, the state railway company paid 400 million euros in wages, and 300 million in other expenses. National railway income was 100 million euros. The average railwayman earned 65,000 euros. The Greeks were once good mathematicians.

When I did finally find an open petrol station, they wouldn't take credit cards – cash only. To fail the credit card test is to become a Second World country. I'd long got used to the Greek cash economy. That morning, I'd loaded up my wallet with notes in Athens. I also made sure to keep a quarter of a tank of petrol in reserve – after a Greek friend told me how many petrol stations had closed down.

My next stop – the ancient city of Sparta – was also buried deep in decay. Here the graffiti artists had little respect for the good old days. On the Roman walls around the earlier Greek city, beneath a lone olive tree, a laconic graffiti artist had written the words 'SEX' and 'boy'. Literally laconic – the word comes from 'Lakon', a person from Lacedaemon, the area Sparta lies in.

Spartans weren't known for their dazzling dinner party conversation. They combined minimum chat with maximum passive aggression. When the Persians told the 301 Spartans at Thermopylae that the Persian arrows would blot out the sky, the Spartan leader, Dieneces, said, 'Brilliant – we'll fight in the shade.'

There was a good reason why that graffiti artist daubed his low-minded thoughts on the Roman walls. There never were any ancient Spartan ones – partly because of Sparta's natural defensive position, cut into the flank of a hill in a steep-sided valley. But also because the Spartans were considered so tough – and thought themselves so tough – that they didn't need any protection. When a Spartan king, Agesilaus, was asked where the city walls were, he said, laconically, 'There,' pointing at his soldiers.

That's why we still use the word Spartan to mean austere. Self-pity was not on the menu. Physical pain had to be disguised, literally: Spartans wore blood-red cloaks to disguise their wounds, as well as their victims'. A Spartan only had his name inscribed on his tombstone if he died in battle.

The other legends were true, too. Spartan children were exposed on the slopes of Taygetus, the highest mountain in the Peloponnese. Those that survived after a week were fit to grow up to become real Spartans. Children stayed with their mothers until they were seven, when they were packed off to a sort of early boarding school – with lots of rugged, character-building sport and drill in a junior corps.

Girls were given physical training, too, wearing so little for their exercises that even the unprudish Greeks were shocked. From time to time, the boys were flogged for no apparent reason in Sparta's Sanctuary of Artemis Orthia, to keep them on the ball. Not unlike British boarding schools until *c.* 1970.

At 20, Spartans became soldiers after a spell in the secret police, the Krypteia. Even when they married, they stayed in barracks, living on rations from their own estates. Between 12 and 18, they were positively encouraged to have affairs with grown-up soldiers, because, as the Greek historian Plutarch put it, that sort of 'love inspires modesty, ambition and a keen desire to succeed'.

Athenian food was hardly great: the usual dinner consisted of two courses, the first a kind of porridge, the second a kind of porridge. But Spartan cuisine was even worse. At a dinner in Sparta, a Sybarite, from supposedly pleasure-loving Sybaris, a Greek colony on the instep of Italy's boot, muttered, 'Now I understand why Spartans don't fear death.'

The idea that Sybarites were a self-indulgent bunch was a Roman fabrication. Dr Johnson adopted the idea in his dictionary – where he told the story of a Sybarite sleeping on a bed of rose petals, who couldn't sleep because one of the petals was folded.

Our use of stoic has also moved away from the original fourth-century BC philosophy school of Stoicism, founded in Athens by Zeno, a Cypriot scholar. The Stoics taught in the Stoa Poikile, or painted colonnade, in the Athenian agora, that gave them their name. The open colonnade offered shelter from the rain and the punishing sun.

Stoics thought happiness could only be produced by your mind, because that was all you could control. The answer was to aim for *apathia* – 'freedom from suffering', as in apathetic – and peace of mind, by rising above the nasty forces of life. As Epictetus, a Stoic philosopher, put it, 'Man is disturbed not by things, but by the views he takes of them' – an idea ripped off in Hamlet's lines, 'There is nothing either good or bad, but thinking makes it so.'

Despite all their Stoic toughness, Sparta declined – not helped by an earthquake in 464 BC, a shrinking ruling class and depopulation. The final indignity came in 425 BC in the Peloponnesian War, when Spartan soldiers – besieged on the island of Sphacteria that encloses the bay of Pylos – did what their mothers told them never to do: surrender. They neither came home with their shields nor on them.

It turned out to be a temporary setback in the Peloponnesian War, fought from 431–404 BC. On one side were Athens, northern Greece and most of the Greek islands. On the other side was the Peloponnesian League, including pretty much the whole of the Peloponnese, led by Sparta.

A plague in Athens in 430 BC didn't help the Athenians much – particularly after it killed Pericles and two of his sons, buried in a tomb near the site of Plato's Academy.

In a disastrous move in 413 BC, Athens attacked Syracuse in Sicily, losing their whole expeditionary force. In 405 BC, the Athenian fleet was thumped by the Spartans under Lysander at Aegospotami, halfway up the Hellespont. A year later, Athens surrendered – and the Athenian golden age was over.

Despite the victory, Sparta didn't fare too well afterwards, either. In 371 BC, they lost to Thebes at the Battle of Leuctra, a few miles from Thebes. The two weakened powers were in no fit state to deal with Philip II of Macedon in 338 BC when he conquered the Greek city states and unified them all – all except Sparta.

A little of the old, tough Spartan spirit lingered on for a while. At one point in the war, Philip II sent a despatch to Sparta, declaring, 'If I enter Laconia, I will raze Sparta.' The Spartans responded, in true laconic style, with the one-word message: *aika*, meaning 'if'.

Even when the whole of Greece was finally conquered by Rome in 146 BC, Sparta was allowed to cling on to its austere military traditions. The self-denying, martial Spartans became a kind of tourist attraction to visiting Romans – like the locals who dress up today outside the Colosseum in centurion outfits and demand payment for photos.

These days, the Spartans have grown as relaxed, easy-going and pleasure-loving as other Greeks. The Spartans of modern Europe are the Germans, as I discovered that evening. I drove on from Sparta to Kardamyli, in the Mani, not far from Marathonisi – the island where Paris first made love to Helen after stealing her from her husband, Menelaus. In Book 3 of *The Iliad*, the island is called Kranae.

As their relationship soured at Troy, Helen nagged Paris for risking his life in battle with Menelaus. A nostalgic Paris referred back to that golden night.

'Let us go to bed and turn to love-making,' Paris pleaded, ever the flashy lothario. 'Never before as now has passion enmeshed my senses, not when I took you the first time from Lakedaimon the lovely, and caught you up and carried you away in seafaring vessels and lay with you in the bed of love on the island of Kranae. Not even then, as now, did I love you and sweet desire seize me.'

I read this passage – in my Loeb of *The Iliad* – under the lengthening shadow of a tree in Sparta. For once, Homer's talk of love and desire left me cold; it only deepened the pain of the first, and the lack of satisfaction of the other. I hopped back into my little hire car.

The Greek radio didn't help my spirits much. On that gap-year trip to the Cyclades in 1989, a school friend told me the golden rule of Greek pop songs: every one contained at least one mention of the word *sagapo* – 'I love you'. The local Mani radio station played a bouzouki number – with plenty of sagapos – as I headed along the spine of the Mani to Kardamyli. This is the handsome little town where the writer Paddy Leigh Fermor lived for half a century until his death in 2011.

Thanks to a friend, I had an introduction to Leigh Fermor's housekeeper, Elpida Beloyannis, who showed me round the place – empty since his death two years earlier at the age of 96. He had left the house to the Benaki Museum in Athens, with an idea to turn it into a writers' retreat. The recession put those plans on hold. And so the house was kept in a state of frozen animation, just as Leigh Fermor left it on the morning he departed for London to die.

Seated on a small hill, overlooking its own tiny bay, flanked by olive trees, rosemary and cypresses, the house reminded me of Goldeneye, Ian Fleming's house in Jamaica. Better designed, though – by Leigh Fermor himself, modelled on Vitruvian and Palladian designs.

The aged roof tiles had been salvaged from ruined houses, destroyed by earthquakes in the Peloponnese. The walls were built out of great, Cyclopean chunks of limestone, flecked with copper and gold. The stone came from the Taygetus mountain range – where those poor Spartan children were exposed. The Taygetus mountains tower over the town of Kardamyli. Inside, the rooms were whitewashed, with little decoration.

Leigh Fermor's wife, Joan – who died in 2003 – had a separate bedroom, some way from his. Peeling, fading postcards covered her bedroom door, showing her favourite pictures: of the ancient boxers at the Minoan palace of Knossos and a Leonardo self-portrait. Evelyn Waugh books were by her bedside.

For a man much celebrated for his writing and his Second World War exploits in Crete, there was an admirable absence of show-off material. In the library, there was a picture of him with his great friend, George Jellicoe, who won the DSO in 1942 for blowing up German planes, parked like sitting ducks on Crete's Heraklion airfield. In Leigh Fermor's will, he made a special request that Jellicoe's descendants should be able to stay in the Kardamyli house whenever they wanted. Down in the cellar, a plaque, celebrating 21 years since Leigh Fermor's Cretan heroics, gathered dust. In one corner of his library shelves, there was a small section marked with a handwritten sign saying 'Own Books'.

High ceilings, and those thick stone walls, kept the house cool in summer; large, ogive fireplaces warmed it in winter. There was only the slightest sign of decay: a single broken fanlight in the shower. That wouldn't have bothered Leigh Fermor – he was determined the house should pass the Mitford test: 'All nice rooms are a bit shabby.' Otherwise, it looked like Leigh Fermor had just stepped out of the house for his daily swim in the wine-dark sea that spread away to the horizon from the broad, deep terrace.

His favourite books – Cyril Connolly, more Evelyn Waugh – filled the other shelves of the library. The Everyman Shakespeare lay by his bed in the small bedroom that led off his work room. Also here were the books written by his great friend, the late Debo, Duchess of Devonshire. Above the fireplace in the lovely library – with its bay window overlooking the bay – there were four phone numbers written on a piece of paper, in three-inch-tall numbers and capital letters: 'DEBO'; 'ARTEMIS', or Artemis Cooper, his biographer and close friend; and two unrecognised Greek names.

'He wrote here every day, all day,' said Elpida as we went next door, into his work room. If he did write here every day, he must have been tortured by the frantic activity that led to so little published work in his last 25 years. The first two books about his 1933 walk from the Hook of Holland to Constantinople took a few years to appear. *A Time of Gifts* appeared in 1977, *Between the Woods and the Water* in 1986. But for the next quarter of a century, nothing about the great walk was published. For day after day, he came into this enchanted room as Elpida tended to him; for day after day, he didn't get very far.

In 2013, after his death, the third book in the trilogy, *The Broken Road: Travels from Bulgaria to Mount Athos*, came out. But it was largely put together by Artemis Cooper, using Leigh Fermor's diary from the walk and a draft he'd written in the 1960s. Little from that last 25 years' work in this room had made it into the final volume.

'He swam round the island every day,' Elpida said, as we left the writing room, pointing from the terrace to Merope, a small island, shaped like a miniature Africa, that lay a few hundred yards beyond the beach below us. Leigh Fermor swum the Hellespont at 70, and managed this admittedly smaller swim in his nineties. It was getting late – and I had to get back to dinner at my nearby hotel. But I determined to do the swim the next day.

Rising at 6.15 a.m. to fit in a dawn swim before a long drive, I thought I'd have the beach to myself. I was beaten to it by three German lady pensioners. The only time the British ever got anywhere first on my odyssey was to dinner in the Kardamyli seaside restaurants the night before.

There was no reserving the sun-loungers for these Germans. They weren't into lounging, just robust, long-distance swimming – naked. I suddenly saw them, standing nude on the beach, as I stepped out of the hanging wood clinging to the hillside. They were extremely polite but unembarrassed, apologising to me in perfect English for not bringing their bathing costumes. They proceeded to zoom at top speed around Merope island, chatting and laughing without losing breath, leaving me in their wake. No wonder they're the kings of Europe.

I made it to the southern tip of the island – about where Cape Town is on Africa – and turned around, defeated, exhausted, back to the beach. As I dried myself, I could still hear the faint, tinkling sound of German laughter on the other side of the island. I noticed they couldn't have reserved any sun-loungers even if they'd wanted to – they hadn't brought any towels with them. That's what I call Spartan spirit.

Poussin's 'Et In Arcadia Ego', 1638. Three shepherds and a shepherdess ponder the inscription: 'Even I am in Arcadia.' But who is the 'I'?

Scylla's Rock in Scilla, the seaside town on Italy's toe. On the other side of the Strait of Messina lies Sicily – and Charybdis, the deadly whirlpool. Odysseus followed Circe's advice and sailed closer to Scylla than Charybdis. Scylla, crouching on this rock, promptly bolted down six of Odysseus's men – raw.

18

Scylla and Circe Get an Italian Makeover

Happiness is a 15-hour train journey from Brindisi to Palermo in an empty carriage, with enough prosciutto and provolone to keep you going.

My booked seat, number 93, was taken, as were its two neighbouring seats, by an enormous, sleeping, middle-aged Italian. A few carriages up, though, lay bliss – an empty, old-style compartment. It got better. What I initially thought was the smell of old BO turned out to be my provolone. Like smelling your own farts, smelling your own provolone is really quite pleasant – and stops anyone else coming into your compartment.

The ferry from Patras, on the Peloponnese's northern coast, took me to Brindisi, high on the stiletto of Italy's boot. And now my gloriously smelly train was taking me through Magna Graecia – 'Big Greece' – the big chunk of southern Italy colonised, along with Sicily, by the Greeks from around 770 BC onwards.

In the unresolved struggle to locate the real sites of Odysseus's original wanderings, the compass often zeroes in on Italy. That isn't as surprising as it sounds to modern ears, now that international borders are carefully demarcated by international law. Ancient Greece was a more fluid concept than modern Greece; its boundaries ebbed and flowed with the centuries.

Still, as soon as I landed in Brindisi, my Odyssean quest seemed a little more dodgy. In Greece, Odysseus visited dozens of named places that still have much the same names today. In Italy, towns like Scilla – the charming little town on Italy's toe – borrowed their name from the legend of monstrous Scylla, long after *The Odyssey* was written, as opposed to vice versa. Most of the Italian places earned their Odyssean associations because they shared geographical similarities with the Homeric lairs of favourite characters – Scylla, Circe, the Sirens and the Cyclops among them. And most of the Magna Graecia spots Odysseus supposedly visited were colonised only a few decades before Homer wrote his epics.

If *The Iliad* and *The Odyssey* were completely made up, Homer probably set them in places that were familiar to his audience. Like a stand-up comedian appealing to the crowd, he could drop in pleasing references to their home town: 'Ladies and gentlemen, you all know that rocky beach on the west coast of Corfu; you know, the one where the stones rip your flesh off like a poor cuttlefish's suckers? Well, that's where Odysseus rocked up – stark bollock naked, only to find Nausicaa, the most gorgeous princess you could imagine, playing beach ball on the sand with her scantily clad maidens.'

Would Homer really set his epic in some newly-founded towns on a faraway Italian shore, rather than in familiar Greek places? Maybe not. Still, why shouldn't Odysseus tackle some famously dangerous rocks and whirlpools off the Italian coast? Particularly when there was a whole new generation of Greek colonists braving these unfamiliar waters. Wouldn't it make sense to set your epic – about a traveller wandering to the ends of the earth – in the farthest-flung edges of the Greek empire?

The Greek presence in southern Italy still feels strong today. Again and again, when my mind wandered a little in Sicily or Calabria, I forgot I was in Italy and thought I was in Greece. I felt the sensation strongly as I climbed the bare, windswept hill to the fifth-century BC Doric temple of Segesta on Sicily's north-western tip. It wasn't just the Doric columns – although they're as good as any in Greece. It was more the combination of intense, dry southern heat, with the lush, fertile valley floor, flanked by mountainsides of bare rock, colonised by hardy, wild, sun-baked scrub.

In Sicilian cities like Palermo and Syracuse – so much poorer than northern Italian ones – there was also a simpler feel; sometimes rougher, sometimes friendlier, often a little lazier. The Italian catchphrase '*dolce far niente*' –

'delicious idleness' – could be the Greek national motto. And there seemed to be a lot more of it in Sicily and southern Italy than in the industrious, industrialised north.

I felt it, too, in the way the locals took their staggering Greek architecture for granted. The best-preserved Greek Doric temples are found not in Greece but in Paestum, just south of Naples. But, still, until 150 years ago, these exceptional sixth-century BC temples were used as stables for water buffaloes producing mozzarella milk. When I visited the temples, they were nearly empty, while, only a few miles north, Pompeii and Herculaneum were crammed with tourists. Tourists like things to be in their proper place: Roman things in Italy, Greek things in Greece.

It isn't surprising that Sicily and southern Italy felt so Greek. The ancient Greeks barely changed a thing – in their architecture, language, diet or world view – when they sailed across the Mediterranean to Italy. They even took their place names with them: in 734 BC, islanders from Naxos founded another Naxos on Sicily.

Sicilians still think the Greek influence is strong, particularly on the east coast – where the Greek colonies were concentrated. Leonardo Sciascia, a Sicilian writer who died in 1989, thought this eastern side of the island had a better sense of humour, thanks to their Hellenic ancestry. The great actors and comic writers, he said, were always from eastern, Greek Sicily, too.

Local Greek feeling is still strong in southern mainland Italy. On a concrete wall overlooking the railway track at Reggio Calabria, the city just under Italy's big toe, I spotted a graffito.

'RHEGION', it read in three-foot-tall capital letters. 'GRECI DI REGGIO'. Reggio – called Rhegion by the Greeks – was one of their earliest colonies in southern Italy, founded in 743 BC by the inhabitants of Chalcis, on the island of Euboea in northern Greece.

In its early, Greek days, southern Italy and Sicily attracted a sophisticated, mathematical crowd. In the sixth century BC, Pythagoras – as in theorem – moved from the Greek island of Samos to Croton, on Italy's heel. Archimedes – as in 'Eureka' – was from Syracuse in south-eastern Sicily. What he really said in the bath was '*Heureka*'. The Greek for 'I've found it' has a rough breathing – a grammatical sign, like a single opening quote mark, which means 'h' in Greek.

Archimedes didn't just work out the concept of volume through displaced bathwater; he also cracked calculus, the accurate value of pi and how to measure a sphere's volume. He was killed in 212 BC when Syracuse was besieged by the Romans. He had devised all sorts of clever machines to protect the city from attack and was studying a mathematical diagram when he was killed by a Roman foot soldier. His last words were '*Me mou tous kuklous taratte*' – 'Don't disturb my circles!'

Magna Graecia was populated with artistic types as well as mathematicians. In 1972, in the waters 200 yards off the little town of Riace – on the ball of Italy's foot – a snorkelling doctor came across an arm protruding from the seabed. At first, he thought it was a dead body, until he touched its hard, bronze fingers. A second bronze figure lay part-buried a few yards away.

These are the Riace Warriors, now on show in Reggio's Museo Nazionale della Magna Graecia. They were cast in around 450 BC – just before the Parthenon was built, that moment when Greek sculpture and architecture clicked into magical, harmonious place. Both men twist their bodies in classic contrapposto style, putting their weight on their back legs, bending their front ones. Where statues a century before held their arms stiffly at their sides, this pair casually hang their left hands in mid-air. They once held shields or spears in their hands – but they look so languid and unmilitary, as if they're about to give you a limp handshake at an upmarket cocktail party in the smartest part of Riace.

They're made of the smartest materials, too: silver for the teeth; copper for the nipples and lips; calcite, a sparkling, quartzy-looking sort of calcium carbonate, for the eyeballs. Bronze was extremely valuable – Pliny the Elder thought Corinthian bronze more valuable than silver, and nearly as grand as gold.

It was a high honour to be granted a bronze statue by your city – but you had to pay for it; 3,000 drachmas in the third century BC, ten times the average wage, and a lot of money, even for a rich man. That high value is why most ancient bronze statues were melted down – those that survive, like the Riace bronzes, were largely found at sea where the melters couldn't get at them.

Sicily and southern Italy may have been the colonial heartland, but the Greeks got much further west. They largely dictated the settlement of much of the Mediterranean, as built on by the Romans and later civilisations. Places that seem quintessentially Roman are often Greek in origin and name. Pompeii was named after the procession – *pompe* in Greek – Heracles led across Vesuvius's slopes after he'd killed some tricky giants and buried them under the volcano. He immodestly named the next-door city – Herculaneum – after himself.

Like Odysseus, the ancient Greeks roved all around the Mediterranean. In 667 BC, Byzas from Megara founded the little town of Byzantium – later to become Constantinople, then Istanbul. For 2,500 years, Istanbul remained full of Greeks, until the Greco-Turkish War of 1919–22, and the 1923 Exchange of Greek and Turkish Populations. Istanbul was exempted from the exchange but the writing was on the wall – and the Greek population began to slide. Still, though, the senior Patriarch of the Greek Orthodox Church has his cathedral in Istanbul, in Fener, an untouristed spot just north-west of the ancient heart of Constantinople.

For the Orthodox Easter of 2012, my ex-girlfriend and I went to the service at the cathedral church of St George – a poignantly small cathedral, if a decent-sized church. At the beginning of the service, the Patriarch, Bartholomew I, with his splendid, great, grey, spade-shaped beard, bustled down the nave, flanked by a retinue of priests, furiously shaking incense censers in our direction.

Bartholomew I, to give him his full title, is 'His Most Divine All-Holiness, the Archbishop of Constantinople, New Rome and Ecumenical Patriarch'. He certainly looked the part. And how stirring it was to hear the Easter Service delivered in the language of the New Testament; unchanged – as far as I could tell, with my ropy Greek – in more than 2,000 years. But, still, the congregation barely touched a hundred – at the most important Christian festival of the year.

It was hard to believe His Most Divine All-Holiness was the spiritual leader of 300 million Orthodox Christians, the *primus inter pares* alongside the other Orthodox patriarchs and the 270th Ecumenical Patriarch, in a line descending from the Apostle St Andrew. The days when Constantinople was the cradle of the Eastern Orthodox Church – and the days before that, when Constantine built his new Christian city here – seemed a long time ago.

The Mediterranean coast was sprinkled with other ancient Greek colonies, whose Greek origins we have long forgotten. Marseille, originally Massilia, was founded by the Greeks in 600 BC. It has retained its foreign flavour: as late as 1914, a quarter of the population were non-French, including a so-called '*clan des Grecs*'. The southern French have a lot to thank the Greeks for – they introduced vines to the region.

Monaco was named after the shrine of Heracles Monoikos, 'Heracles who dwells alone'. Nice was originally Nikaia, or Victory. Antibes was once Antipolis, 'the City Opposite [their original colony, Nice]'. And Naples began life as Neapolis, or 'the New City'. Even the Romans called southern Italy 'Oenotria' – Greek for 'the land of wine'.

Today's northern Italian prejudice against the south is an inversion of the ancient position: the smart south was settled by the sophisticated Greeks; the downmarket north was the land of the barbarian. Southern Italy remains rich in Greek references. The local version of the Mafia in Calabria is the 'Ndrangheta, from the Greek *andragathia* – 'manly virtue'. Some villages in the toe of Italy's boot still speak a Greek dialect.

After that 15-hour trip, I finally got to Palermo – itself derived from the Greek *panormos*, meaning 'complete port'. Much of the journey was spent waiting for the whole train to be loaded on to a ferry at Villa San Giovanni, the town just under Italy's big toenail.

My old map confidently proclaimed, in dotted lines, that a bridge was to be built in 2012 across the two-mile Strait of Messina. But, so the rumour went, the Mafia put paid to that, diverting the stream of national bridge-building cash into its own pockets. Still, the lack of a bridge meant I could recreate Odysseus's sea journey – even if I was foolishly sailing from Scylla to Charybdis, as opposed to charting a careful course between them.

As the train-boat made its sluggish course across the water, you could see why euhemerists were certain Odysseus came here. The stretch of water is so narrow – 1.9 miles at its narrowest – that you can always see both sides; even at dusk, as I climbed out of my carriage and stood on the top deck. Homer wrote of the two sides being a bowshot apart.

On the Sicilian side of the strait lies the harbour of Messina, given to choppy waters – hey presto, the whirlpool of Charybdis! Even more helpfully for us euhemerists, Messina was an eighth-century Greek colony. It was originally called Zancle – from *zanclon*, Greek for 'scythe', thanks to Messina's harbour, scythe-shaped today.

The coast directly opposite, on the Italian mainland side, is fairly flat and open. That, presumably, is why euhemerists, in search of Scylla on her crag, roamed a few miles further north to the first big, freestanding rock, just at the lower edge of the toenail of Italy's big toe.

I went to Scilla before I took the ferry across to Sicily. Overlooking the town, her huge rock shoots 240 feet up in the air from the flat coastline, visible from the sea for miles around. It was even taller before an earthquake sliced off its top section in 1783. The rock looks right across the water to the Punta del Faro, the north-easterly tip of Sicily. Surely this must be the boulder on which the monster Scylla perched, selecting the tastiest members of Odysseus's crew to munch?

Odysseus's ex-girlfriend, the witch Circe, had warned him to sail closer to Scylla. Yes, she said, six of your men will be gobbled up by a cannibalistic monster, but that's better than losing the whole ship to Charybdis.

Next time you're told by someone in a quandary that they're between Scylla and Charybdis, tell them to head for Scylla. When caught between a rock and a hard place, Odysseus wisely chose the rock. He took Circe's advice and, as she predicted, lost six men to Scylla: 'They writhed, gasping, as Scylla swung them up her cliff and there, at her cavern's mouth, she bolted them down raw – screaming out, flinging their arms toward me, lost in that mortal struggle.'

Scylla's rock was such a good tactical spot, overlooking the strait to Sicily, that the Saracens built a castle there in the ninth century. The Normans took it over in the eleventh century. In 1806, it was occupied by the British, after victory over the French at the Battle of Maida, 60 miles north-east of Scilla – Maida Vale in north London was named after the battle.

Today, Scylla's Castle is a lighthouse and Italian naval base, the Marina Militare Faro Di Scilla. I headed for the castle from the little railway station of Scilla. The Fascist-minimalist station is built of handsome travertine blocks. 'Scilla' – the Italian version of Scylla – was spelt out in 1930s metal letters, in a sans serif front, on one pristine wall. The main concourse, though, was covered in graffiti: fat, squashy, New York subway-style letters, in garish red, green and sky blue.

Much of Scylla's castle was still fenced off, with signs saying, '*Marina militare comando zona fari divieto di accesso zona militare*' – no entry, in other words.

But, still, I could climb to the top of the rock, past the castle's mini-lighthouse, and take in heavenly views over the Strait of Messina. Despite those heavenly views, the fortress was empty – except for a single Russian tourist, a pretty bleached blonde, who asked me to take her photo in front of the naval base's main gate, with the rock in the background. Odysseus would have taken her photo, slept with her and spent the next couple of years with her, holed up in this dramatic fortress, with its sandy beach and string of fish restaurants. I took her photo, she took mine and we parted company.

At Scilla, more than anywhere on my travels, I saw best how Odyssean myths developed in certain ideal spots. OK, Scilla is a little north of the narrowest bit of the strait but, otherwise, it's perfect for euhemerists in search of genuine geographical features to fit the myth.

Myths also developed wherever there are lots of people. Look at the map of urban sites in the Roman Empire, and the Odyssean sites are usually found in areas that were well populated even then. The more people lived in an Odyssean spot, the quicker the myth spread, the stronger the Odysseus association with that town.

Romantic southern Italians have been keen euhemerists for centuries. They even embellished the stories in *The Odyssey*. South of Naples, near those Doric temples of Paestum, locals say the headland of Punta Licosa is named after the Siren Leucosia. In the new, improved Italian version, she threw herself into the sea after failing to lure Odysseus to his death. It's a good twist on the tale: the Sirens may have been tempting, but not half as tempting as Odysseus, the hot Greek hunk.

The Scilla naval base wasn't the only *Odyssey* destination taken over by the armed forces. More than 250 miles north, near Anzio, lies Circe's mountainous home, San Felice Circeo, named after the gorgeous witch who seduced Odysseus for an arduous year.

Once a wild, remote island, San Felice Circeo is now a headland connected to the mainland by flat, alluvial earth, washed down from the Tiber. Today, the pretty little Roman settlement is a prominent pimple on the coast, looking north towards Rome and south to the Bay of Naples. Its other claim to fame is that Lepidus – who once shared power in the Roman triumvirate with Augustus and Mark Antony – was exiled here by Augustus in 36 BC.

When I visited San Felice Circeo, after my Sicilian tour, there was no sign of Lepidus on the streets. The town's Odyssean connections were proudly trumpeted – in Via Omero, Via Virgilio and the Odisseo knick-knack shop. On the outskirts of town stood the Maga ('witch') Circe Hotel, an upmarket, neatly whitewashed place, sheltered from the road by a delicate, wrought-iron gate.

The wilderness lair of the town's favourite witch has not been so well treated. Once clearly a bewitching peak, overlooking the Tyrrhenian Sea, it's not quite so alluring these days. The 1,800-foot-high summit is another Italian army base, crowned with a bristling array of towering satellite dishes.

Still, though, the surrounding woodland was thick with a yellow-flowered garlic, *Allium moly*. Its name comes from the drug, 'moly', given by Mercury to Odysseus as an antidote to Circe's drug – the drug she used to turn Odysseus's men into pigs. He only slept with Circe on the understanding that she turn them back into humans.

Today, Circe's idyll is off-limits. At the wooded spot where she dallied with Odysseus, a sign attached to a big wire gate read, '*Zona militare Limite Invalicabile*'. Just outside the military exclusion zone, there was a teenage hangout spot, plastered with graffiti tags, scrawled by 'SAGE' in outsized, curving red and white letters. A local girl had overwritten Sage's work with the declaration, 'MICHY, TI AMO SEMPRE X SEMPRE', in purple spray paint.

Opposite the graffitied wall, a concrete platform, looking out to sea, was littered with Carlsberg beer bottles – just at the spot where Circe drugged Odysseus and his men with her magical potions.

It's not as if the Italian armed forces – and the Saracens, Normans and British who occupied the castle on Scylla's rock – were staunch euhemerists. They didn't pick their bases for their ancient classical connections. It's more that they were independently drawn – like Odysseus – to similar, prominent geographical features on the coast. You can completely see why armies and navies colonised these easily defensible lookout points, overlooking the coast to north and south.

As he was bounced from side to side of the Mediterranean like a crazed pinball, Odysseus was no longer at war, unlike the Saracens, Normans and the British. But he did need to navigate his ship by prominent features on land, particularly when he was in trouble. Again and again, on my trips at sea, as I approached one harbour or another, I could see exactly why it was where it was.

Istanbul is at the near-meeting point of Asia and Europe – with the Black Sea on one side, the Dardanelles on the other, and the Golden Horn estuary leading off to one side. Ithaca's capital, Vathy, is securely tucked away from the winds. To dock in Vathy, the *Corinthian* first entered one great bay, facing the sea, before taking a left into the narrow port; a harbour within a harbour. What's more, Vathy has unusually deep water; it took its name from *bathus*, Greek for 'deep'. Greek 'b's are pronounced like 'v's. Dubrovnik is a peninsula stretched out in parallel to the coastline, forming its own natural harbour in the gap between the peninsula and the mainland.

I only understood how deeply revered Apollo's shrine at Delphi was when I arrived there by sea. The journey from the modern port of Itea to Delphi makes for a beautiful drive through Greece's biggest olive grove, but it is a hellishly difficult climb up the steep mountainside.

You see why all the main Greek cities were within 25 miles of the coast – any further and they became logistically impossible to run. Only if you felt a really strong religious pull to a place would you build your shrine halfway up a mountain, subject to earthquakes and landslides. That's why so many of the vast pillars at Delphi's Temple of Apollo are now on their side, their column drums tumbling away from each other like a mammoth, sliced cucumber.

Delphi did have lots of spring water bursting out of the side of the mountain, in two places. It still does – as our coach traversed the mountainside, we kept on meeting the great pipe that carried the water down to more parched areas of Greece. Spring water alone wasn't enough to explain the attraction of the site to the ancient Greeks. Only religious power could account for the conviction that Delphi was the *omphalos*, or 'navel', of the ancient world.

Back in Scilla, I could see, more clearly than anywhere else, how towns hardened their Odyssean connections over the centuries. The Romans made the earliest connection; Pliny called it *oppidum Scyllaeum* – 'Scylla's town' – in the first century AD. By the time I arrived, there was a Hotel Le Sirene, a Ristorante Lo Scoglio ['rock'] di Ulisse and a Ulisse Bed and Breakfast.

The Italian love of beauty – and naked girls – is so great that there wasn't a single restaurant or hotel named after the poor, ugly sea monster who gave the town its name. There was one bust of her – the centrepiece of the town fountain, a Doric temple wrapped around a grotto. But she looked less a hideous monster than a supermodel, channelling the wet look. The fountain water came pouring out of her pouting lips, splattering down on to an oversized shell.

Near the railway station, Ristorante Ulisse had a charming, hand-painted, blue and white sign. It showed a tousle-haired Odysseus, flanked not by hideous Scylla but by three generous-breasted Sirens with mermaids' tails. The Sirens were said to hang out 200 miles further north up the Italian coast, in Positano. But when did the Italians let the truth – or legend, for that matter – get in the way of a picture of an attractive, topless woman? An image of a man-eating monster, however charmingly painted, wasn't going to get the punters in.

Those hot, sweet-singing chicks have made it to Dublin, too: to the Sirens Bar at the Ormond Hotel on the Liffey. The Ormond was the setting for the Sirens chapter in James Joyce's *Ulysses*. The chapter – where Joyce's Odysseus, Leopold Bloom, dines with his uncle – is rich in musical references, in honour of the Sirens.

As the financial crisis hit Ireland, the Ormond Hotel fell apart. The pink plaster on the handsome, classical façade has cracked and peeled, revealing great stretches of the brickwork beneath. The only thing in good nick was the 'SIRENS BAR' awning on the ground floor. Here, in reverent Ireland, there were no pictures of large-breasted women. Drink references were OK, though: the black and white awning, sponsored by Guinness, was liberally sprinkled with the brewer's name.

Maga Circe – 'Circe the Witch' – Hotel, in San Felice Circeo, near Anzio, Italy. Circe's lair – now a teenage drinking den – is on a hill overlooking the town.

The Ulysses Restaurant in Scilla. Rather than showing Odysseus with the hideous Scylla, the restaurateur has surrounded him with topless mermaids.

The Cyclops Trattoria in Taormina, Sicily. Polyphemus the Cyclops is flanked by two Trinacria symbols. The Trinacria – 'a triangle', referring to the shape of Sicily – is on the island's flag. It shows the head of Medusa, with three legs, and three stalks of wheat to signify Sicily's fertility.

19

The Sicilian Cyclops

I crossed the Strait of Messina at dusk.

The twin gods that now ruled the waves were Health and Safety; yes, even in Italy. As night fell, you couldn't see Scylla's rock any more; but you could see, on the Italian mainland, a big, flashing red light.

On the Sicilian side, there was no sign, as yet, of Charybdis's whirlpool; but there was a corresponding green light – like the one at the end of Daisy Buchanan's Long Island pier in *The Great Gatsby*. Unlike Jay Gatsby, the gin palaces, passing either side of the painfully slow train ferry, weren't lured to the green light. One vast cruise ship, the *Equinox*, slipped north ahead of us, its lights blazing, noiselessly drifting by, a tower block on castor wheels.

When I looked around Messina a few days later, I went in search of Charybdis in her traditional spot, the town's harbour. Earthquakes have shifted things about over the millennia, and some say Charybdis lies further north along the Sicilian coast. I must say, I didn't see signs of any whirlpools in Messina Bay – even though tidal currents of four knots have been reported here when the moon is really tugging away.

I had to spend quite a lot of time at the harbourside, staring at the water, before I even spotted a few ripples. The water was roughened, yes, but into furrows no more than four inches deep. If I had jumped overboard off the train ferry, I could have swum the last 50 yards into Charybdis harbour pretty easily.

There's a suggestion that the Charybdis whirlpool was distorted by the passage of those mega-cruise ships rolling through the strait – but presumably those ships would only have deepened the disturbance, not eradicated it. These days, I wouldn't take Circe's advice to dodge Charybdis; a monster on top of Scylla's Castle would be much more life-threatening.

Apart from the lacklustre whirlpool, euhemerists have it all by the Strait of Messina: near-perfect geography; a lot of Greeks around at the right time; and plenty of arty, bookish colonists, who'd be delighted to appear in the pages of Homer.

The northern Sicilian coast was even more pleasingly Odyssean. When I took the return trip from Palermo, trundling along Sicily's northern coast, I got occasional glimpses of the Aeolian Islands. Further west lay the other Aeolian Islands. Hidden by the hill of the horizon, they revealed themselves, one by one: Vulcano, Lipari, Salina, Filicudi, Alicudi, Panarea... And then there was Stromboli – like a child's drawing of a volcano, an isosceles triangle with a scallop-shaped indentation at the top of the cone.

The Aeolian Islands were ruled by Aeolus, god of the winds – thus the Aeolian harp, its strings plucked by the air. In Book 10 of *The Odyssey*, Aeolus gave Odysseus a firmly sealed bag of winds so that, at last, he could sail back to Ithaca. Needless to say, it's not as simple as that: convinced the bag was full of riches, Odysseus's men ripped it open, only to let loose the wind that sent them racing back towards Sicily.

West of the Aeolian Islands, 30 miles north of Palermo, lies another claimant to the title of Aeolus's royal island: Ustica. Once a prison island – used by Mussolini to jail his enemies and by the Italian government to lock up Sicilian Mafiosi in the 1950s – Ustica is a wild, isolated speck of land.

As my half-empty ferry from Palermo approached Ustica, the growing speck formed itself into two big humps – like a fat man lying in the water, one hump his upturned head, the other his rounded belly, connected by a low neck of land. The only big town, also called Ustica, trickles down the fat man's neck to the harbour – a streak of orange roofs on the otherwise undeveloped island. On the apex of the fat man's belly, there perched a telecoms sphere on its stand, a vast golf ball on a tee rooted in his tummy button.

Right on cue, as the twin humps hoved into view, some modern Aeolus opened his bag of winds. The millpond-flat waters of the Med were instantly flecked with white horses, flanked on either side by deep barrel vaults of blue-black water, reflecting the angry, lowering heavens above.

I had not slept well the night before. I'd stayed with my friend Hannah in the Palazzo Conte Federico, a twelfth-century, Norman-Arabic palace built on Palermo's Roman walls. Its owner, Count Alessandro Federico, was descended from Sicily's thirteenth-century ruler, the Holy Roman Emperor, Frederick II.

The palace had had its good times in the eighteenth century when it was decked out with baroque ceiling frescoes. Its surroundings had slipped a little in the last 300 years. Not far from the train station, the palazzo was in a neighbourhood largely inhabited by recent arrivals from North Africa.

Sicily and its neighbour, the little island of Lampedusa, 100 miles south, are now the entry point to Europe for thousands of desperate refugees – the latest in countless waves of new arrivals to Sicily, from the Greeks to the Normans to Count Alessandro Federico's ancestor, Frederick II.

Many of those refugees washed up against the ancient walls of the Palazzo Conte Federico. They were broke but not starving. There were no beggars, just a lone prostitute, twerking away on a street corner to a nearby bar's rap music as I made my way to the palazzo from the station at midnight.

The current Conte Federico can't have been short of cash – he had devoted much of his life to vintage car racing. His study was plastered with pictures of him at the wheel of a post box-red, open-top, 1930s Fiat Balilla 508s, negotiating hairpin bends across Europe. The gleaming car now sat in the middle of the palazzo's open-air courtyard.

'Do you know the Prescott Hill Climb in Gloucestershire?' asked the count when we came across him in his study on the palazzo tour.

In recent years, the Federicos had turned their attentions to bed and breakfast. My bedroom – the 'Marvuglia' room – was grand enough, with a four-poster bed, ancient shutters and a fine, fourteenth-century, coffered ceiling. The problem was that on the other side of that coffered ceiling stood the kitchen. And that night, the Federicos also rented out the state rooms of the palazzo for a gala evening.

According to the palazzo's website, the 20 guests got a 'Guided tour through the palace; Apéritif in the torch-lit Arabic-Norman tower; Candlelight dinner and concert in the Baroque dancehall. (First-class singers, together with the Countess Federico – soprano from Salzburg – entertain the guests between the different courses of the gorgeous meal and perform songs of the finest operettas and thrilling Neapolitan melodies.)'

By the time I got to bed at around 11 p.m., the evening was still young for the *jeunesse dorée* of Palermo. I caught a glimpse of a tall, slim blonde in a silvery, scaly dress, shimmering across the inner balcony of the *piano nobile*, overlooking the courtyard and the Conte's Fiat Balilla 508s. The good looks of Sicilians are said to derive from their mix of Norman and Arab blood.

Until four in the morning, the girl in the shimmering dress and her pals shuttled from baroque dancehall to the kitchen and back. Lissom as she was – and her pals presumably were – she teetered on impossibly high, impossibly thin stiletto heels.

I remembered my maths teacher at prep school explaining the concept of pressure – 'Pressure = mass over volume' – via the example of the stiletto heel. As Miss Elgar taught me in 6 EJ, 30 years before, a ten-ton elephant exerts less pressure with his four-foot-square feet than a ten-stone woman does with the quarter of a square inch platforms of her stiletti. Miss Elgar hadn't expanded on the noise implications of high pressure – but I could have given her a pretty impressive lecture on the subject, after the equivalent of ten outsized elephants helped themselves to Prosecco in the room above me.

Several frantic phone calls to the count's charming, frantic son didn't stop the elephantine clattering. He apologised profusely but there was nothing he could do. There were 20 of them, paying for the full gala evening, and there was only one of me, paying for a B-list room.

So, the next morning, I sat, fully zombified in the ferry restaurant, reading a newspaper and cradling a double macchiato – ferry restaurants are the only place in Italy where you can't get good coffee. I could hardly feel too sorry for myself. The newspaper I'd bought at the ferry terminal, *La Sicilia*, told the bleak story of another journey across the Mediterranean.

The day before, 3 October 2013, a migrant ship from Libya sank a quarter of a mile off Lampedusa. As the ship foundered, one of the migrants, who were mainly from Eritrea, Ghana and Somalia, lit a blanket to attract attention, which had blown up into a deadly fire. 155 people survived; more than 360 are thought to have died. Eight days later, another boat, full of Palestinian and Syrian migrants, sank 75 miles off Lampedusa. Thirty-four people were killed.

In 2014, an estimated 230,000 migrants tried to cross the Mediterranean to Europe, with 167,000 of them landing in Italy.

More than three thousand years after Odysseus managed to sail across the Mediterranean, lots of people still don't make it – not least the 32 victims of the *Costa Concordia*, wrecked on the rocks of Isola del Giglio in Tuscany, thanks to the blundering antics of Captain Francesco Schettino in January 2012.

In all these tragic cases, the weather was calm enough: human error did for the *Costa Concordia*; engine trouble and grotesquely overcrowded, antiquated boats were behind the Lampedusa disasters. Even when Aeolus or Poseidon aren't turning the heavens black and the seas white, the Mediterranean is a place of heightened danger.

The morning after our Ustica trip, my friend Hannah and I drove to Polyphemus the Cyclops's cave in Trapani – at the far western end of the northern coast of Sicily.

Trapani has been associated with Odysseus for centuries. But few people have been as certain as Samuel Butler, the writer of the 1897 book *The Authoress of the Odyssey – where and when she wrote, who she was, the use she made of The Iliad and how the poem grew under her hands*. Butler was convinced, not just that Homer was a woman, but also that she was a 'young, headstrong and unmarried' girl from Trapani in Sicily – where he thought the Cyclops's cave was.

Like Shakespeare, Homer's identity shifts according to the passions of his fans. Nicholas Stampilides – director of Athens's Museum of Cycladic Art, and curator of a 2015 exhibition on ancient Greek medicine – thought Homer could have been a military doctor. According to Stampilides, a mere poet couldn't have given such a brilliant analysis of the human organs.

Butler wasn't entirely the feminist he sounds. Homer, he thought, must have been a girl because she made such silly blunders, like thinking ships have two rudders. Homer repeated the mistake twice in Book 9 of *The Odyssey*.

The Cyclops's cave was easy to find – on the outskirts of the semi-industrialised town of Trapani, at the end of a cul-de-sac, Via del Ciclope. The small grid of post-war suburban streets had Odyssean names: Via Polifemo and Via Calipso among them.

You can see why Butler was captivated by the cave. Its entrance had a pleasing symmetry: mouth-organ shaped, with curving sides to the void that ate into the cliff, with a flat ceiling and floor. Just the sort of neat entrance a Cyclops could close off with one enormous stone that no man can move. That's why Odysseus couldn't kill the Cyclops inside the sealed cave – he and his men could never have got out alive.

Instead, the devious old brainbox got Polyphemus drunk and, while he was sleeping, blinded his single eye with a sharpened olive-wood trunk, hardened in the cave's fire. Odysseus and his men then escaped by hiding under the bellies of the sheep as they were counted out of the cave by the blinded monster.

On top of all this, Odysseus came up with the brilliant wheeze of introducing himself as 'Nobody'. When Polyphemus later complained to the other Cyclopes that he was under attack, he screamed, 'Nobody, my friends, is trying to kill me by violence or treachery.' And so the other Cyclopes pushed off, convinced Polyphemus was merely very ill.

Fifty feet up the side of the hill, the cave was easily accessible by a path, with far-ranging views over the sea towards Sardinia. I could easily have imagined the Cyclops hurling boulders at Odysseus, as he fled in his ship. Polyphemus bellowed at his father, Poseidon, to curse Odysseus – as Poseidon dutifully did, adding yet more trials to Odysseus's journey.

There was still a selection of different-sized boulders conveniently piled up outside the cave entrance. What's more, the top of the hill above the cave had an even, flat surface – fitting Homer's description of Polyphemus 'shattering the crest of a tall cliff' and hurling it at Odysseus and his men. Too good to be true!

Samuel Butler was so convinced that he fell over himself to find a factual counterpart to everything in *The Odyssey*. He even calculated that the cave was perfectly fitted out for producing large blocks of feta cheese. Homer didn't specify that the Cyclops made feta, though he did write about baskets full of cheeses in the cave, alongside pails and bowls for milking, swimming with whey. Feta is made from sheep's milk – and the Cyclops had his own flock of sheep that he kept in his cave. There's plenty of the salt needed for feta, too, in the salt flats only a few miles from the cave.

Still, today, Trapani is a salt town, its southern fringes an eerie, flat, white landscape of shallow, saltwater pools, fringed with windmills and interlocking pyramids of salt. The main visitor attraction is still the Museo delle Saline – the Salt Museum. Only a few miles out to sea from the saltwater pools lies

Favignana, a kidney-shaped island, called, in antiquity, Aegusa – Greek for 'goat island'. Favignana, so the legend goes, was the island Odysseus visited before encountering the Cyclops:

> A fertile island lies slantwise outside the Cyclopes' harbour, well wooded and neither close to, nor far from, shore. Countless wild goats inhabit it, since there is nothing to stop them; no hunters to suffer the hardship of beating a path through its woods, or to roam its mountaintops. There are no flocks, and no ploughed fields: but always unsown, and untilled, it is free of mankind and nurtures only bleating goats.

Bingo! Again, it all fits.

As the biggest island in the Mediterranean, Sicily is bound to provide lots of coves, hills and mountains that chime with places in *The Odyssey*. In fact, the island as a whole, with its distinctive three-cornered shape, was said to be the inspiration for Homer's Thrinacia – roughly, 'the three place', or a triangle. Thrinacria is the island in Book 12, home to the cattle of Helios, the sun god. Still, today, Messina's football team is called Trinacria Messina. It's in the Hotel Trinacria, on the Palermo seafront, that the prince dies at the end of Giuseppe di Lampedusa's *The Leopard*.

The one thing Odysseus and his men were told is: don't eat the cattle of the sun god. You can guess what happened next. The starving men broke their oath not to eat the cattle. Odysseus may have been extremely clever, bloody; violent and great in the sack; he wasn't much cop at authority.

Cue more divine punishment. On Helios's request, Zeus zapped the whole crew, except for Odysseus, with a killer thunderbolt. Odysseus's punishment was to spend the next seven years on Ogygia – thought to be Malta – with Calypso, she of the inexhaustible sexual appetite.

Taormina – the town colony on Sicily's eastern coast, founded by Greeks from Naxos in 734 BC – is said to be home to the cattle of Helios; for no obvious geographical parallel I could discern. I think it won its Odyssean claims more through its significance as a major ancient Greek town; and through its natural advantages, perched as it is on the edge of a cliff overlooking Mount Etna on one side, and the underside of Italy's toe on the other.

If I was in the nostalgic vein, this was the place to be. My grandparents spent their honeymoon in Taormina in 1938. I had my twenty-first birthday here with my family and a friend of my sister's, Tommaso. From an aristocratic family in Tuscany, Tommaso travelled with my sister by train down the west coast of Italy, shaking with fear. He'd been brought up on the idea that Sicily was less the home of Mafiosi monsters and more the lair of Homeric monsters, savages that bore no resemblance to the sophisticates of northern Italy.

In the 20 or so years since my twenty-first birthday, mass tourism had arrived in Taormina, stamping its internationally uniform look on a once unique place. The pointless knick-knack of 2014 was a little jellified orange blob you flung on the ground; it momentarily flattened itself on the tarmac before reblobbifying. From Athens to Rome to Taormina, Asian and African hawkers spent their days demonstrating the blob's life cycle. I never saw a single tourist buy one.

Taormina tourists, too, dressed like all other tourists on my travels: in jauntily coloured T-shirts and shorts with trainers, flip-flops or sandals. They were usually equipped with water bottles, even though they were fed and watered like babies by their guides. They moved en masse, locked together physically by a desire for security, and mentally by wireless headsets. They were in a state of semi-exhaustion and semi-terror – of being ripped off, looking like a fool, getting lost and not being understood.

The tourists were bored, too, by what they'd travelled thousands of miles to see: history. In Rome, I saw a group of tourists thrilled by the excellent gelato shop in Torre Largo Argentina; they were thrilled, too, by the cats that roamed the ancient ruins in the big piazza. The ruins themselves – where Caesar had been murdered by Brutus, Casca and the other senators – were of little interest.

Still, they looked perfectly at ease in their national skins. They had none of this effete Englishman's impossible ambition to be mistaken for a native. Wherever I went in Italy or Greece, I opened up conversation with a '*Buongiorno*' or a '*Kalemera*'; I took photos surreptitiously. I wore trousers and long-sleeved shirts, too, even on the hottest days, as I'm wearing on the cover of this book – all in a bid to avoid the 'I'm on holiday' look. How it annoyed me to see occasional Italians and Greeks wearing the sort of hoodies and dayglo singlets sported by tourists; they were letting the side down.

Who was I kidding? My native-born look was a patently see-through act. I was pale-skinned, taller than most Greeks and Italians, and barely capable of taking a conversation beyond *buongiorno* or *kalemera*.

It wasn't entirely snobbery and cultural cringe that got me behaving like this. I never wore jeans, shorts or T-shirts in London, either – but perhaps that's all part of the same snobbery. I hated to be part of a crowd – metaphorically and literally speaking. And that applies in London, too – where I only drop into the National Gallery when it's deserted, for the last ten minutes before closing.

The empty gallery ruse first occurred to me when I lived in Florence 20 years ago. I nipped into the Uffizi at half past six, 20 minutes before closing, and had Botticelli's *Primavera* to myself for a heart-stopping quarter of an hour. Tourists always allow themselves too much time for a city's greatest hits – and push off to the nearest café long before their allotted time is up. That's the time when we emptiness addicts pounce.

It wasn't just the Uffizi that emptied while the rest of Florence filled up. Wherever the tourist crowd went, it travelled, as it did in Taormina, in one vast river, flowing down the major boulevards. Wherever the flood went, it spotted and faded the beauties of the places it had travelled thousands of miles to revere. Wherever locals were hit by the flood, they were brutalised by the attendant, repetitive, mercenary demands of mass tourism.

Move one street west or east of those boulevards, though, and you find the real, half-empty life lived by the natives. There's a logic to the two lives, the tourist's crammed one and the local's empty one. When we're out of our comfort zone, we seek the proximity of fellow concerned foreigners, driven by a collective purpose – surely they must be making for the Duomo, too? When we're in our own home towns, we follow deeply individual routes – from the dry-cleaner, to work, to a favourite bar – dictated by nothing but our own wishes.

I suppose I was desperate to be an individual, not part of a crowd. That's why I was delighted at the limited menu in Davy Byrne's pub in Dublin – when I was following the Ulysses trail at the beginning of 2015. James Joyces's protagonist, Leopold Bloom, had a Gorgonzola cheese sandwich and a glass of Burgundy at Davy Byrne's. When I visited, the Gorgonzola delivery man had failed to turn up. Thank God! So I could go off the Joyce pilgrims' menu and have what I really wanted – crab and salmon sandwiches, and a pint of Guinness.

The same urge to be an individual explained my strange behaviour in Ithaca. At the Hexedra bar in Vathy, all the tourists in shorts sat outside in the evening warmth. The grizzled, Ithacan pensioners, in trousers, were playing cards inside, watching Panathinaikos, the big Athenian football team, lose on the bar telly.

'Outside?' said the ancient waiter, also, consolingly, in trousers like me.

'Inside, please,' I said, throwing in a '*eucharisto*' – Greek for 'thanks' – to flaunt my insider credentials.

Neither the tourists outside, nor the card-players inside, paid the slightest attention to me, as I took up my little table in the middle of the restaurant and stared at the telly gloomily, like a veteran Panathinaikos fan.

It was easy enough to behave like an individual when I was travelling as one, but much more difficult when part of a group – as I was for my three-week lecture trip on the *Corinthian*. I had been on countless holidays with family and friends, but never on one where I had to get along with a different set of strangers at every meal. My lecture contract stated that I had to attend every communal meal – all 63 of them. There was no chance of grabbing a plate of sandwiches and skulking off to my cabin.

Forced communal dining should have been excellent therapy for a heartbroken, sociopathic loner. Instead, at breakfast and lunch – both buffet meals – I often waited until the end of the appointed meal period before nipping into the emptying room, just like I did at the Uffizi. Uplifting banter is never easy in the morning, or without a drink. The formal, sit-down dinners were much less stressful, for both reasons.

Normally, in my single, self-absorbed life, I never had to do anything I didn't want to do. The trickiness of fitting in with other people's schedules on the *Corinthian* could be trying.

At one point on the cruise – touring Diocletian's extraordinarily intact fourth-century AD palace in Split, Croatia – we had a particularly slow guide. My teeth ground together; my fists clenched; my irritation boiled. I had planned to whip round the palace and hire a moped to see the Roman city of Salona, three miles from Split. At this pace, I would never get to Salona before the *Corinthian* sailed. But then, an indulgent guardian angel appeared, in the form of Heather, a lady in her eighties, who'd slipped on Diocletian's greasy Roman marble floor and hurt her knees.

'I'm so sorry,' she said, 'but is there any way you could accompany me back to the ship? I really don't think I can go on.'

I'm not a Catholic. I don't know if there's a word for a sin that masquerades as a holy act – the holy sin of disingenuousness? Whatever it's called, I committed it in spades, as I told the thunderingly dull guide, 'I'm really sorry, but one of the group has hurt herself really rather badly. I'm going to have to take her back to the ship.'

What joy! What selfish, wicked joy, wrapped in humble altruism, at being magically returned to my customary state of selfish singledom. I walked Heather back to the ship, discussing the recent trip she'd taken round the early Byzantine churches of Greece with a thrill in my heart. It took me ten minutes to get her back on board. I then had all the time in the world to hire a moped and take in the sprawling ruins of Salona, with its fine baths, bridges and amphitheatre; all the finer by contrast with its neighbours, grim tower blocks dating back to the Tito years.

Heather wasn't the only angel aboard the *Corinthian*. Of the 60 crew and 87 passengers, there was only one shocker. Just as every club must have its bore, every cruise must have its professional complainant – often accumulating a dossier to present at the end of the trip, to justify a full or partial refund. This man – a well-dressed, tall, imposing figure in his eighties – was so dedicated to complaining that I almost admired his talent for coming up with new gripes.

To be fair, on our second evening – the night of the captain's cocktail party – he had quite a lot of ammunition. The loos on board the boat had packed up, and the air-conditioning wasn't working in the Nautilus Club, where the drinks were being held.

'So there's no air-con, there's no loos and there's no internet,' he said. The last one was true, too – although the internet is always patchy at sea. 'It wouldn't happen on the *Queen Mary*, would it?'

I didn't know – I'd never been on the *Queen Mary*. Also, I was in a strange halfway house when it came to on-board hierarchy. I was the cruise lecturer, being paid by the company, but I didn't have any official role beyond that.

'I'm so sorry,' I said, 'I'll pass on your complaints to the cruise director.'

'I've already complained to him,' he said. 'I want to know what YOU are going to do about it.'

Absolutely bugger all, was my unsaid answer. Not because I didn't want to help him – or me. My loo had packed up, too. After a day without facilities, it transpired that a passenger had dropped a face towel into the sensitive vacuum system – contrary to the pre-launch briefing that 'You should only put down the toilet what the good Lord intended'.

I was rather desperate to use the internet, too. And I was also sweating a bit at the captain's cocktail party, in my cream linen jacket and tie. I wasn't wearing any socks – it saved on laundry – and so came the closest I've ever got to dressing like Julio Iglesias. It was the sort of Eurolothario look a modern Odysseus would sport when seducing a modern Circe or Calypso.

The outfit even had a certain Eurolothario effect. Later that evening, as night cooled the Nautilus Club and I stopped sweating for a brief interlude, a French widow in her eighties ran her right hand down my shoulder, above the breast pocket of my jacket, and whispered, 'Ooh, you do scrub up well.'

This incident apart, I'm afraid the sexual advantages of coming from a fairly rich, capitalist nation – as we travelled along the Albanian and Croatian coasts, as well as the bankrupt Greek one – proved to be sadly diminished these days.

The complaining man got more inventive as the trip progressed. After my first evening lecture – 'The story of *The Iliad* and the ruins of the city of Troy' – he came up to me, as I was packing away my computer and microphone.

'I've got no idea what's in *The Iliad* and *The Odyssey*,' he said. 'You must pitch your lectures at our level.'

By 'our', he meant 'my'; there were several ardent classicists aboard. I wondered why he'd chosen to come on a cruise tellingly called 'In the Footsteps of Odysseus'. But I said nothing – except for various repeated combinations of 'Sorry'/'I quite understand'/ 'How very kind of you to tell me.'

His finest hour came towards the end of our trip, as we were pulling slowly into Corfu harbour. The whole of Corfu Town opened up to us, building by building, in the sharp, early morning light: from the medieval citadel, the Palaion Frourion, to the Liston, the elegant French arcade overlooking the lush, green cricket pitch, popular with visiting teams from Malta and Britain.

Corfu is the epicentre of Greek cricket, providing 11 out of the 14 teams in the whole country. The star Corfu player – and Greek national captain – in recent years has been Nic Pothas, the former Hampshire wicket-keeper, a South African of Greek ancestry.

The scoreboard on the edge of the pitch had all the details in English – the total, number of overs played, last man's score, and the last innings. Only the name of the league was written in Greek: the 'Ellenike Omospondia Kriket', the Hellenic Cricket Federation. Omospondia, or federation, comes from the lovely ancient Greek word *omospondos* – 'sharing in the same cup or drink offering'.

'Is there a delay?' came a familiar voice at my shoulder, as I gazed towards the cricket pitch.

'I'm very sorry – they're waiting for a pilot to guide us into Corfu harbour,' I said.

It was good to have a concrete answer to give him for once. While we waited 15 minutes or so for the pilot to lead us gently into our berth, there were few prettier views on earth to while away the time. 'So there's a delay,' said my complaining friend, who would have made a good cross-examining barrister.

His imperviousness to beauty was matched only by that of a wonderfully grumpy lady when we finished our trip in Venice. As the *Corinthian* slipped into the Venetian lagoon, the faint dawn sun strengthened and lit up the sleeping city's monuments one by one: the dazzling white marble façade of the church of San Giorgio Maggiore; the faint pink Gothic pinnacles of the Doge's Palace.

'Why do cruises always finish in Venice?' said the grumpy lady. 'It's so BORING!'

I was speechless – not with rage, but hidden joy at her last-minute triumph in trumping the Corfu complainer for sheer, self-obsessed philistinism.

Back – on my own – in Taormina, it was easy enough to escape the crowds, by climbing to the top ring of seats in the Teatro Greco – strictly speaking a Roman theatre, on Greek foundations.

As I took in the stirring views down the coast, I was hit by a wave of nostalgia: for my youth, and for my grandparents' younger days, too. It was a pleasant kind of nostalgia – if that isn't a tautology, given that the literal translation of nostalgia is 'pain in looking back'. There should be a different word for pleasure in looking back – 'nosthedone' perhaps; *hedone* is Greek for pleasure.

I felt only nosthedone at Taormina. The bleaker kind of nostalgia didn't need a formal invitation to return, though, at my next stop: Syracuse, 70 miles further south down the coast, in the bottom right-hand corner of Sicily.

It wasn't as if my ex-girlfriend and I had been there before. I was having a perfectly jolly time, bicycling round the city, dropping in on its charming cathedral, built around the Doric skeleton of a Greek temple to Athena. Syracuse was founded by Greek colonists from Corinth and Tenea in 734 BC.

I was reading all this in my guidebook when I was brought up short by something it said. The little headland I was racing around on my hired bike had once been an island, Ortygia. The island lent its name to the upmarket Sicilian soap company, Ortigia, founded in 2006. Some say Ortygia was the original Ogygia – Calypso's island.

My ex-girlfriend had been keen on Ortigia products. A bottle of Ortigia shampoo stood, a holy relic, in the metal caddy in my shower for a year after we split up. I would have used it if I could – I bet Odysseus would have slathered it all over his lovely, thick hyacinth-locks without a care in the world. But my bald head had no need of it. The Ortigia shampoo greeted me every morning that year – a daily Proustian stab – as I woke up and showered. Until, one morning, the accumulation of wounds got too much – and I flung it in the little chrome pedal bin in the bathroom.

Little stab wounds like this awaited me everywhere we'd been. I could hardly throw dozens of restaurants and boutique Mediterranean hotels into my pedal bin. But anything small enough to fit in it was better there than in the outside world, winking at me, forever sharp, forever prone to attack.

As I neared the end of my journey, the pain was as acute as ever.

The scoreboard by the cricket pitch in Corfu Town. The Greek at the bottom reads 'Ellenike Omospondia Kriket' – the Hellenic Cricket Federation. Omospondia – 'federation' – comes from the ancient Greek, omospondos – 'sharing in the same cup or drink offering'.

Straight out of the Asterix and Obelix School of Architecture – the Cyclopean walls of Odysseus's Palace on Ithaca. Below is Frikes Bay – from phrikes, the Homeric word for ripples on the surface of the sea.

20

Going Home to Ithaca

Travel doesn't free the mind. It does free up lots of time to feel sorry for yourself.

On the long road to Ithaca, there were none of the occasional drinks with friends that punctuate the boredom of life; none of the opening of the post, no putting the bins out, no mowing the lawn to fill up the great lengths of lonely time.

And yet there was no one calling me back home. Since I had broken up with my ex-girlfriend, I had taken a momentary break from my customary pattern of going out with girls, running away from them and making them – and me – miserable.

Still, when I finally got to Ithaca in September 2014, I felt the siren call to go home: partly because I had been travelling, and working on this book, on and off, for three years; partly because Ithaca is the Western European mythical and literary code word for home, however far you are from your real home.

Ithaca is a strange combination: a remote, foreign, strange island that reminds you of home; an island that makes you long for home, while its surpassing beauty invites you to stay for ever.

When Byron got to Ithaca in 1823, he said, 'If this island belonged to me, I would bury all my books here and never go away.' I could see Byron's point, as the *Corinthian* tracked Odysseus's route from Corfu and turned into that great natural harbour of Ithaca. Homer's epithet for Ithaca is *kranae* or 'rugged' – and it was certainly that, with its cliffs sliding sheer into the water practically all the way around the figure-of-eight-shaped island.

Since the economic crisis hit, Ithaca, in the Ionian Sea, on Greece's western shore, has grown more remote. Budget cuts meant the Athens ferries had slowed down to save on fuel. It now took a day to get to Piraeus from Ithaca and the number of daily ships had been reduced. Agony for Ithacans; but, for ruthless tourists like me in search of Homer's empty, ancient Greece, pure ecstasy, in its original Greek sense, *ekstasis* – a removal of yourself to elsewhere.

Even before the crisis, Ithaca was depopulated. Its population has shrunk, from 10,000 a century ago to just over 3,000 today. Lots of Greeks have emigrated over the years, particularly from Ithaca, thanks to its rugged, inhospitable landscape. And the Ithacans, just like Odysseus, have always been terrific sailors. By legend and reputation, they yearn to rove the world, just like the aged Ulysses in Tennyson's poem:

> I cannot rest from travel: I will drink
> Life to the lees.

Government cuts also meant the supposed site of Odysseus's palace, in the north of the island, lay unguarded, unfenced and open to the elements. It was almost too good to be true – not only to have the place to myself and three friends but also for the palace to fit the myth so well.

The site was uncovered in 1994. For 16 years, archaeologists from the University of Ioannina carried out research. In 2010, they declared the palace to be the right date for Odysseus's home.

For us euhemerists, there was already plenty of other proof, if that's the right word. Far below the peak on which the palace perches, I looked down on Frikes Bay – from *phrikes*, the Homeric word for ripples on the surface of the sea. A little further down the coast was Aphales harbour, named after the Homeric term for white horses at sea. The sea was the great name-giver in *The Odyssey*, even to the gods: Aphrodite was named after *aphros*, Greek for sea foam.

All circumstantial evidence, of course. But, still, there was plenty more of it in this delightful spot. The palace had easy access to three harbours – the supposedly royal harbour of Polis, used by Odysseus, and the two common harbours of Aphales and Frikes. Odysseus's palace was built in position A, with its stellar views across the Ionian Sea. It stands on solid bedrock, able to withstand the earthquakes that ravage this corner of Greece. And the site is blessed with a natural well, still overflowing with water when I climbed down into it at the end of a long, parched summer. Just down the road from the palace, there's a modern fountain from which locals still pick up their water.

The mighty Cyclopean walls of the palace – straight out of the Asterix and Obelix School of Architecture – were still in terrific nick, with the uneven edge of each stone meticulously locked into the uneven edge of its neighbour. Just as in Homer's description, the palace was built on two flat, terraced, rock beds, one above the other, connected by a surviving stone staircase.

Terracotta urns, a Mycenean bath and a graveyard have all been discovered on the site. Entranced, I could well believe that lovely Penelope – Helen's first cousin, she must have been a looker – had undone her tapestry work every night within the palace's Cyclopean walls, to keep the suitors at bay.

Still visible, beneath a rudimentary modern roof, were the moulds of a metal-working workshop. Was this where the 12 axe heads were made, the ones lined up in pairs to form a super-narrow passage – which Odysseus fired a bronze-tipped arrow through, to prove his vast martial superiority over the suitors? I certainly thought so.

Not far away, in a cave sanctuary in the Bay of Polis – investigated, inevitably, by Heinrich Schliemann in 1868 – an ancient inscription on a mask has been found. '*Euchen Odyssei*', it reads: 'My vow to Odysseus'. Nearby, on the old path to south Ithaca, a rock is inscribed with the ancient letters O and Δ – the first two letters of Odysseus's name. Scholars think Odysseus was worshipped in a hero cult at an extremely early stage, by sailors who revered the ultimate seafarer.

Towering over Ithaca is Mount Neriton: '*Neriton einosiphullon*' ('Neriton with its trembling foliage'), as Homer called it. Today, the island is thick with gnarled old olive trees – the sort Odysseus built his indestructible bed around. It is by telling Penelope about the bed's history that Odysseus convinces Penelope it is really him who has returned home after 20 years away. Of course, there are olive trees all over Greece; lots of ancient, gnarled ones, too. But, still, the evidence kept on mounting, wherever I pointed my little rental car.

I had a blissful evening swim – like swimming through silk – in Phorcys Bay, where Odysseus was carried, in a deep, exhausted sleep, by the friendly

Phaeacians from nearby Corfu after that original thrilling meeting with Princess Nausicaa on the beach. It was late September, when the Mediterranean is at its warmest after a long summer of baking heat.

Whenever I swam in the sea on my odyssey, I felt closest to the natural forces that have whipped those waters, and shaped those coasts, since Odysseus sailed the same seas 3,000 years ago. I swam in the tiny bay of the Greek island of Nisyros, protected by a breakwater, smugly staring just a few yards beyond me, where the unprotected water was whipped up into angry white horses. In the not-so-pretty Turkish port of Kuşadasi, I had a heart-in-mouth moment, battling even bigger rollers – the remnant of a storm brought on by the robust northern winds.

The sheltered bay of Phorcys was unruffled by wind, even if it didn't look exactly like Homer's description: 'At its mouth, two projecting headlands sheer to seaward, but sloping down on the side towards the harbour.' But, still, it was close enough to the description.

As soon as the *Corinthian* turned into the main bay of Ithaca – formed between the two loops of the figure-of-eight shape – the brisk westerly wind dropped. It was just like in *The Odyssey*, where two headlands 'keep back the great waves raised by heavy winds without but, within, the benched ships lie unmoored when they have reached the point of anchorage'.

There was even a cave at the head of the bay – which I winched myself down into on a tattered rope. It was the living image of Homer's 'pleasant, shadowy cave sacred to the nymphs that are called Naiads'. A 20-year-old Edward VII visited the cave on his Grand Tour-cum-gap year in June 1862, when Ithaca was still a British protectorate.

I didn't find the Naiads' mixing bowls, springs, jars, honeycombs or the stone looms on which the gorgeous nymphs weaved purple-dyed webs. But, still, there was a charming little graffito of an ancient trireme painted on the wall – a little more recent than the Naiads, I felt. Certainly more recent was a graffito in the collapsing old guard's hut: 'Nekrobastard was here,' it read, 'November 2011.'

There is one great stumbling block to the theory that modern Ithaca is ancient Ithaca. At one point, Homer wrote, 'Low-lying Ithaca is furthest out to sea, towards the sunset, and the others are apart, towards the dawn and sun.'

That, I'm afraid, isn't true. Directly west of Ithaca, and further out to sea, is the island of Cephalonia. This anomaly led a British writer, Robert Bittlestone, to suggest that Paliki, a peninsula on the north-west coast of Cephalonia, is in fact Ithaca. According to his theory, the isthmus connecting Paliki to the main island was once submerged, leaving Paliki an independent island. An earthquake later raised the isthmus to its current elevation, Bittlestone says.

It isn't just Cephalonia that claims Odysseus. Dimitris Paizis-Danias, a former captain in the Greek merchant navy, has written several books arguing that his home island, Ithaca, is Odysseus's Ithaca. In his latest book, written in 2013, the charming biographical sketch reads, 'Paizis-Danias is Ithacan by birth but, at times, he becomes a Cephalonian, according to the theory of Kourouklis (1893), a Dulichian [from the mysterious, ultra-fertile Homeric island of Dulichium] according to Volteras (1903), Tsimaratos and le Noan (2003–4) and Bittlestone (2005), a micro-Ithacan according to Goekoop (1908), a Samian according to Livadas and Campanis (1998) and Cramer-Metaxas (2000), and no one in particular, according to Apostolatos (2001).'

Wherever there's any doubt about great literary figures, the conspiracy theorists leap in – just look what they've done to poor old Shakespeare's lineage and life story. It's worth noting that the earliest conspiracy theorist on the list is Kourouklis in 1893. Until then, the world was happy to take modern Ithaca for ancient Ithaca.

I'm still happy to do so. How likely is it that, one day, all the islanders on Ithaca declared that, from henceforth, they were moving to a new Ithaca on the next-door island? Wouldn't the next-door islanders be pretty peeved at having to rename themselves? Wouldn't there be records of that previous name on what is now Ithaca? The attachment to place and place names is an extremely strong, natural human emotion. Who would go along with such a madcap scheme?

If the name change did take place, the islanders would have to have done it very early on. Already, by 350 BC, coins, showing Odysseus and a ship, were minted on what is now modern Ithaca. By the Hellenistic period, Ithaca's parliament was called the Odysseion. At the same time, a popular 'game of the bridegrooms' was played on Ithaca. It was a dating game based on draughts – the winner ended up marrying Penelope.

It's more likely that Homer got his geography a bit wrong when he said Ithaca was the most westerly island; much more likely than all the strange twisting of history you have to do to make Cephalonia Ithaca. More likely, too, than Shakespeare being the Earl of Oxford, or George W. Bush blowing up the Twin Towers.

But no evidence could impress as much as the calm of the palace; the being in the moment, the unchanged look. When I first saw the remains of Odysseus's palace, I felt almost sick with exhilaration. Even if the stones had been eroded down to neck height – and all on a footprint smaller than most British villages – enough remained. Though much had been taken, so much abides.

It wasn't just like going to Odysseus's home, or coming to the end of his odyssey and mine. It was also going back to the beginning: to before *The Iliad*, to the kingdom Odysseus ruled before the Trojan War broke out. It took me back, too, to the beginning of my school life, to the age of nine, when I started learning Latin, and a year later when I started Greek and the whole world of Odysseus; when the nouns, verbs, optatives, gerundives and all the rest of it first started flooding in.

I had never chosen Classics. Classics chose me. I knew nothing of the thrills of Classics when I started learning Latin and Greek at my north London prep school, on the northern edge of Regent's Park. Latin and Greek were obligatory at my prep school; and Latin was obligatory at Westminster, in the first year anyway. But, even when both languages were optional, I made little conscious choice to do Classics. My older brother did it at Westminster and Magdalen College, Oxford – and, therefore, so did I.

I dutifully did my work at Oxford but never realised quite how staggering the classical world was. On my first visit to the ruins of Knossos, on my gap year in 1989, I shared Evelyn Waugh's view on seeing the Minoan pictures 60 years earlier.

'Only a few square inches of the vast area exposed to our consideration are earlier than the last 20 years', Waugh wrote. 'And it is impossible to disregard the suspicion that their painters have tempered their zeal for accurate reconstruction with a somewhat inappropriate predilection for covers of *Vogue*.'

On my last visit in 2014, I was deeply excited by those same pictures. I even came up with a pet theory – looking at the paintings of the Minoan columns – that, in their simple, huge, rounded, tapering way, they were the precursor of Greek Doric columns 700 years later.

That last visit to Knossos also saw the lowest, most shameful point of my trip – the closest to that moment when Odysseus was shipwrecked, naked, on the skin-ripping shallows of Corfu; when, as George Chapman translated it, 'The sea had soak'd his heart through.'

For the second ten days of the cruise, there were 87 passengers on board – 20 more than during the first ten days. And so, when we got to Knossos, I was asked to do some head counts – a possibility I'd signed up to in my contract. I was delighted to do it. All it meant was sitting in the front of the coach for the short journey from Heraklion port to Knossos, giving the guide and coach-driver their tips, and counting the passengers off and on my coach.

Easy enough. We had a delightful morning, studying the finest surviving fragments of Minoan civilisation in existence, at King Minos's palace – the best place on earth to see what Greece was like in the pre-classical age, from around the twenty-seventh to the twelfth century BC.

Here – in the Knossos wall paintings Evelyn Waugh hated – were the first depictions in art of a human figure on a chariot, found by Sir Arthur Evans in his excavations 115 years ago. Here, in theory, the terrifying Minotaur, half-man, half-bull, munched his way through generations of Greek youths; before Theseus killed him and found his way out of the labyrinth thanks to the ball of twine given to him by his new girlfriend, Ariadne.

Knossos is the epicentre of Greek myth. Daedalus, the skilled builder of the labyrinth, was imprisoned here by King Minos to stop him leaking the secret of the perfect prison; thus his attempt to escape Crete with his doomed son, Icarus.

On previous trips, I'd taken all these overfamiliar stories for granted. This time, I felt a renewed thrill. I didn't necessarily believe the legends. But my heart leapt at the legends' real-life counterparts: the fresco of a bull, which showed how venerated the animals really had been in Minoan Greece; the ruined passages of the palace, still thick with labyrinthine twists and turns.

Perhaps those twists and turns didn't quite correspond with Ariadne's advice to Theseus on how to crack the labyrinth – look straight ahead, go downhill and never look left or right. But, still, I was in a state of fevered, Classics-loving excitement as I counted Group A back on to Bus A.

'Twenty one off, twenty one on,' I mumbled to myself, as I stood at the foot
of the bus door, staring over in the direction of Villa Ariadne, the house Evans
built in the grounds of the dig. During the war, the villa was inhabited by
General Heinrich Kreipe – the Nazi officer kidnapped by Paddy Leigh Fermor
in 1944 in one of the great feats of wartime derring-do.

As the last of the *Corinthian* passengers climbed aboard Coach A – '… 19,
20, 21 …' – I pondered the protean nature of the Greek myths, their near-
infinite capacity for reinvention through the ages.

The story of wicked Theseus, deserting Ariadne on Naxos, has produced
endless lovely permutations: an exceptional Catullus poem; Titian's
Bacchus and Ariadne in the National Gallery; a Richard Strauss opera; and
a constellation named after Ariadne. The tale of silly Theseus, forgetting to
change the sails of his returning ship from black to white, gave the Aegean Sea
its name. His father, Aegeus, was so distressed at the black sails, suggesting his
son had died, that he flung himself into the sea below. Aegeus also bequeathed
to us the word 'archipelago' – an Italian corruption of the Greek words *Aigaion
pelagos*, 'Aegean Sea'.

'Bus A is back, Peter!' I said cheerily to the cruise director, spirits lifted by
my pumped-up love of the classical world, when we got back to the ship.

'Yes, Bus A is back,' said Peter in a resigned, friendly way. 'But you've left a
passenger behind in Knossos car park.'

In my self-indulgent dream world, while I'd been musing on the Villa
Ariadne, I'd counted wrongly. Only 20 passengers had got back on Bus A.
The twenty-first – Beata, a 92-year-old retired conference organiser from
Germany – had returned to the car park to find Bus A had gone.

Thank God, Beata had the initiative to ring up the boat, despite the panic
and the baking heat of the exposed tarmac of the car park at midday in late
September. You could see why Icarus's wings melted so easily in the punishing
Cretan heat, somewhere just above that car park. King Minos's palace at Knossos
had been designed to deal with the heat: light was let in, diffused, through timber
colonnades and light wells. Step into the direct sun, though, and you were toast.

A taxi was sent to pick Beata up from the cruelly exposed car park. Once
she got back on board, the crew had the decency not to blame me – but I
blamed myself, as I should have.

At my lecture that evening – 'A Very Relaxed Latin Lesson' – I wasn't very relaxed, particularly when I saw Beata sitting calmly in the audience before the lights went down in the Nautilus Club. I went up to her, more ashamed, and more terrified of anyone, than I had been in years.

'What happened today was entirely my fault,' I said. 'I'm extremely sorry.'

'Sorry ...' Beata said in a steely, measured tone, lightly inflected with German precision, '... isn't good enough.'

I have spent my life playing the Englishman's trick – saying sorry and not meaning it. This was the first time I'd said it, meant it and had my apology refused. I would have bought her a drink, paid for her cruise, anything ... But she was too decent to be swayed by mere money.

'I'm so, so sorry,' I said. 'So extremely sorry.'

Beata sat there silently, staring into the middle distance. After what seemed to be several days, she said, gently, 'Thank you.'

Chastened as I was by Beata's thoroughly justified anger, the day at Knossos still lingered in the mind for reasons other than my idiocy. It was the day my decades of classical education – that useless thing I'd derided for so long – clicked into place. It had been an ultra-slow-release thing: years, decades, in the dogged accumulation of the seeds of knowledge; even more years in the appreciation of the plants, now fully grown.

I had been quick to learn all those optatives but ever so slow to show any desire for the juicy meat and marrow of Greek and ancient Greece; for what Odysseus, Homer, Pericles and all that squad were really like. Instead, I just sat there at school, dutifully learning the declensions and conjugations I'd been told to learn. I'd always been the good boy who did what was expected of him. At school, anyway; I was a grumpy little thing at home.

I remember going on a school trip to the Rijksmuseum when I was 11. Everyone else lurked around the insalubrious parts of Amsterdam. They bought flick knives, sneaked a look at the live peep shows, teased the two teachers for flirting – even though Mr Elwyn Jones with his bushy moustache, and hair *en brosse*, was not the sort to go out with Miss Smith, the Rubenesque English teacher. When we went round the Rijksmuseum, the other children rushed to hog the banquettes in each gallery and chat away with each other. Only I sought out the pictures – not because I loved them, not because I wanted to show off. But because that's what I thought I ought to do.

'I ought' still came before 'I want' at 19, when I was doggedly sitting my Classics Mods at Oxford – held up as the longest exams in the world apart from the Chinese Civil Service exams.

For my revision, I'd taken to visiting different libraries, to spice up my life in the smallest possible way. One day, I'd go to Hawksmoor's library at All Souls – Gothic without, classical within. The next day, I'd go to Rhodes House – where the Rhodes Scholars studied. There, in the lobby one day, I spotted a sign saying '*Meh kapnetai*' – 'No Smoking' in ancient Greek. 'A don's joke,' John Betjeman called it.

I must say, I didn't find it very funny at the time. I thought it showed the worst side of classicists; their conviction that they are an intellectual breed apart – because they're told they are, and because they tell themselves they are.

The Rhodes House joke depended on the classicists' smug self-assurance that they were studying the cleverest, obscurest, most exclusive of all languages. Only then could such a workmanlike, modern, practical instruction be funny. It wouldn't have been funny in German or French – languages that weren't freighted with the same heavy baggage of seriousness and grandness.

Us classicists at the university had to cling hard to the myth that we were so clever, because it was so much easier to get into Oxford to do Classics than any other subject. The ancient universities had largely been built on Classics-teaching; and so there remained a lot of places for classicists, even though fewer and fewer schools taught the subject. The upshot was that around 70 per cent of classicists who applied to Oxford got in, compared to around 30 per cent of lawyers and medics. We justified this to ourselves by implying or, more often, declaring, that classicists were a self-selecting bunch of geniuses.

I still fall for the delusion. The other day, I met a PR man from Somerset whose intelligence suddenly glowed more brightly when he let slip that he'd read Classics at university. Classicists are always more likely to read Classics at university than study it. But, still, for all my self-delusion, he was clever.

And classicists of a certain vintage, before the rigour of the subject fell apart – always after your own time, of course – do bear a certain mark: of having gone through an old-fashioned sort of education, which produced an understanding of how languages work; of knowing the beginnings of things; of appreciating the worth of education for education's sake; of knowing things that are useless, practically speaking, but crucial to your intellectual make-up.

Halfway through university, I cracked. 'I ought' gave way to 'I want' – and I changed from Classics to history, a subject I read then for pleasure. Admittedly, it was ancient and modern history – not that far removed from Classics – but, still, far enough removed for me to find a great deal of joy in it. I had tired of the Thomas Gradgrind approach to Classics – of learning the conjugations and declensions, of toiling through Homer in the original Greek, of reading dry-as-dust articles by Oxford dons and regurgitating them in my essays.

In 2008, I handed back those essays to my old college library at Magdalen, but not because they were fans of my work – my old philosophy tutor, Dr Ralph Walker, was horrified to hear my essays were coming back to the college. Magdalen wanted any old undergraduates to hand back their essays as a memento of the days when work was handwritten. When I was there, between 1989 and 1993, I was in the last generation to use the pen rather than the keyboard. I had become a museum piece in my lifetime.

Looking back on my old essays that day, I was disturbed by how boring they were. 'Hadrian was the most interesting of emperors – do you agree?' was the title of one of them. One of the most interesting of emperors, yes; the dullest of essays.

I still have a copy of the thesis that got me into Oxford, too: 'Heracles – Internal & External Hero'. The first soulless sentence could stand in for the next several thousand words: 'Sophocles and Euripides chanced upon or chose a very stimulating period in the history of Heracles in which to pen their studies of the hero, and subsequently did much to enhance this history.'

I'm not sure I was that stimulated at the time.

The funny thing is that, ever since giving up the subject, a genuine love of Classics has slowly emerged and grown. Give me a holiday on a Greek beach nowadays and I genuinely long to be climbing up through the mosquito-haunted, hanging wood above the sea at Ithaca, tracking down those chunks of battered limestone – all that's left of Odysseus's palace. And entirely because I want to, not because I ought to.

As a teenager, I used to laugh at diagrams in old guidebooks to Greece. They showed the tiny, surviving scraps of old stone in continuous, bold lines;

while the rest of some imaginary, fabulous Doric temple was marked out with dotted, extremely conjectural, far more extensive lines. Now I fill in those dotted lines in my head on site, and thrill at the thought of what isn't there but just might have been.

My revived love of Classics has its downside. I worship the ancient at the expense of the modern, or even the really quite distant past. On one trip to Athens and the Peloponnese in 2013, I noticed myself rushing past anything built after 1000 AD, in search of the smallest fragment of pediment or column drum. Worship of the ancient is an incurable condition but, still, it has its uses. What survives from any ancient civilisation, 2,500 years or so on, is intriguing. And, in Greece, what survives is strikingly consistent – temples first, theatres second, houses third.

The dogged survival of ancient Greek temples answers Philip Larkin's question in 'Church Going': 'Wondering, too, when churches will fall completely out of use, what we shall turn them into'? If Greece is anything to go on, they will be revered more by architectural obsessives than spiritual followers of any description. I don't imagine any of my fellow ruin addicts, scrambling over those temples, actually believed in Athena or Zeus.

If you are going to become obsessed with one historical period, I do now finally agree with my Classics teachers of 25 years ago: you're best off learning Greek history. Learn about the Second World War, and your mind naturally gravitates to the tiny gap between 1945 and now. Learn about Greece, and you think about the yawning millennia in between. It helps, too, that the amount of surviving Greek history and literature is relatively limited. With a little bit of reading, you go quite a long way.

In my cynical days, I used to pump out a dull line about the Greeks and the Romans – amazing for the time, yes, but, really, aren't we much more sophisticated now? Dwarves on the shoulders of giants and all that. Well, yes, our telly's better and, flippancy aside, so are our plays – those really are the territory of those dwarves climbing higher and higher on the back of their ancestors. Alan Bennett is funnier than Aristophanes, and almost as filthy.

But other things haven't got much better in the last two or three millennia. I'm writing this two hours after gazing at the statues in the Naples Archaeological Museum; I'm still deeply stirred by them. The Greek second-century BC statue of the Farnese Bull, supposedly carved on Rhodes, is of a size and beauty I still don't think any sculptor could match today.

I'm afraid I did used to think that Homer was a dwarves-on-the-shoulders-of-giants merchant, and I still do occasionally when I read some of his simpler verse. But what a giant. And what a lot of dwarves.

And how extraordinary that it has survived at all. At an evening of Sappho poetry reading in a Mayfair gallery in the summer of 2014, I stared at the fifth-century BC statue of Persephone, queen of the underworld, that stood centre stage in the lecture room. Her statue was old by the time of Jesus, positively ancient when William the Conqueror won at Hastings. Like Homer, exceptional just by her survival.

That astonishment snowballed as I travelled around Greece, Italy, Turkey, Corsica and Sardinia, with my two little green Loeb translations of *The Odyssey* in my bag. In my Classics-mocking years, I used to ask ex-classicists whether they'd ever taken down a Loeb from the shelf for pleasure since leaving university. Most didn't; a few said they did and I shamefully didn't believe them.

I do now.

A bull fresco at Knossos, Crete, home of the Minotaur. The Minoan columns – from 1400 BC or earlier – were reconstructed by Sir Arthur Evans a century ago. They're similar to Greek Doric columns around 700 years later.

LOEB CLASSICAL LIBRARY

HOMER

ODYSSEY

BOOKS 1–12

With an English Translation by

A. T. MURRAY

Revised by

GEORGE E. DIMOCK

A lifesaver for generations of child classicists. The Loeb – invented by James Loeb, an American banker, in 1912 – has the Greek, or Latin, on the left-hand page; with the English translation on the right.

21

Calypso's Lament

I took those two little green *Odyssey* Loebs on my last trip, to Ramla Bay on
Gozo, thought to be the site of Calypso's cave on Homer's island of Ogygia –
'the navel of the sea', as he called it. It was on the sands of Ramla Bay that
Odysseus was washed up, clinging on to the last plank from his fleet before
clambering up to Calypso's cave, where he took refuge with the knockout,
golden-voiced nymph for seven years.

The reddish-brown sands of Ramla Bay were crammed with sun-
worshippers. Malta and Gozo had just had a big double dose of healthy PR.
Brad Pitt and Angelina Jolie were shooting a film on Gozo, and had hired a
secluded pebble beach for the summer. It had also just been announced that
the Duchess of Cambridge would make her first visit to the island for the 50th
anniversary of Maltese independence in September 2014 – morning sickness
meant she ended up sending Prince William instead.

Maltese tourism had never been so big. But only a handful of tourists
bothered to drive up to Calypso's cave through the strange landscape: part
deserted fields, crammed with cacti; part vineyards, producing the upmarket
Marsovin Antonin red wine. Calypso's cave sat next to a gun battery built by
the Knights of Malta. The knights also built a wall across the bay to prevent
Napoleon invading; the clever little Corsican invaded via the undefended gully
next door instead.

None of the tourists dared climb over the high fence around the cave
entrance. The cave has been closed for three years now; the little boys who
used to rent out candles to guide you down into its labyrinthine depths

are long gone. I waited for the other tourists to trickle away, climbed over the fence and let myself down into the cave, lined with frayed, collapsing cobwebs. An iron bar had been set into the rocks to let you descend another level. I didn't need a candle. The light from the cave mouth above me was strong enough to light up an old packet of King Edward VII tobacco on the cave floor.

I sat in the cave for a while; long enough to hear another little group of German tourists turn up and gather round the cave mouth above me. Unlike the last lot, they were keen to hang around, chattering. Should I wait for them to go? Or should I risk giving them a shock by suddenly emerging from the closed-off cave – the foreign oddball in trousers and long-sleeved shirt on a hot day in high summer?

A few years ago, the fear of embarrassment would have meant I'd have waited for them to leave. But that fear had gone – through growing age, confidence and eccentricity. I clambered out of the cave, looking straight ahead as the Germans went quiet at the strange sight of an Englishman wrapped in cobwebs, emerging out of Calypso's cave. Or was it the trousers that astonished them? I didn't stop to find out. I got back in my hire car and headed for the ferry back to Malta, to the airport and home.

The cave may have been nymph-free – but, still, I'd loved Valletta and its terraced houses, with their delicate balconies carved out of Malta's two limestones, one an off-white, the other a golden yellow. So I was in a grumpy mood as I returned home on the Gatwick Express at around midnight. I was made even grumpier by the fool tourist at Victoria who'd got his oversized holdall clamped in the jaws of the ticket barrier. There was no Penelope waiting – at Victoria, Gatwick or Heathrow Terminal 5.

It was a Friday night, and my bike ride back across Oxford Street had all the worst hallmarks of London life: drunks shouting at each other, some with anger, some with crazed pleasure; more fool tourists ambling across Regent Street without looking. But then I crossed Marylebone Road and made my way up the Outer Circle of Regent's Park. The road is closed to cars – but not bikes – on Friday nights. So I had the Outer Circle to myself. The only lights were the sparse, old-fashioned gas lamps, trailing away in a long enfilade ahead of me.

When I'd left two days earlier, London had been in the sort of heatwave that doesn't suit the city – muggy and close, even at night. That oppressive heat had lifted, and there was a cool undercurrent to the gentle wind in my face – perfect bicycling weather.

As I made my way along the edge of the park, I noticed a large, half-moon-sized puddle obscuring the double-yellow lines to my left. London had been through one of its rare tropical drenchings and the air was rich with *petrichor* – the smell of rain on earth, from *petros*, 'stone', and *ichor*, 'liquid'. The Outer Circle felt like I feel after a shower – invigorated, fresh, light.

Please forgive the vulgar analogy, but Kingsley Amis said the essential elements of a hangover cure must include a shower, a shave, an evacuation of the bowels and bladder, and, ideally, the sexual act, self-applied if necessary. Once these steps are taken, you begin the journey back to a modicum of healthy self-respect.

I wasn't hungover. I'd only had half a bottle of gently resinous Marsovin Antonin wine the night before in my Valletta hotel – from the grapes growing in the vineyards beneath Calypso's cave. But, as I'd exited Victoria Station, I had been bathed in the mild self-loathing – and humanity-loathing – that often accompanies hangovers.

I hadn't had a shower – or any of the other Amis recommendations. But London had had a shower – and its improved mood improved mine. My heart hadn't lifted on my immediate return to London – the architecture of Gatwick Airport, and the hell of its passport queue, guaranteed that. But a while later – after the 15 minutes it took to bike from Victoria to Regent's Park – my heart lifted, even though I came home as I left it – alone.

Still, my ex-girlfriend had been my semi-permanent, invisible companion throughout. Suddenly – once, memorably, out of nowhere in the Mediterraneo bar on the harbourside in the Dodecanese island of Symi, over calamari and a Mythos beer – she would return, unbidden, to mind. I would flinch, pulling my lips between my teeth and gently biting them. 'Please stop haunting me,' was the unspoken thought behind the flinch.

She was my default memory – as my brain automatically clicked back to the last time it properly felt something. Even though she wasn't with me, her attitude to Greece was. She had persuaded me out of an intellectual approach to the ancient world and guided me towards an emotional one.

As a teenager, hauled around Greek and Roman ruins, I had often thought, 'Different city, same stones.' By now, I knew what I hadn't as a teenager: that most Greek sites were not abandoned. They were built on; from Marseilles to Athens, from Nice to Syracuse, the Greeks had got there first. The trail they blazed was permanent.

Soon after I got back from my odyssey, I read a newspaper interview with Cardinal Gianfranco Ravasi, President of the Pontifical Council for Culture, and the best classicist in the Vatican.

'You don't study Latin or Greek to speak them,' he said. 'You do so to come in direct contact with the civilisation of two peoples who were the bedrock of modern society, that is, you study them to be yourself and to know yourself.'

That was the sort of thing my Classics teachers told me at school – and I used to scoff inwardly at the overblown claims for a pair of dead languages. Now I had begun to appreciate the truth of the things repeated to me incessantly by those teachers 30 years earlier – the Greeks had created the modern European world, as well as the modern European mind.

Poor, battered, modern Greece may have fallen far since the days it ruled the Mediterranean, since it emerged as the early cockpit of Western art, architecture, literature and democracy. But, in the shadow of the Parthenon, in the ruins of Odysseus's palace on Ithaca, beneath the towering, sloping walls of Troy, the old, colossal ghosts of the greatest civilisation of them all flickered into real, tangible life.

The whimsical – possibly fictional – foundation of my trip hadn't been so flimsy a basis for a journey after all. Perhaps Odysseus never existed; but the places that claim a connection with him most certainly do. And what a wonderful, random collection of places they are. A more precise itinerary – to bag all the Munros in Scotland, say, or to visit the last outposts of the British Empire – would have been less fanciful. But it would have been circumscribed by fact, predictability and lack of romance.

Odysseus's wild route had taken me not just to a random assortment of new places: Corsica, Malta and Gibraltar, among them. He had also taken me on my first cruise. He had directed me to unfamiliar bits of familiar towns. I've been to Dublin dozens of times – but I'd never been to St Peter's Terrace, James Joyce's childhood home, in a small nineteenth-century cottage north of the Georgian city I'd never strayed from before. I'd been to Sicily plenty of times – but I'd never sailed between the real-life seaside town of Scilla and Charybdis. I'd never travelled down a nondescript cul-de-sac on the outskirts of the untouristed town of Trapani, where the Cyclops made his feta cheese in his cave.

The old adage of travel is that, wherever you go, you have to take boring old you with you. But how much newer things are when it's not boring old you who's deciding where to go, but a 3,000-year-old genius, love-rat and strongman; or, failing that, a bunch of fifth-century euhemerists.

For all the freshness of my journey, it was hard to dodge one maddeningly familiar companion: a default mood of melancholy and failure, not least since *The Odyssey* is soaked in melancholy. As well as being the original of all stories about returning home, it's also the quintessential story about leaving a loved one behind.

Just as I was finishing this book, I got a text from my ex-girlfriend, saying she was getting married to her boyfriend. I was undone once more. I was on the battlefield of Waterloo at the time, writing an article for the *Daily Mail* about the 200th anniversary of the battle. A charming ex-Guards officer was showing me round the farmhouse of Hougoumount, where the heat of the battle was at its hottest, when I got her text.

But I was sort of OK. I kept on talking about the Duke of Wellington to the Waterloo expert – with genuine interest. But the dagger, unnoticed at first, had sunk deep. After too many drinks in a Brussels art nouveau bar with the ex-Guards officer – and several more drinks on the Eurostar home – I came home, and burst into unprecedented floods of tears; the sort of impressive output not seen since childhood. It's easy – and fatuous – to say it was a kind of shrieving. Stupid word, anyway. But some sort of agonising, yet effective, and final, farewell had taken place.

Even as Odysseus was heading back to Penelope, he was constantly deserting others, chief among them Calypso – who he deserted after seven years on Ogygia, or Malta, where I'd just returned from.

In her song, 'Calypso', Suzanne Vega described the deserted girl on the beach – left alone on the island at dawn, as Odysseus sails away after one last night together. In Vega's lyrics, Calypso recognises her lonely life ahead, but she doesn't ask Odysseus to return. Instead, she stoically accepts the inevitable – she must let him go.

I, too, had been a serial deserter – of girlfriends, jobs, emotions. Odysseus returned home eventually – to his wife, to his destiny as King of Ithaca, to his natural world. I still haven't found a wife, a destiny or a natural world.

His journey only lasted 20 years. Mine has been 43 years and counting. Surely it can't go on for ever. Can it? I still don't know.

But my ex-girlfriend, who came up with the idea for this book and this journey, had unwittingly provided me with a Mediterranean escape route from the awful sadness of our parting.

I have let her go.

Scylla's view – Looking down from Scylla's Rock, across the Strait of Messina, to Sicily.

Bibliography

Beard, Mary, *All in a Don's Day* (London: Profile, 2012)

—— and John Henderson, *Classics: A Very Short Introduction* (Oxford: OUP, 1995)

Bebbington, David, *The Mind of Gladstone: Religion, Homer and Politics* (Oxford: OUP, 2004)

Betjeman, John, *An Oxford University Chest* (London: John Miles, 1938)

Bittlestone, Robert, James Diggle and John Underhill, *Odysseus Unbound: The Search for Homer's Ithaca* (Cambridge: Cambridge University Press, 2005)

Bradford, Ernle, *Gibraltar: the History of a Fortress* (London: Rupert Hart-Davis, 1971)

——, *Ulysses Found* (London: Hodder & Stoughton, 1963)

Lord Byron, *Don Juan* (London: Penguin, 2004)

Byron, Robert, *Europe in the Looking-glass: Reflections of a Motor Drive from Grimsby to Athens* (London: Routledge, 1926)

Chaline, Eric, *The Temple of Perfection: A History of the Gym* (London: Reaktion Books, 2015)

Clifton-Taylor, Alec, *The Pattern of English Building* (London: Faber, 1972)

Conan Doyle, Arthur, *The Memoirs of Sherlock Holmes* (London: George Newnes, 1894)

Crook, J. Mordaunt, *The Greek Revival* (London: John Murray, 1972)

Dickey, Eleanor, *The Colloquia of the Hermeneumata Pseudodositheana* (Cambridge: Cambridge Classical Texts and Commentaries, 2012)

Dover, Kenneth, *Greek Homosexuality* (London: Duckworth, 1978)

Eyres, Harry, *Horace and Me* (London: Bloomsbury, 2013)

Fermor, Patrick Leigh, *Words of Mercury* (London: John Murray, 2003)

Finley, M. I., *The Ancient Greeks* (London: Chatto & Windus, 1963)

Freely, John, *A Travel Guide to Homer* (London: I.B. Tauris, 2014)

Gailey, Andrew, *The Lost Imperialist: Lord Dufferin, Memory and Mythmaking in an Age of Celebrity* (London: John Murray, 2015)

Grafton, Anthony, Glenn W. Most and Salvatore Settis, *The Classical Tradition* (Cambridge, Mass. Harvard University Press, 2010)

Gwynne, N. M., *Gwynne's Latin* (London: Ebury Press, 2014)

Hilton, James, *Goodbye, Mr Chips* (London: Hodder & Stoughton, 1934)

Hitchens, Christopher, *Hitch-22* (London: Atlantic, 2012)

Homer, *The Iliad*, Book XXIV, ed. C. W. MacLeod (Cambridge: Cambridge University Press, 1982)

——, *The Odyssey*, Volumes I and II: Books 1–12. Translated by A. T. Murray. Revised by George E. Dimock. (Cambridge, Mass. Loeb Classical Library, Harvard University Press, 1919)

——, *The Odyssey*, translated by E. V. Rieu (Oxford: OUP, 1946)

——, *The Odyssey*, translated by Robert Fagles (London: Penguin Classics, 2006)

——, *The Odyssey*, translated by T. E. Shaw (Oxford: OUP, 1955)

Hood, Jane, *The Classics Magpie* (London: Icon Books, 2014)

Jacobovici, Simcha and Barrie Wilson, *The Lost Gospel* (New York: Pegasus, 2014)

Johnson, Boris, *The Churchill Factor* (London: Hodder & Stoughton, 2014)

——, 'The secrets of London's Athenian golden age', *Spectator*, 13 September 2014

Jones, Peter, *Eureka! Everything You Ever Wanted to Know about the Ancient Greeks but were Afraid to Ask* (London: Atlantic, 2014)

Joyce, James, *Ulysses* (Paris: Shakespeare and Company, 1925)

Kazantzakis, Nikos, *Zorba the Greek* (London: Lehmann, 1952)

Kitto, H. D. F., *The Greeks* (London: Penguin, 1951)

Kristol, Irving, 'The Neoconservative Persuasion', *Weekly Standard*, 2003

Lampedusa, Giuseppe Tomasi di, *The Leopard* (London: Collins, 1960)

Lanchester, John, *How to Speak Money* (London: Faber, 2014)

Lane Fox, Robin, *Alexander the Great* (London: Penguin, 1973)

——, *Travelling Heroes in the Epic Age of Homer* (London: Penguin, 2008)

Levi, Peter, *Atlas of the Greek World* (Oxford: Phaidon, 1984)

Lewis, Michael, *Boomerang: The Meltdown Tour* (London: Allen Lane, 2011)

Liddell, Henry George and Robert Scott, *A Greek-English Lexicon* (Oxford: OUP, 1843)

Lodwick, Marcus, *The Gallery Companion: Understanding Western Art* (London: Thames & Hudson, 2002)

Luce, J. V., *Celebrating Homer's Landscapes* (New Haven, Conn.: Yale University Press, 1998)

Mahaffy, J. P., *Greek Pictures* (London: The Religious Tract Society, 1890)

Marozzi, Justin, *The Man Who Invented History: Travels with Herodotus* (London: John Murray, 2008)

McGilchrist, Nigel, *McGilchrist's Greek Islands* (London: Genius Loci Publications, 2009)

Mount, Ferdinand, *Full Circle: How the Classical World Came Back to Us* (London: Simon & Schuster, 2010)

Munro, H. H., *The Collected Short Stories of Saki* (London: Wordsworth Classics, 1993)

Nicolson, Adam, *The Mighty Dead: Why Homer Matters* (London: William Collins, 2014)

Ostler, Nicholas, *Ad Infinitum: A Biography of Latin* (London: HarperPress, 2007)

Paizis-Danias, Dimitris I., *Throwing Light on Homeric Ithaca* (Ithaca: Koinofelis Omilos Stavrou Exhibition Catalogue, 2013)

Paxman, Jeremy, *Great Britain's Great War* (London: Penguin, 2014)

Pope, Alexander, *Preface to The Iliad of Homer* (1715)

Raven, Simon, *Come Like Shadows* (London: Blond & Briggs, 1972)

Roose, Kevin, *Young Money* (London: John Murray, 2014)

Rossiter, Stuart, *The Blue Guide to Greece* (London: Ernest Benn, 1973)

Rubens, Beaty and Oliver Taplin, *An Odyssey round Odysseus* (London: BBC Books, 1989)

Severin, Tim, *The Ulysses Voyage* (London: Hutchinson, 1987)

Shay, Jonathan, *Odysseus in America: Combat Trauma and the Trials of Homecoming* (New York: Scribner, 2002)

Stark, Freya, *Ionia – A Quest* (London: John Murray, 1954)

Tartt, Donna, *The Secret History* (New York: Knopf, 1992)

Vinke, Jacoline, *Small Hotels in Greece* (Athens: A. Papasotiriou, 2013)

Waugh, Evelyn, *Brideshead Revisited* (London: Chapman & Hall, 1945)

——, *Scott-King's Modern Europe* (London: Chapman & Hall, 1947)

Weil, Simone, *The Iliad, or the Poem of Force* (Marseilles: Les Cahiers du Sud, 1940)

Wilson, A. N., *Victoria: A Life* (London: Atlantic, 2014)

Wood, Michael, *In Search of the Trojan War* (London: BBC, 1985)

Wright, John, *The Naming of the Shrew* (London: Bloomsbury, 2014)

Acknowledgements

I would never have gone on this journey but for two people. One is Robin Baird-Smith, my friend, publisher and North Star. With the lightest touch on the tiller, he has gently steered me in the right direction whenever I headed for the rocks.

The other came up with the idea in the first place. When she suggested it, the thought was that we would do the journey together. The small part of the trip we did do is scorched into the memory. That we didn't complete it together is an enduring, deep sadness. That I did it at all is entirely thanks to her. This book is dedicated to her.

Many thanks to all my family, particularly Ferdinand and Julia Mount, William Mount and Mary Mount. My thanks to the late Mary Clive and the late Violet Powell, my great-aunts, and my great-uncle, the late Frank Longford, for sharing memories of their father at Gallipoli. Many thanks to Thomas Pakenham, for letting me reproduce his photograph of Thomas Longford.

Thanks to all at Bloomsbury, particularly Jamie Birkett, for his extraordinary attention to detail, and to Laura Brooke, Nick Fawcett, Maria Hammershoy and Emily Sweet. Many thanks, too, to my fearless agent, Peter Straus. Many thanks to Emily Faccini for her terrific map.

Particular thanks to Robert O'Byrne for entertaining me so generously at Ardbraccan House in County Meath, when I bicycled round Dublin in search of James Joyce's *Ulysses*.

Deepest thanks to Hannah Betts for accompanying me to Polyphemus's cave and for her photos of the Hellespont swim. Thanks to Ned Cranborne for sharing the walk – and cab ride – from Marathon to Athens, for leading the way across the Hellespont, and for identifying the chukar partridges at Sunium.

Thanks to Alice Boyd and Rosemary Fitzgerald for identifying the flower growing on my great-grandfather's grave. Thanks to Richard Ehrman for showing me around the Corfu Literary Society. Thanks to Artemis Cooper and Justin Marozzi for arranging my visit to Patrick Leigh Fermor's house in Kardamyli; thanks, also, to Elpida Beloyannis for showing me round.

Thanks also to Liz Anderson, Lola Armstrong, Sarah Baxter, Mary Beard, Adam Beresford, Rachel Billington, Mark Bostridge, Rob Bruno, Charlie Byron, Robin Byron, Alexander Chancellor, Alex and Eliza Chisholm, Tom Chivers, Robert Colvile, Johnny Cornwell, Armand D'Angour, Peter and Genevieve Davies, Justin Doherty, Lindy Dufferin, Daisy Dunn, Kate Ehrman, Coco Ferguson, Deirdre Fernand, James Fletcher, Flora Fraser, Laura Freeman, Tanya Gold, John Goodall, Catriona Gray, Freddy Gray, Drue Heinz, Charlotte Higgins, Richard Ingrams, Martin Ivens, Ian Jenkins, Boris Johnson, Rachel Johnson, Stanley Johnson, Paul Keegan, Mary Killen, Ben and Sasha King, Sam Leith, Joshua Levine, the late Angus Macintyre, Robert Malone, Derwent May, Eleanor Mills, Tim Moore, Cristina Odone, James Owen, Valerie Pakenham, Giorgos Papakonstantinou, Jamie Philippsohn, Barnaby and Nicole Phillips, Archie Powell, Stuart Reid, Mika Ross-Southall, Sarah Sands, Liz Sawyer, Brian Sewell, Nicholas Shakespeare, Charlie Smith, Camilla Swift, Inigo Thomas, Damian Thompson, Lorne Thyssen, Dionyssia Trohoulia, David and Liz Uren, Jacoline Vinke, Mary Wakefield, Justin Warshaw, Molly Watson, Heather Wells, Frances Wilson and Alice Yates.

Many thanks to Harry Eyres for letting me use his translation of the Horace ode and Horace's letter about the Greeks.

I'm very grateful to the editor of the *Spectator*, Fraser Nelson, for letting me reproduce an article I wrote for the magazine. From the *Daily Telegraph*, many thanks to Neil Armstrong, Lorna Bradbury, Andrew M. Brown, Sally Chatterton, Harry de Quetteville, Will Heaven, Luke McGee, Charles Moore and Nick Trend.

Christopher Howse's help with the languages spoken by Jesus was invaluable. My thanks to the editor of the *Sunday Telegraph*, Ian MacGregor, for letting me adapt an article I wrote for the paper.

My thanks to the editor of the *Daily Mail*, Paul Dacre, for the same kindness. Also at the *Mail*, my thanks to Leaf Kalfayan, Andrew Morrod,

Matt Nixson, Mark Palmer, Laura Pullman, Emma Rowley, Suzy Walker and Andrew Yates.

My thanks to Steven O'Brien for letting me adapt an article I wrote for the *London Magazine*. Thanks, too, to Luke Coppen, editor of the *Catholic Herald*, for the same kindness. Thanks to Will Schwalbe, formerly of Hyperion, for letting me adapt the passage on Greek fraternities at American universities from *Carpe Diem*, the American edition of my book *Amo, Amas, Amat and All That*.

With deepest thanks to the American Academy in Rome for providing me with the loveliest rooms in the city, in the Villa Aurelia. Thanks, too, to the Vatican Apostolic Library. The staff of the London Library were extremely helpful.

Many thanks to all at Noble Caledonia cruises – particularly Victoria Brittain, Chantal Cookson, Peter Graham, Judith La Rocca and Thomas Pankkoke – for letting me lecture on board the *Corinthian*; and to James Pembroke for coming up with the idea of approaching Noble Caledonia in the first place.

Permissions